Cheating

Cheating

Gaining Advantage in Videogames

Mia Consalvo

The MIT Press Cambridge, Massachusetts London, England

MIT Press books may be purchased at special quantity discounts for business or sales promotional use. For information, please email <special_sales@ mitpress.mit.edu> or write to Special Sales Department, The MIT Press, 55 Hayward Street, Cambridge, MA 02142.

This book was set in Rotis Sans and Janson by The MIT Press. Printed and bound in the United States of America.

Library of Congress Cataloging-in-Publication Data

Consalvo, Mia, 1969–
Cheating : gaining advantage in videogames / Mia Consalvo.
  p. cm.
Includes bibliographical references and index.
ISBN: 978-0-262-03365-7 (hardcover : alk. paper)
1. Cheating at video games. 2. Video games industry—Corrupt practices.
3. Video games—Moral and ethical aspects. I. Title.
GV1469.34.C67C66 2007
798.8—dc22

                                                                    2006030942

10   9   8   7   6   5   4   3   2   1

Contents

Acknowledgments

There are many people who I need to thank in relation to this project, and as my dissertation advisor Professor Sue Lafky once told me, you can never go wrong when thanking people, repeatedly, for the help, ideas, and support they've given along the way. And even thanking them repeatedly doesn't seem enough, as I literally could not have completed (or even started) this project without the help of others—the players who volunteered to talk with me, the game developers and publishers who freely shared information with me, and my friends, colleagues, and family members who all helped me sharpen my arguments and refine my ideas as well as offered wonderful advice and suggestions. I'm listed as the author, but only because I stand on the shoulders of many terrific people as I do so. And of course, the mistakes within are my own, probably despite the good advice of those I've consulted as I've done this research.

A few of the following chapters are much revised and expanded versions of material published elsewhere. Small portions of chapters 1, 2, and 3 appear in "Cheat Codes, Strategy Guides, and Walkthroughs: Official and Unofficial Sources of Cheating and Help in the Digital Game Industry," a chapter in *Digital Games Industries: Work, Knowledge and Consumption*, edited by Jason Rutter, forthcoming; an earlier version of chapter 4, "Gaining Advantage: How Videogame Players Define and Negotiate Cheating," appeared in the *Changing Views: Worlds in Play* proceedings of the 2005 Digital Games Research Association Conference, Vancouver; and segments of chapter 8 first appeared in "Rule Sets, Cheating, and Magic Circles: Studying Games and Ethics," *International Review of Information Ethics*, vol. 4, December 2005.

There are quite a few people from the game industry who have contributed directly to the information I've gathered here. I enjoyed talking with all of them, and they offered valuable perspectives that have helped me in understanding the evolving nature of the digital game industry. Those individuals include David Waybright of BradyGames; Andy Rolleri of Prima Games; Tony Ray of Even Balance; Will Leverett, Charlie Porter, and Phil Cimoch of NCsoft; independent strategy guide writers Bart Farkas and Mark Walker; Ben Sawyer from Digital Mill; Steven Davis of IT GlobalSecure; Jennifer Sun of Numedeon; and Tom Odell, Jim Hughes, Rick Johnson, and Bobby Duncanson of Raven Software.

I also greatly appreciate the game industry folks who provided general perspectives, detailed information in related areas, and ideas and encouragement to me throughout this project. They include Sheri Graner Ray, Sheri Pocilujko, Clarinda Merripen, Eric Marcoullier, Marty Poulin, Noah Falstein, Cory Ondrejka, Daniel James, Dave Weinstein, Mike Steele, Neil Kirby, Brad King, and Victor Jimenez.

In addition to the players I formally interviewed while conducting the research, there are also the players that I spent time with in game, particularly in *Final Fantasy XI*. That includes, most of all, the individuals in CantaPerMe, "the finest role-playing linkshell" on my server. Those people include Akuma, Tobias, Xenedra, Wriath, ShiroMiro, Alveen, Ayvaen, Keiro, Vyce, Wendell, Richelle, Psylight, Psylite, Kaahi, and Unikatze.

When it came time to discuss, analyze, and critique what I was working on, I again found people willing to help and encourage me. At both Ohio University and the University of Wisconsin at Milwaukee as well as when visiting other parts of the world, I had (and still have) the privilege of working with amazingly smart people who made my work so much better. They include Tasha Oren, Stewart Ikeda, Nola, Karen Riggs, Roger Cooper, Amy Mattson Lauters, Casey Hayward, Courtney Cole, Keiko Yanagiya, Chris Curley, Nathan Dutton, the students in all of my digital games classes over the past few years, and especially Erica Butcher, who offered me the term "gaming capital" to encapsulate what I had been thinking about in relation to gamers and their knowledge.

Further afield but closer discipline-wise, there are many game studies folks who I have looked forward to talking with at conferences, over IM, and any chance I get, really, about cheating and games, and they include Ren Reynolds, Ian Bogost, Jason Rutter, Aphra Kerr, Julian Kücklich, David Thomas, T. L. Taylor, Dmitri Williams, Tom Malaby, Ted

Castronova, Charles Ess, and Matthew Weise, who must take some of both the blame and credit for getting me interested in studying games.

Likewise, my family has always been there for me, and I have been extremely lucky in that regard. They have consistently encouraged my interests and passions, and have been unwaveringly supportive in their belief that I can achieve whatever I desire. I can never repay that debt, but plan to keep thanking them often and frequently. To Mom and Dad, Jen, Blair, Matante, Uncle Rusty, Nana and Grampy, and Cleo, thank you for your love and support.

Finally, there are the ones who were physically there throughout it all, including the endless research, writing, rewriting, editing, waiting, and completion. Without the love, support, meals, walks, ideas, critiques, and company, this book would still be a pile of paper somewhere, an interesting idea never completed. To Jasper, Georgia, Malcolm, and most of all Bill Reader, thank you for everything—this book is for you.

Cheating

TO CHEAT OR NOT TO CHEAT: IS THAT EVEN THE QUESTION?

On Christmas Day, 1980, videogames invaded my home. My younger sister and I received a joint gift from our parents: an Atari 2600. When we unwrapped the gift and saw what it was, my sister was almost ecstatic with glee, clearly excited by the thought of playing with the Atari. On the other hand, I was happy, but definitely not to the same degree. Was I less excited? Not really; I was probably even more demanding in my wishes for the system. Yet I had cheated. So eager to confirm that my parents had indeed acceded to my desires, I had searched their room one day earlier in the month and had found the Atari system unwrapped, under their bed.

That knowledge satisfied my desire to know, yet at the same time it extinguished something maybe even more vital: my capacity for surprise at the future unveiling of the gift. My tempered happiness on Christmas Day was the result of my foreknowledge of the event, and my trading of that knowledge for the later surprise. Although it's not a big deal, certainly nothing to lose sleep over, from that point on I never searched for presents again—I had learned my lesson: that the surprise was worth more to me than early knowledge of what I would receive.

That experience is definitely not the same for all people; some of my friends continued peeking and searching for gifts as long as they continued to receive them. Nevertheless, those experiences have valuable things to say about how different individuals approach the pursuit of information, and the costs they are willing to pay to acquire that knowledge. It also says something about what those costs are, and how they operate.

Like peeking at Christmas gifts, reading a puzzle solution for the adventure game *Dreamfall: The Longest Journey* at GameFAQs.com can help a player find the solution, but it also ends up negating the surprise that may come from working it out on one's own. It can also diminish the sense of achievement earned by solving the puzzle for oneself, rather than reading to find the answer. Although trivial to some, elements such as surprise and earned achievement in a digital game are important and worthy of study. Similarly, but generally needing less justification, practices such as "real-money trade" or the buying and selling of in-game accounts, items, and money, need further examination. Who buys such things, and why? Why do some players consider it one of the worst forms of cheating, while others see it as of little relevance to their own experiences? How players choose how to play games along with what happens when they can't always play the way they'd like are the beginning points of exploration for this book. Such activities by players challenge the notion that there is one "correct" way to play a game, or that games can have specifiable "effects" on players.

Game players and the broader game industry have created different ways of playing and enjoying games. Such ways can give players a wider range of experiences, can reward superior players, and can challenge game companies in understandings of who controls the game space. Although I began this project primarily interested in the phenomenon of cheating, how players define that term has opened up a huge range of activities that demanded investigation, from both the player and industry perspective. What that investigation found is a cultural history of gameplay that puts player activity and peripheral industries at the center of analysis. That foregrounding reveals how player agency is central to understanding games as well as the development of the wider game industry. Yet additionally, it is crucial to keep in mind how power moves along those pathways, through individuals as well as industry professionals. Just as players exercise agency, they aren't doing so in a vacuum. Along the way, various industry elements work to constrain certain readings or activities, promoting certain ways of seeing gameplay and ways of playing that are valued over others.

Such power systems must be carefully delineated, however, lest this account slide into a false celebration of player agency at the expense of understanding the more complex, dynamic push-pull of industry and player currently at work in the gaming universe. The development and circulation of *gaming capital* takes into account such an interplay. That concept is developed in this book to seek out how multiple structures, relations, commodities, and groups of players have been central to its development and deployment.

To get a grasp on such complexities, this book investigates a wide range of player behavior in relation to digital games, including cheating alone and in groups, how cheating is defined, and how the industry has helped create a system of cheating and help that has ultimately worked to stabilize (and occasionally destabilize) itself.

This book utilizes as well as develops several themes and theories to advance its arguments. Most centrally, it defines and develops the concept of gaming capital. It also brings in past literature and theorization about cheating, drawing on past studies from human and animal behavior, philosophy, and ethics. Such theoretical frameworks undergird and help provide various lenses for the arguments advanced. Finally, the concept of "paratext" as developed by Gérard Genette is expanded on as a way to better understand the multiple elements involved in the larger game industry, and how those elements contribute to shaping the industry.[1] Here, I introduce these theoretical concepts, and then preview the structure and content of the book.

Gaming Capital

One way to describe player activities both in games and generally could be to conceptualize players as members of a particular "subculture," as originally articulated by Dick Hebdige.[2] In that sense, players could be identified as belonging to a particular group that shared similar practices, beliefs, and a sense of style. Certainly some gamers do seem to belong to a culture distinct from mainstream society. The term *subculture*, however, is too limited to adequately explain the broader world of games and game players that currently exists.

For example, the argument could be made that *EverQuest* players constitute a subculture, as they create fan fiction about the game, have conventions to meet each other, and often play the game together for many hours a week. But where would the avid *Counter-Strike* player fit in that scenario? A subculture, to be identified as such, must share common symbols, through such things as fashion, music, or aesthetics. Although individual games or genres may spawn such subcultures, games as a whole are too varied to paint their players with such a broad brush. And to trace an adequate history of gameplay, we must confront differences between players—in genre preferences, play styles, and many other areas. For those reasons, the concept of the subculture cannot work satisfactorily to explain gamers and gameplay. I believe instead that gaming capital captures the dynamism of gameplay as well as the evolving game and paratextual industry.

Thus, one of the themes running through this book is the development of gaming capital as a central element to serious gameplay. That term is a reworking of Pierre Bourdieu's "cultural capital," which described a system of preferences and dispositions that ultimately served to classify groups by class.[3] Of course such a system was not apolitical, but Bourdieu's intention was to investigate how certain interests, pastimes, or preferences were conveyed (and kept) among groups, while kept carefully distinguishable from other interests or pastimes.

I believe that the concept of gaming capital provides a key way to understand how individuals interact with games, information about games and the game industry, and other game players. The term is useful because it suggests a currency that is by necessity dynamic—changing over time, and across types of players or games.

Games aren't designed, marketed, or played in a cultural vacuum. I would argue that it is somewhat futile to talk about the player or a game in the abstract, as what we know about players can change over time, and be dependent on such elements as player skill or age. Likewise, even the most linear game can be experienced in multiple ways, depending on a player's knowledge of past games in that genre or series, including previewed information from magazines or Web sites, and marketing's attempt at drawing attention to certain elements of the game. All of that knowledge, experience, and positioning helps shape gaming capital for a particular player, and in turn that player helps shape the future of the industry.

Specific segments of the game support industry have shaped important elements of gaming capital over the past several decades. The contents of game magazines and strategy guides as well as the development of Game Genies and mod (short for "modification") chips have had critical impacts on how all gamers evaluate, play, and talk about games.

And players themselves further shape gaming capital, especially as new media forms offer individuals more opportunities to share and the game world grows even larger. This book explores that coevolution of gaming capital, and its impact on the world of games as well as digital culture in general. It does that by examining the role of such things as magazines and mod chips along with players' own contributions to and articulations of gaming capital.

What Is Cheating?

This book takes cheating as a central point of departure for its look into how players understand and enact gameplay practices. How they define cheating in their own terms is my main intent. It is useful, however, to consider how the concept has been defined and debated over time to better contextualize player definitions. But context *is* all we should draw from such a discussion. I believe it's important to keep our understandings of what cheating is or might be open to interpretation as well as debate.

Although not written about extensively, a few individuals have considered the concept and act of cheating in history as well as contemporary culture.[4] J. Barton Bowyer writes that cheating "is the advantageous distortion of perceived reality. The advantage falls to the cheater because the cheated person misperceives what is assumed to be the real world."[5] The cheater is taking advantage of a person, a situation, or both. Cheating also involves the "distortion of perceived reality" or what others call "deception." Deception can involve hiding the "true" reality or "showing" reality in a way intended to deceive others.

Bowyer also argues that cheating has been around since ancient times; in his *Cheating*, there are pictures of hieroglyphs found in Egypt that suggest ancient Egyptians played the "shell game" that can still be found on the streets of any major city. He also states that although U.S. society (and many others) pays lip service to the idea that "the honest person never cheats or lies," in actuality cheating is pervasive and often expected in areas such as war, politics, and espionage. As an example, he describes the Trojan horse and how deception was an integral part of strategy by the Greeks. Bowyer also maintains that the need to cheat "arises out of the nature of power," meaning that when one is faced with a more powerful opponent and desires to win, cheating can become a viable option to help "even the score."[6] Certain such ideas about cheating can extend to beliefs about gameplay. On a discussion board for *Final Fantasy XI* on Allakhazam.com, many players debate the topic of cheating in the game and what activities deserve (or don't) that label. I will explore some of those discussions in chapter 7, but here it is essential to mention that although most posters claim to be against whatever activities they have decided are cheating, they are also fairly sure that such activities are widespread in the game. The many discussion threads about such issues, including gil selling and power leveling, seem to lend further weight to these beliefs.

If cheating is a deception, what is the purpose of the deception, and what are the ramifications of it? Moral philosophers can help us in figuring out how truth and deception function to keep societies, whether real or virtual, stable or in chaos. Sissela Bok observes that when we deceive others, we communicate messages that we ourselves don't believe.[7] Eventually, those who are deceived learn that they have been deceived, and there is a gradual erosion of trust, leading to a collapse of society, with all individuals relying only on their own information for survival. Lies or deceptions "can affect the objectives seen, the alternatives believed possible, the estimates made of risks and benefits. Such a manipulation of the dimension of certainty is one of the main ways to gain power over the choices of those deceived," notes Bok.[8]

And what if you live in such a society but aren't actually lied to yourself? Bok believes that doesn't really matter, as the ramifications of the deception are felt "by all those who feel the consequences of the lie, whether or not they are themselves lied to."[9] Even if you aren't lied to personally, if you live in a society where lying is routine, you will come to regard most or all speakers as suspicious, thus affecting how you judge objectives, alternatives, risks, and benefits. So deception can have far-reaching effects beyond one cheater and the person who is cheated. For example, in my own gameplay in *Final Fantasy XI*, I have not encountered any individuals that have tried to scam me out of in-game items of value, yet the subject comes up frequently on Allakhazam.com's game boards. The repetition of the message that scammers exist works to increase suspicion in the game, regardless of whether players have individually experienced such events for themselves. Additionally, popular media attention to cheating in online games strengthens such feelings and suspicions.

Rules of the Magic Circle

Johan Huizinga argued that play occupies a time apart from normal life (when one is playing a game, the rules of normal life aren't supposed to intrude), and when a game is played it creates a space apart from regular space—the playground or "magic circle" where a special sort of order is created. That order is also dependent on rules. As Huizinga writes, "Rules in their turn are a very important factor in the play-concept. All play has its rules. . . . [T]he rules of a game are absolutely binding and allow no doubt. . . . [A]s soon as the rules are transgressed the whole play-world collapses. The game is over."[10] So just as play involves a special time and place, it also requires specific rules for its continuation and practice. Still, with the development of entire genres of games such as Alternate Reality Games (ARGs) that are played across time and space, and player interest in games that extend beyond the simple playing of a game to activities such as creating walkthroughs of games, writing fan fiction, or developing character skins for particular games, can we always say that play involves a special time and place?

While it may be helpful to consider that there is an invisible boundary marking game space from normal space, that line has already been breached, if it was ever there to start with. My point is not to contend that such boundaries are necessary (or unnecessary) but instead to point to the most important boundary marker for games: their rules. Rules keep a game distinct from other games as well as other parts of life. Paradoxically perhaps, it is the rules that make a game fun and entice an individual to play. Rules, then, are a central component of games, and their significance for cheating (or its various expressions) cannot be understated.

Players then have the options of following the rules, refusing to abide by the rules overtly, or secretly not abiding by the rules (although appearing to do so) and thus cheating. Different outcomes occur in each situation, and Huizinga claims that we attach different meanings and penalties to each of the latter. He states:

The player who trespasses against the rules or ignores them is a "spoil-sport." The spoil-sport is not the same as the false player, the cheat; for the latter pretends to be playing the game and, on the face of it, still acknowledges the magic circle. It is curious to note how much more lenient society is to the cheat than to the spoil-sport. This is because the spoil-sport shatters the play itself. . . . [H]e robs the play of its illusion.[11]

The belief that the spoilsport is worse than the cheater is supported by Bowyer, as he argues that cheating is a "normal" part of society or culture, present in most aspects of life. It begins early: "all the way from

Peek-a-boo to their card game of Cheat, children learn the principles of cheating."[12] And it pervades our world: "to be is to be cheated."[13] Bowyer also agrees that cheating is transgressive and alters the game being played to give power to the cheater; "to cheat, not to play the game that reflected the norm, indicated that there was another world, the world of deception, in which people did not play *the* game, *your* game, but their own."[14]

How does that relate to videogames? As long as there have been videogames, people have cheated while playing them. But now we arrive at the point where we must turn to players themselves, because only they can tell us what it means to cheat in a videogame.

Paratext

Before a videogame is ever released, communication and artifacts relating to it spring up like mushrooms, much of it (the noncommercial side at least) with little planning or overall design from the game's developers. Fans of a game series post updates to a blog, mailing list, or chat site. Previews of the game, including screen shots, trailers, and interviews with the developers, appear on television and in magazines. Slots for the game, to allow potential players to preorder it, are created on Amazon's and GameStop's Web sites. Rumors may fly. A strategy guide may go into production. Shelf space and advertising are secured.

Before a player loads a game on to a console or computer, the opportunities to learn about that game have become vast. And once a game is released, that steady stream of information becomes a flood. Reviews (both commercial and noncommercial), ads, cheat code releases, G4 TV specials, walkthroughs, discussion board topics on GameFAQs.com, and perhaps the opportunity to pay more real money to upgrade your game experience all appear.

In two decades, we have moved from a trickle to a torrent of information, and it all plays a role in shaping our experiences of gameplay—regardless of the actual game itself. Yet how can we make sense of such a system? This system isn't the game industry but is closely related to it. To call it peripheral dismisses or ignores its centrality to the gaming experience. Whether we admit it or not, we have learned how to play games, how to judge games, and how to think about games and ourselves as gamers in part through the shaping of these industries. How best to capture that system?

Writing originally about printed works and the surrounding materials that frame their consumption, Genette introduced the concept of the paratext.[15] He argued that the paratext, which could include a table of contents, a title, and a review (among many other things), all helped shape the reader's experience of a text. And centrally, the paratext helped give meaning to the act of reading.

Peter Lunenfeld later took that concept and applied it to digital media, writing that the boundaries now are even more fluid, and the paratexts are often more interesting than the "originary" texts.[16] I believe that the peripheral industries surrounding games function as just such a paratext. Gaming magazines, strategy guides, mod chip makers, the International Game Exchange, Even Balance and other companies, and industry segments work to shape the gameplay experience in particular ways. Those ways have played a significant role in how gameplay is now understood. Yet not all such shaping—or attempts to shape—went unchallenged, either by the game industry or the players themselves. I will explore that history throughout this book. The central tendency remains, though: the creation of a flourishing paratext has significantly shaped games and gamers in the process of creating new markets.

Book Structure and Chapter Preview

Part I: A Cultural History of Cheating in Games

Part I looks at the cultural history of cheating in videogames. It examines how the act began, from the desire of game designers to put in "Easter eggs" for players to find, to the implementation of cheat codes to help designers in constructing the game. The chapters in this part chronicle how those items migrated to several paratextual industries, such as game magazines, tip lines, and cheat books, to GameSharks and mod chips. The focus concerns how the packaging and selling of cheats was developed into a market, and how that market helped define particular modes of playing games that go beyond simple cheating. That growth also spurred the development of subindustries not working together with designers and publishers that actively pushed for player activity outside the bounds of what is deemed fair play. The part ends by asking how contemporary videogame players conceive of cheating: how do they define it in their own terms, and how do or don't they engage in those practices?

Chapter 1: Creating the Market: Easter Eggs and Secret Agents
This chapter chronicles the history of cheats, including how and why they appeared, and the types of things that they did. It explores how at first cheats were largely unmoored from the business of the game industry, even if they were a part of games. Cheats existed, but as insider knowledge among game creators and a few committed players. Initially, cheats were seen as having no place in a game. The chapter examines how and why that changed, and the beginning of a market for those cheats in early magazines such as *Nintendo Power*. It then argues that this magazine in particular helped institutionalize cheats and the act of cheating, normalizing it for the player, and turning it into an expected and profitable part of gaming for the player and the industry.

Chapter 2: Guidance Goes Independent: The Rise of the Strategy Guide Publishers
Chapter 2 goes beyond the early days of *Nintendo Power* to study how cheats and other game help moved outside Nintendo (and just game creators themselves) to create another fledgling industry. The analysis considers the development of print and electronic strategy guides, and explores the process of creating guides as well as the strength of publishers Brady and Prima. Additionally, the chapter discusses how such guides continued the function of teaching players how to play games, but also further developed stylistic approaches to offering guidance as well as conventions concerning what game-related items should and should not appear in guides. The contribution of these guides to the culture, and how their presence raised expectations for what is found in games, is detailed.

Chapter 3: Genies, Sharks, and Chips: The Technological Side to Cheating
Chapter 3 concludes with the backlash of the growing paratextual industry as against the core game industry itself. As gamers' appetite for more knowledge and help with games grew, so too the industry responded with products that the core industry objected to—items such as the GameShark (and earlier Game Genie) and mod chips to install (illegally by players) in PlayStations. The chapter explores how those items were received by gamers and the game industry, and how peripheral makers walk a fine line between legal and illegal, acceptable and unacceptable help for use in games. The chapter ends by asking how players themselves see those items in relation to their gaming activities.

Part II: Game Players

The second part of the book discusses the actual game players, and their views and behaviors relating to gameplay generally as well as cheating in particular. The chapters in this part focus on how players define cheating, what activities they engage in related to their stated definitions, and how those choices can be understood. Cheaters in online games are given special attention, from their evolving activities to their justifications for such actions. A study of the Massively Multiplayer Online (MMO) game *Final Fantasy XI* is undertaken to understand online cheating in context, and the responses of game developers and publishers—both positive and negative—to such actions are examined.

Chapter 4: Gaining Advantage: How Videogame Players Define and Negotiate Cheating

This chapter explores how different individuals actually play games, and how they draw from various sources available to help them play as well as have more fun (and occasionally cause trouble). It examines how players themselves differentially define cheating, and whether or not they engage in those activities and why. Through extensive interviews with game players of varying ages and ability levels, a typology of player activity in games is presented, thereby explaining the differences between how various individuals conceptualize the boundaries of the game and its related materials, such as walkthroughs and cheat codes. The key reasons for cheating (as well as not cheating) are also delineated. Ultimately, this chapter argues that players choose to cheat or not cheat in order to enhance their gameplay, and that cheating is a dynamic concept that cannot be easily defined or limited.

Chapter 5: The Cheaters

This chapter looks at the behaviors associated with online multiplayer games that most everyone considers cheating. These behaviors include practices such as hacking the code of a game for various purposes and gaming the system along with more debated practices such as griefing and the use of exploits. Are such behaviors the hallmark of a typical sort of player—the cheater—or more fluid behaviors that different players engage in at different times, for different reasons? Is the cheater an identifiable playing position, a personal identification, or something else? To investigate such questions, evidence is drawn from interviews with players that cheat as well as popular accounts of cheating and industry reactions toward it.

Chapter 6: Busting Punks and Policing Players: The Anticheating Industry
This chapter studies how different game-related companies have responded to cheating—including game developers and publishers as well as new businesses that have been created to combat cheating such as Even Balance and IT GlobalSecure. The chapter also examines how such practices work to define, stabilize, and secure specific definitions of cheating that occasionally may be at cross-purposes with each other as well as with player interests and activities.

Chapter 7: A Mage's Chronicle: Cheating and Life in Vana'diel
This chapter draws from an online ethnography of the MMO *Final Fantasy XI*. It provides a closer look at how cheating and its practices are debated and defined in an ongoing, dynamic manner. The chapter provides a detailed account of the design implications of a particular virtual world, and how such designs attempt to limit certain player activities in addition to allowing for others. I explore, through the eyes of my avatar Leiya, the gameplay and player activities on the Lakshmi server. Specific practices such as real-money trade, bot use, and power leveling are discussed in terms of design limitations as well as players' perceived knowledge of those activities and their own feelings about them. Player responses to those activities are also delineated and studied in order to better understand how players can help maintain game worlds that have agreed-on norms as well as systems for ensuring that such norms are adequately enforced.

Part III: Capital and Game Ethics

Chapter 8: Capitalizing on Paratexts: Gameplay, Ethics, and Everyday Life
The concluding chapter explores the growing corporatization of the para-textual industries, read through practices such as the 2005 purchase of the MMO-focused Allakhazam.com site by RPG Holdings, which also owns real-money trade giant International Game Exchange. Such practices

suggest that the paratext is gaining ground on the primary game industry, and thus the paratext becomes critical to consider as a way to understand gameplay as well as the business of digital games.

Additionally, this chapter brings together final thoughts on gaming capital and what cheating means for gameplay as well as digital life. How we use and think about digital games are expressions of ethical choices. Likewise, digital games are spaces for play and experimentation, and are systems with (perhaps) fewer consequences for actions taken there. How we use such spaces, experiment and play with them, and then relate that use elsewhere, is crucially important, and the subject of this last chapter.

Part I

A Cultural History of Cheating
in Games

CREATING THE MARKET: EASTER EGGS AND SECRET AGENTS

It all started with an Easter egg. Although game scholars and fans can debate the start of the digital game industry, or when it became truly established, the key occurrence that gave rise to the ever-expanding videogame market was Warren Robinett's secret inclusion of his name in flashing colors in the 1978 Atari 2600 game *Adventure*.

Upset that game programmers and designers did not receive publicity for the games they created, Robinett decided to take matters into his own hands. Given that he was designing and coding the game on his own, that wasn't much of a problem. Robinett created a secret room, and the key to it was a dot—"a single gray pixel in the center of a wall of the exact same color. If your cursor touched the single interactive dot on that non-interactive wall, it would indicate that you could pick it up."[1] If you picked up the dot and carried it to another location, it would open a chamber that led to the room where his name "filled the screen like a throbbing, multicolored movie marquee."[2] Robinett kept the secret of his special room from Atari executives and his friends until the game was in production. But soon enough, some players discovered the secret, and a new form of gameplay was born: the hunt for secret elements. Game secrets, and the industry that evolved to support them, began with that dot.

This chapter investigates the role of that first Easter egg, the rise of such items, and the emergence of game magazines as an integral part of the history of the game industry. Those elements helped create, structure, and maintain a loyal gamer market, and "produced" identifiable demographic niches for easy product promotion by the game industry. While later chapters consider such matters as player activities and beliefs, it's also important to examine the early industry actions that helped to shape what we now see as a range of acceptable as well as unacceptable player responses to games. Game magazines did important work in shaping later player expectations about games and gameplay. The revealing of secret rooms or god mode codes, along with reviews that taught readers how to tell a "good" game from a "bad" one, were key contributions of early game magazines, which demand critical analysis. Those efforts, explored in this chapter, provide an early snapshot of the formation and proliferation of gaming capital, and how such a system operates in more contemporary times.

In this chapter, I also bring in Genette's formulation and Lunenfeld's later development of the paratext.[3] The concept helps us understand how elements related to games became a central part of the industry, and also how game players were drawn into game culture through the cultivated desire to possess "gaming capital."

Gaming Capital

Bourdieu originally wrote of cultural capital and taste as helping to define "the systems of dispositions (habitus) characteristic of the different classes and class fractions. Taste classifies, and it classifies the classifier."[4] Going beyond Bourdieu's high/low divisions, other researchers have explored how cultural capital is gained, expressed, and used to delineate identities and groups in relation to popular media and everyday life.[5] Along those lines, I have reworked the term into gaming capital, as mentioned earlier, to capture how being a member of game culture is about more than playing games or even playing them well.[6] It's being knowledgeable about game releases and secrets, and passing that information on to others. It's having opinions about which game magazines are better and the best sites for walkthroughs on the Internet. Easter eggs gave rise to some of the earliest gaming capital, and one role of game magazines was to push the envelope about what could be considered part of gaming capital. In the following sections I'll look at the rise of each phenomena, and analyze how each form helped shape the larger game industry as a paratext, ultimately codifying what is now considered to be obvious knowledge for gaming capital.

Cooking the Egg: Shaping the Industry

The first Easter egg was a useless hidden bonus. It didn't give you an extra life or allow you to change your appearance. It was just there, waiting to be found; nothing bad would happen if you never found it. How could such a simple dot, and a hidden room with a flashing name, change the industry? That dot and other such elements were originally inserted into games in secret, to either communicate something to the player, get back at management, or both.

Although many early eggs were largely ornamental—designed for display rather than being functional to gameplay—they began to pop up in various places. In addition to Robinett's original egg, other programmers inserted their names or initials into games such as the Atari ports of *Missile Command* and *Defender*, and the original Atari game *Raiders of the Lost Ark*.[7] Taking the secrets to another level, games such as *Space Invaders* allowed the player to "hold down the reset button while powering up the game" to get a double shooter, while other games gave extra lives or similarly enhanced powers for pressing the right key combinations either on start up or while playing the games.[8] So already a rough taxonomy of eggs began to appear, as designers went beyond the decorative to the functional in egg design and placement. While functional eggs have since branched off to become more aligned with cheat codes and other functional gaming "enhancements," purely decorative eggs still appear in games, either as stand-alone items or rooms to discover, or as found abilities that do little or nothing to gain advantage in gameplay, except increase enjoyment. Players now may ride bicycles around town in *Crazy Taxi* rather than cars, or they may launch cows from catapults (rather than explosives) in *Age of Empires*.

Yet in addition to the decorative and functional eggs, game developers have also inserted eggs that attempt to make a larger statement about the game itself or the game industry, but only on rare occasions. One of the most famous is the inclusion of "muscular bikini-clad men" that would appear on certain days and kiss each other in the Maxis game *SimCopter*.[9] Programmer Jacques Servin inserted the figures to make a fun statement about the lack of gay images in games. Designers before and since then have mostly stuck to less inflammatory content for players to seek out or stumble on, with part of the challenge being getting it past company management and testers, and part being creativity in its design and execution.[10] Whatever the reason for its design and whatever the function of the egg, players have taken up the challenge of finding those game elements, often taking pleasure in being the first to discover them in new games and proudly noting their discovery in public.

The enthusiastic drive by players to find such items caused the game industry to pause and take notice; the inclusion of such items could drive the popularity (and playtime) of a game, and perhaps its sales. But in the beginning, there was no real way for players to find out about such elements other than word of mouth.

That seemed to be the way that most information about games spread in the early 1980s. No organized and established game press existed, let alone Web or online space, for players to find unbiased information about games other than the marketing information found on the game box.[11] How could players find out if a game was great or a dud? What would even define what great or dud meant? And as playing a game is an interactive experience, what if players got stuck along the way? What or who could help them out, other than perhaps a friend who happened to be playing the same game? The Easter egg and its eager reception set the stage for a paratextual industry to spring up, to alert players about what to look for in games, help them through the games, and in the process, shape and stabilize a game market that would need assistance after the crash of the industry in the early 1980s.

What came out of this industry was a clearer picture of what the "ideal" gamer should know and expect from games. That player was then groomed by the industry, encouraged to identify as a power gamer or a member of the gaming elite because of their expertise in gaming and knowledge of everything related to games. That knowledge was a basis for gaming capital, and Easter eggs, secret information, strategy tips, and the latest news all formed the basis of this new form of capital, marketed and sold to a growing audience of (mostly) adolescent boys. One key element of that paratextual system was game magazines.

Games and Paratext

Various media theorists have attempted to explain the relationship between a primary text and those peripherally related to it—such as a television show, its reviews, cast profiles, promos airing before a new episode, and the like. Is the division between these different texts useful? How do they work to sustain each other? John Fiske argues that as part of actively reading or viewing a text, individuals readily draw meanings from these related or intertextual forms, and oftentimes the primary texts themselves draw from prior media culture, such as when *South Park* mocks *The Passion of the Christ,* or when William Shatner is replaced as Priceline spokesperson by his old friend Leonard Nimoy.[12] But the concept of inter-textuality does not adequately account for the system-as-a-whole that can result, as it frequently refers to media relations at the broadest possible level—often searching for breadth rather than depth.

A better way to think about the game industry and the texts (and the industries) that surround it is through Genette's conceptualization of the paratext, which constitutes all of the elements surrounding a text that help structure it and give it meaning. Although for Genette paratext is mainly textual and in the service of singular printed works, his arguments about its significance to the central text can also be adapted to signify and explain larger sets of paratexts. Genette believes that such paratexts are more adaptable than the original text referenced, and can ultimately become critical to the success or failure of the primary source. He writes that

the paratext provides an airlock that helps the reader pass without too much respiratory difficulty from one world to the other, a sometimes delicate operation, especially when the second world is a fictional one. Being immutable, the text in itself is incapable of adapting to changes in its public in space and over time. The paratext—more flexible, more versatile, always transitory because transitive—is, as it were, an instrument of adaptation.[13]

Although games are not immutable in the sense that there is only one way to play them, they can be more static and fixed than their surround-ing discourse. And that discourse is much easier to change, amend, update, or retract than even a patch—arguably a paratext itself—to a computer game. Lunenfeld takes the concept one step further, maintaining that in the contemporary media universe, "it is impossible to distinguish it [the paratext] and the text. . . . [W]ho is to say where packaging begins and ends in a medium in which everything is composed of the same streams of data?"[14] Lunenfeld contends that digital media are perhaps the best at this collapsing of text and paratext, and we are in an age where the backstory to the creation of objects is often more interesting than the texts themselves.

What might have begun as the peripheral aspects of the game industry (magazines, strategy guides, and so on) can now be recognized as such a paratext quite easily. The hype surrounding the release of id Software's first-person shooter *Doom 3* might have eclipsed the actual game for some fans, and certainly, the interest in the ill-fated shooting game *Daikatana* was far more robust than the eventual release. Centrally then, a significant piece of gaming capital has become knowledge of the paratext itself. Knowledge of release dates and secret codes may have nothing to do with actual gameplay itself—but that doesn't really matter, if the paratext and text are now functioning as an interrelated unit.

In addition to seeing magazines and guides as aspects of the paratext, they serve a specific role in gaming culture and for gaming capital: they instruct the player in how to play, what to play, and what is cool (and not) in the game world. In that way, they function much like teen or women's magazines do, instructing the reader in "how to" achieve a certain role or look. Feminist critics of *Seventeen* and *Glamour* argue that such magazines play an ideological role in teaching readers what the important parts of life are: looking good, getting a guy, and being successful at work.[15] Although these periodicals offer different levels of sophistication, their role is the same: selling readers products, based on creating needs that are carefully cultivated.

Gaming magazines, when viewed through this prism, function in the same way. They tell interested readers what the best games are, and why they are the best. They imply that readers need to be constantly buying games, or else they will miss out on these wonderful advances and milestones in gaming history. They also create an average or perhaps ideal gamer that is young, male, and heterosexual, with plenty of disposable cash. Although the end result is the production of a gamer, the person who is hailed successfully by this discourse has been taught "how to be a gamer" just as well as women are taught "how to be feminine" by women's magazines. Of course, actual reader interpretations will vary, given the role of active audiences, but the pedagogical functions of these types of magazines are not far apart at all.

The Rise of *Nintendo Power*

One of the earliest developed peripheral industries that supported the sale and use of digital games was the print magazine industry. Although home game consoles were commercially popular in the late 1970s, it wasn't until 1981 that the first dedicated videogame magazines appeared—*Electronic Games* in the United States, and *Computer & Video Games* in the United Kingdom. Over the next few years similar publications started up across the United States and Europe, but many folded after the industry crash of 1983, and it wasn't until the end of the decade that the magazine industry began to successfully exploit as well as stabilize and shape an identifiable game market niche: the power gamer.[16]

Several game magazines of the time contributed to this creation, with *Nintendo Power* and *Electronic Gaming Monthly* as two of the longest running of those publications.[17] Each magazine had its own style of production, and the approach and ownership of the two—the first targeting Nintendo products by Nintendo versus the second, which offered a multiplatform focus from an independent publisher (Sendai Publishing Group)—markedly differed, even though the larger result was essentially the same. Both magazines helped contribute to a growing culture of gaming, creating a space for game players to learn about upcoming titles, read reviews, and gain strategy tips and hints for the games they had just bought. The particular way that this was done differed with each magazine, but *Nintendo Power*'s approach, its particular offering to readers of game capital that could be easily grasped through a careful reading of the magazine, and the opportunity to flaunt that capital in various ways set it apart from the rest on the rack.

Nintendo's first efforts at publishing started with a free newsletter for its console owners that covered Nintendo-produced or licensed products exclusively. Related publications such as *Electronic Gaming Monthly* faced a more difficult task, as during the late 1980s there was little competition for the Nintendo Entertainment System (NES), and so an insider's publication had a much greater edge. Once competing console systems did appear, there were soon so many of them that coverage of each (and its games) was by necessity fragmented, and the game player was likely as confused as *Electronic Gaming Monthly* editors sometimes were about the future of the industry.[18]

Electronic Gaming Monthly and similar game magazines of that time period labored to create an image of games as "cool," in response to first Sega's and then the larger console industry's push to market "up" in age and reach individuals with greater amounts of disposable income.[19] Yet no other successful commercial publication went to the lengths that Nintendo did to solicit reader input, and make readers feel as if they were contributing to the magazine and the game culture, rather than simply reading about the newest games.

Fun Club News *Turns Powerful*

After the game market crash in the United States, Nintendo approached the market cautiously. With a successful launch in Japan, the Famicom was revamped and released in the United States in 1986 as the NES, and quickly became a best seller.[20] Yet Nintendo's success did not rest solely with its ability to make a sophisticated console or quality games. It also strategically created a publication that stood out for what a magazine could do to help construct a market, shape player expectations for gameplay and game help, and continuously use this information to strengthen the position of the major industry contender at that time.

Nintendo Power magazine began publishing in 1988, but was actually the successor to the earlier free quarterly *Nintendo Fun Club News*. The *News* started as a twelve-page publication in 1987, yet kept growing due to game player requests for more game news and hints. Keen to capitalize on that demand, Nintendo turned the *News* into a subscription-based magazine.[21]

The magazine was initially offered six times a year, with strategy guides alternating the regular, general-format magazine. Subscriptions were $15 per year, and by 1989, more than one million people had subscribed.[22] A year later, the magazine claimed that more than six million people read the periodical each month.[23]

Critics have derided the magazine for being nothing more than a promotional tool for Nintendo, which it largely was, as the magazine did not run advertising, and heavily promoted new and future Nintendo games and systems as "the best" that was out there; negative reviews were nonexistent. Yet through the various feedback elements that were constructed, the magazine also worked to establish a community of players that could both gain gaming capital and display it, either nationally in the magazine or more locally through friendship circles. Whichever route a player took, *Nintendo Power* was there to guide and shape expectations about the proper gaming capital, and the proper way to play (and win) videogames.

Nintendo's magazine functioned in ways that independent magazines could not as well as in the traditional ways—as a promotional tool to sell games and next-generation systems, a source of free or subsidized player feedback, and a way to keep game licensees in line (with the promise of game coverage or the threat of withholding it).[24] It created an enclosed space for readers to inhabit, where Nintendo was the only console around, and all the games coming out were the "best and most exciting" to ever be released.

That space helped to stabilize the game market, providing a ready feedback circuit for game players to give their preferences as well as offer them room to "claim ownership" (if only in a small way), and develop and display the cultural capital on offer in the magazine.

Learning How to Play

In its early days, *Nintendo Power* magazine was a young game players' delight. It featured interesting and varied graphics, extensive details on how to play games and beat them, and news about the latest games to be released for the various Nintendo systems. Although such magazines seem commonplace today, at the time *Nintendo Power* stood out for its unified message: teaching players how to be the best around. Doing so meant loyal readers, and more important, loyal Nintendo game and hardware buyers.

Rather than assess the features of various games, the magazine gave its prime coverage to games it had already deemed "great" and spent its time instructing readers in the best ways to play them. That approach is more akin to what strategy guides now do, but at the time, facing a young audience and a relatively new medium, the approach worked extremely well in teaching players how to play and what to expect from a game (as well as magazines) as a "good" experience.

Game coverage during the early years of *Nintendo Power* was usually dedicated to three or four high-profile games each month. These games would receive between six to twenty pages of coverage, which could also extend to a pullout map or poster featuring additional maps or game visuals. Each game "guide" functioned largely as a mini–strategy guide—explaining the basic story and character information to the player, showing pictures of helpful movements or items to collect or avoid, and displaying monsters that would appear throughout the game. These guides varied widely in their stylistic designs, but each game had a consistent design template for its particular section of an issue. So, for example, the design of *Mega Man III* might be a futuristic space motif, while the design for *Little Nemo* had graphics and a layout suggesting bedtime (moon, stars, a bed, and so forth), and a more childlike atmosphere.

By making the guide for each game distinct, the magazine could reinforce a sense of each game as a consistent, unique world unto itself. It also helped construct such worlds in the game player's imagination, as game graphics in the late 1980s and early 1990s were quite limited. Oftentimes screen shots in the magazine were enlarged, with certain items in them depicted separately in a drawn graphic to better show the player what one could expect when facing the television screen and its tiny pixels.

In addition to being colorful and consistent, guides were oriented toward getting a player through a game from beginning to end, but although the pages provide a linear progression through the various levels of a game, the information was provided in easily digestible (or searchable) "chunks" rather than a narrative, with a few exceptions. So the reader could learn that "bees hate to bathe" when reading about *Little Nemo: The Dream Master*, and further discover that "you can't get any farther than the third big pond as the Bee. As Nemo, take a swim to find a secret passage deep underwater that will take you to the end."[25] By doing that, *Nintendo Power* could help the player who did not wish to follow the guide from beginning to end but might only need help at one particular moment or section.

Likewise, the design emphasized several key elements, with the depth of focus depending on how many pages were allotted to the game. A game such as *Super Mario Bros. 2* featured many pages of coverage, and included elements I term warm-ups, maps, single-panel lift-out screens, screen series, and enhanced graphics. The warm-ups provided the reader with some basic information about the game: the key characters to control, including their strengths and weaknesses, some important items, and a preview of early bosses and monsters. While such information was not critical to helping a player improve, it did supply the curious player with additional facts about the game, which could be used to a player's advantage as gaming capital in later conversations with friends.

The more crucial elements of the guides were the maps and lift-out screens that explained various aspects of gameplay. Generally, a series of maps showed how the scrolling world looked in its entirety—a view that the player facing the television screen never got to see. Furthermore, that map provided the central keys to finding significant items, the locations of monsters, and "secret hints." It was here that the guide proved its worth for the player, as access to the extra or bonus elements of the game were revealed. Lift-out screens detailed where to find hidden doors or entrances, or could also be used to better illustrate the key item being obtained, as often they were hidden from view. While a nonguide reader may have chosen not to seek out the hidden materials most players already suspected were in the game, the guide reader was confronted with that information almost as a challenge—it was right there; why not go after it? And in gaining the knowledge of where the secrets were, the player could achieve a higher level of credibility in the (wider) gaming community.

Likewise, the strategies offered for how to deal with various challenging monsters and terrain provided the player with critical knowledge—not just to complete the game but to tell others how to complete the game. And if the player chose not to finish or go much further in the game, reading about what comes next could keep the player in the loop with friends who played (much like readers of *Soap Opera Digest* can keep current on missed episodes and still talk about a series with their friends). Many of these strategies were detailed in the screen series that were ubiquitous throughout the guides, boxed off from larger maps. Consisting of two to three screen shots showing an action and the result of that action, they functioned as a time series analysis of the strategy offered by the guide—attempting to show dynamic procedures through a static medium. So, for example, these sequences show readers how to "escape from Phanto" or some other monster, or how to "use bombs effectively" if players haven't already figured out how to do so. If they have, the tip provided a different sort of information for the reader: confirmation that one was already in the know or on the right track, and did not need complete hand-holding throughout gameplay.

In addition to detailing how to get through specific games, the guides offered more general instructions for readers on how to play digital games in the abstract. Again, as these may have been newer players, their knowledge of such a medium was likely limited (and if not, they got to feel superior), and so while guiding the player through the game, the magazine also taught players how to play generally, what to expect from a game, and how to evaluate games.

For instance, the guides were faithful in pointing out the differences between regular monsters and "big bosses." Players learned that bosses generally appeared at the end of each level, and the biggest boss awaited the player at the end of the game. Similarly, and consistent with this, gameplay in the game got gradually harder. The text above early screens and maps for games often reminded players "the first area will be easy to win." The implication (and later warnings) let the player know that later areas were moderate to difficult to complete. Yet the later parts of guides always encouraged players to keep going: "the World of Deserts seems extremely difficult when you are not used to it. . . . However, the jars are closer together, the quicksand is faster, and you have a smaller area to move around in."[26]

Players thus learned that gameplay should progress from easy to difficult, and with diligence (and perhaps help) they should be able to beat any game. The player was frequently reminded that exploration, persistence, and strategizing were essential to succeed in the given game. Still, these challenges were presented as exciting obstacles to be overcome—not work to be slogged through. Guides walked a fine line in convincing players that the activity should be fun—not a chore. And the guides also (worked to) help keep the games fun, which was one of their essential functions. For if a particular element of gameplay became too difficult, players may have given up in frustration and complained about the game to others.

If the game guides were not enough help, the player could also consult the "Counselor's Corner" later in the magazine, where players asked specific questions about how to proceed in a tough situation. For example, questions about the game *Maniac Mansion* included "How do I open the safe?" "How do I send the demo tape or manuscript to the publishing company?" and "How do I call the meteor police?"[27]

Additionally, later game guides, such as one for *Castlevania III*, introduced the idea of different paths through the game for players of differing abilities. Segmented as "apprentices," "devotees," and "masters," the guide advised players on routes of varying difficulty and length how to reach Dracula's castle, although all players had to engage in the boss battle at the end with Dracula himself. This segmentation worked to carefully allow readers to "choose their own adventure" through the maze of caves and dungeons, and did so in a way that was adaptable to their own playing level. It avoided categorizing less skilled players as newbies (or any other potentially derogatory term), but if newbies were so inclined, they may have attempted the more difficult route anyway, because the strategy hints were already in place. The guide also alerted players to the fact that there were multiple paths through the game, and those paths varied in difficulty. But more important, the magazine made visible a key activity: delineating the varying skill sets of players, and carefully playing to each of these groups. In doing so, it also kept the replayability of the game high; apprentices who successfully completed the route may have been encouraged to replay the game, first exploring the devotee route and finally progressing to the master level.

The magazine also subtly encouraged the reader to categorize and therefore separate different types of information or help regarding games. So the guides for games contained the location of secret items, and maps and strategies for getting through the game, but they did *not* include any cheat codes for altering game options or outcomes. That information was presented separately, in either the "Counselor's Corner" or more likely the "Classified Information" section. It was here that the player could find out that in many Konami games, the "Konami Code strikes again."[28] The player was advised that after pausing the game, one could press "up, up, down, down, left, right, left and right on the control pad. Next press the B button and the A button. Your Energy Meter will fill up to maximum! Use the code wisely. You'll be able to Power-Up only once per game."[29] While the Konami Code was one of the best-known secrets in gaming, that sort of information was what could commonly be found in the "Classified Information" section of *Nintendo Power*.

What's especially noteworthy is the separation of that information from the larger review. The codes were created during the game production process by the developers and could have easily been included in the game's original guide. But their placement in later issues of the magazine helped keep interest in the game strong; players already finished or perhaps just struggling with the game had a renewed reason to pick it back up.

Moreover, the idea that players could participate in (and be rewarded for) helping find the secrets of games likely kept readers interested in looking for such secrets themselves, in hopes of having their own "Secret Agent" byline within the "Classified Information" section of the magazine.[30] Whether *Nintendo Power* actually used readers as Secret Agents isn't really relevant; the idea that they might be doing so helped readers believe in their importance, and the addition of a separate section devoted to reader knowledge gave the magazine further credibility.

Yet regardless of the actual or stated reasons, the separation of codes and additional secret information from the flagship review established that such information was actually peripheral to the central gameplay experience. It was certainly legitimate—legitimized by its inclusion in the magazine—but it was set apart from regular gameplay. And while regular gameplay demanded knowledge of strategy as well as the multiple game paths and bonus/secret objects, codes were constructed as discursively apart—an addendum or even superbonus part of gameplay, but not the core of the experience.

In doing so, *Nintendo Power* tried to shape players' expectations about the elements of core gameplay, and what exceeded those bounds. The codes found in "Classified Information," and now other places, might exist, but they were not the equivalent or equal of the sanctioned methods for gameplay. They were a central part of gaming capital, but for actual gameplay, players could choose whether to incorporate their use or not.

What's a Good Game? Nintendo Power *Can Tell You*

In addition to instructing players in how to play games, the magazine also instructed readers in what made a game great. Ratings for individual games were absent from the first issues of *Nintendo Power* but appeared in 1991, when a feature titled "Power to the Player" explained how games were rated by the magazine and how players could best use those ratings in choosing different games. For example, the article noted that there were eight original measures by which a game was judged, and these were condensed into four ratings that appeared next to games: graphics and sound; play control; challenge and lasting interest; and theme and fun.[31]

The inclusion and resulting codification of components or segments of games that could be individually evaluated and rated worked to create for readers a tangible system for comparing games, and ultimately making purchases (or not). The magazine thus helped create the illusion that games *could* be divided up into discrete parts available for individual analysis—teaching readers that while the graphics and sound might be poor, for example, the story and play control of a game might be superb. While the magazine argued that the player was left to decide which rating elements to ignore and which to attend to, the simple presence of the ratings helped set in place a rubric for evaluating games and a value system for determining just what was worthy of an evaluation or not; so, for instance, violence is not a measure, nor is the complexity of the game's artificial intelligence in a particular game.

Finally, the presence or absence of game coverage in *Nintendo Power* implied in itself a rating. Games deemed average or poor never even appeared on the pages of the magazine, except perhaps in the "now showing" or preview sections, as a small blurb and a screen shot or two. Thus, a two-layered value system was installed: *Nintendo Power* deciding which games were above a certain baseline competence, and then a review system to help readers "figure out" which games of those in the magazine they might prefer.

The magazine reinforced those lessons in quality through other reoccurring features, such as the annual game awards that asked readers to vote for, and then later read about, the winners in such categories as the best graphics and sound, challenge, theme and fun, play control, and the like, which are (of course) identical to the magazine's own game-rating elements. Finally, a player could get her name in the magazine for doing well at another feature of each game—either a high score or game completion. Each issue, lists of the players achieving high scores for various games were run, and readers were encouraged to submit their own scores, after properly recording it with a camera with the flash turned off. Although not explicitly portrayed as a "best" category, the potential recognition coming from achieving a high score likely had the same effect in conveying to readers the importance of mastering or completing a game.

Nintendo Power's *Inclusion of Reader Input*

Part of the value of having gaming capital is being able to display it. While reader contributions to mass-market magazines are always controlled, *Nintendo Power* did manage to create in readers the sense that they were more than mere fans or readers; they were actively taking part in game culture, gaining and displaying their own growing gaming capital. To that end, *Nintendo Power* offered readers several ways to contribute to the magazine, directly as well as indirectly. The most straightforward of these elements included a letters section ("Player's Pulse"), a scoreboard ("NES Achievers"), and running tabulations for the "Player's Poll," which was a way to win prizes for answering marketing questions.

Yet similar elements could be found in most game magazines, including in *Electronic Gaming Monthly*, at that time as well. Where *Nintendo Power* stood out, and where its creation of a game culture really began, was in elements such as "Classified Information." Each issue, several pages of the magazine were devoted to "secret" information about various games, such as ways to get more lives for a character or secret areas to locate. The information was (allegedly) provided not by the magazine but by Special Agents, who were identified only by a three-number code (such as Agent #333). Readers of the magazine were invited to become Special Agents, and write in and share their tips and strategies for the games they were playing. By doing so, they not only gave free content to the magazine but also participated in creating the magazine and the knowledge it conveyed to readers.

The construction of the game player with knowledge as a Special Agent gave players in the know a piece of gaming capital—as someone who was a good enough player to be published in a major magazine. That information then became important to know if one wanted to be thought of as a "power gamer," and reading *Nintendo Power* became a way to gain that knowledge as well as have your status as a knower confirmed.[32]

Nintendo Power also kept close tabs on its readers through the regular "Counselor's Corner" section, which provided questions about difficult parts of various games along with detailed answers. In the beginning years of the magazine, the section also included counselor profiles, which contained pictures and brief biographies of four counselors working for *Nintendo Power* at the time. That personalization probably encouraged avid readers to imagine their own futures as game counselors, as most of the workers appeared to be only slightly past high school.

Nintendo Power was building and shaping a market for Nintendo's games and game hardware. It saw the value in (carefully) revealing game secrets, and paying attention to player questions and complaints. But its influence went much further by defining game culture generally. Such early elements as its game guides, "Classified Information," and "Counselor's Corner" (among many others) worked together to help create a game player who possessed critical pieces of gaming capital: the player knew about the newest soon-to-be-released games and their general content; what advances were coming in game hardware; how high a high score should be in order to be impressive; what secret codes and tricks could be used in the latest games; why such elements as controls and graphics were important; and how to play and finish specific games. That power gamer would become the ideal consumer of games and game magazines, and has shaped how the game industry has responded.

The Evolution of Nintendo Power

Over the years *Nintendo Power* has freshened its look, but many elements remain largely the same. One notable difference is the presence of outside advertising for games that the magazine does not choose to provide a guide for or review. Many of the ads are for multiplatform games, with the design and marketing for the game coming from the game publisher, rather than the editorial office of *Nintendo Power*. While readership for the magazine is still strong, the addition of a new revenue stream makes it a more solid financial risk for Nintendo, which is seeing more competition now than ever before.[33]

When looking through the pages of a 2002 issue, what is readily apparent is how much *Nintendo Power* has *not* changed, especially in comparison with earlier peer gaming magazines. While the average age of an *Electronic Gaming Monthly* reader has risen, *Nintendo Power* sits squarely in the youth demographic. That could be due to Nintendo's continued strength in attracting younger players through more family-friendly content for its consoles and handhelds, but part of it is likely strategic as well.[34] Although the reviews are more savvy than in the past, and the "Classified Information" section no longer invites readers to write in and become a Secret Agent, the tone of the magazine still caters to the younger game player. But with more gaming magazines appearing to clutter the racks, *Nintendo Power* can at least stand out with a clear focus as a subniche publication.

While most other magazines are no longer carrying the in-depth, didactic guides that instruct the reader in how to play, *Nintendo Power* still takes up that role. The magazine now also runs negative reviews of games, although these games are not given extensive coverage, and the criticisms are fairly tame compared to other reviews found on the Internet or in similar mainstream publications. And although volume 170 featured a detailed review of *Enter the Matrix*, it still extolled the game, seemingly unaware of the rest of the gaming community's overwhelmingly negative reaction to the game.[35]

Nintendo Power has continued to modify its content to stay current, yet it has shrunk in influence in the game magazine market. Yet what is most important is the early start *Nintendo Power* gave to the game industry in sustaining a readership of millions, and creating in that audience an expectation for certain types of knowledge: not only previews and reviews of games but detailed strategies and help for troublesome parts of games, including lavish pictures, intricate maps, and secret codes. That knowledge and that audience were successfully transferred to another growing area of the peripherals industry: the strategy guide segment. Nevertheless, *Nintendo Power* isn't the only successful videogame magazine being published, and other periodicals have also helped to contribute to the creation of gaming capital.

Game Magazines Today: More Than Just Fanboy Publications?

Electronic Gaming Monthly in particular stands out as one of the longest-running, successful multiplatform videogame magazines still in publication. It also began in the late 1980s, and has continued to do well in circulation, growing to approximately six hundred thousand copies sold per month.[36] It too has evolved over time, even more so than *Nintendo Power*. During its early years of publication, *Electronic Gaming Monthly* also solicited the younger game player (the central demographic at that time), running previews and reviews of games, including reader letters, detailed strategy sections, and cheats and tricks for recently released games.

Yet the early period of the game industry almost seemed to conspire to ruin such magazines. While *Nintendo Power* suffered from no shortage of focus, it could be criticized for being simply a mouthpiece for Nintendo. *Electronic Gaming Monthly* was independent, but that meant being an outsider to (and second in line behind) official magazines that might get information about games and new systems first. *Electronic Gaming Monthly* attempted to distinguish itself by touting its unbiased and independent reviews of games as well as its comprehensive coverage of the console industry. At some points, however, that comprehensiveness was more likely a curse than a blessing. For example, in the May 1992 issue, the game consoles with games to be reviewed included the Super Nintendo Entertainment System (SNES), the NES, Sega Genesis, Nintendo Game Boy, TurboGrafx 16, GameGear, Atari Lynx, Neo Geo, the Sega Master System, and the JVC Wonder Mega (on sale in Japan). The coverage might touch each system, but it was thinner overall by necessity.

As the console industry has consolidated, so too has magazine coverage. Multiplatform games also make reviews and previews a more manageable task, with occasional exclusives (such as *Grand Theft Auto III*'s initial release for the PlayStation 2) making larger news. Over time, though, *Electronic Gaming Monthly* has reconfigured what it considers proper gaming capital, with an older, more affluent demographic in mind—and one that is increasingly online as well. Strategy sections are largely gone, and tricks and codes were for a time relegated to the back of the magazine, but now are absent from its pages entirely.[37] More emphasis is placed on profiling the development of particular games, multireviews of games, and entertaining information about the game industry and its personalities.

That shift has been largely echoed in the wider game magazine industry, although now magazines have been forced to slice up the sections of the game-playing demographic into smaller pieces. In addition to focusing on one platform, being independent or official, or adding computer games or not, magazines now go after different age demographics as well. And growing industry consolidation allows corporations to easily slice and dice markets to reuse product and workers as necessary, but with careful modification for each individual market.

For example, IDG Entertainment owns both *GamePro* and *Code Vault*, magazines that target the "core gamer," who accounts for $4.5 billion of the $7.1 billion spent yearly on video and personal computer (PC) software sales.[38] *GamePro* claims a readership of three million gamers per month with a rate base of a half million copies sold monthly. Of its readers, 43 percent are sixteen and under, and 57 percent are seventeen and older. *Code Vault* has a smaller rate base of only three hundred thousand copies bimonthly, yet delivers the young gamer—the average reader is fourteen years old. But both demographics are easily reachable for advertisers, who can choose package deals by advertising in both *GamePro* and *Code Vault*, or receive even greater synergy by also placing ads on the gamepro.com Web site.[39]

Other synergies appear within publishing houses as well. For example, *Electronic Gaming Monthly* often includes game reviews by staffers from sister publications owned by Ziff Davis, such as *Official PlayStation Magazine*, *GMR*, and *Xbox Nation*.[40] Finally, other publications such as *Game Informer* attempt to position themselves not only as competitive with other gaming publications but also as a men's general-interest periodical, due to their overwhelmingly male readership. In doing so, they cross over fairly successfully, as *Game Informer* has a rate base of 1.6 million, compared to *Maxim*'s 2.5 million or *Stuff*'s 1.2 million.[41]

Beyond their growing circulations and competitive differences, though, game magazines overall perform important functions for the larger game industry. For instance, most game magazines have an overwhelmingly male readership, usually in the 90 to 95 percent range.[42] That readership is also considered the central core of game purchasers—they regularly buy more console games and spend more money than most other demographic groups.[43] Magazine publishers know that, and play to that demographic above all else—making self-comparisons to *Maxim* not really all that surprising. What results is a product that excludes almost as much as it includes, in part to help define such a small segment of society. That naming of a group also helps define gaming capital—and who is likely to want or possess it. Those excluded by magazines' address are also more likely to be excluded from wanting or possessing gaming capital. It's not intentional; it's a by-product of the system.

And finally, the larger magazine industry, faced with more game releases and branded titles to cover, makes decisions about how and what to cover, and what to exclude. Since only so many pages exist for coverage, what should be included? Console makers already have high standards for console games to be released, yet not all get reviewed or even mentioned in game magazines. Decisions about what to give featured reviews to, what to preview and what to ignore, although usually made on a case-by-case basis at each magazine, tend to look increasingly similar over time. Which magazine didn't have a review of *Grand Theft Auto: San Andreas?* Which could afford to ignore it? But by including some, others are left out, and they gradually disappear from the larger gaming culture if no other outlet exists for bringing them to players' attention.

Prior to the establishment of game magazines and their information, where could game players or potential game players go for information about the newest, best, and worst games? Before magazines, the choices were severely limited—either reading the back of a game box, or asking friends or store clerks. Clearly, game magazines filled a need, and for both sides of the industry—publishers as well as players. Magazines were a way for publishers to promote new titles and reach potential consumers, while readers found a space to learn about new games in development, read reviews of recently released games, and increasingly, learn about strategies (or get tips or cheat codes) for enhanced play of their newly purchased games.

In providing these services, magazines walked a fine line, and many have been derided as nothing more than either public relations rags for the game industry or fanboy publications that lack serious journalism. Both charges contain some truth, although that doesn't seem to decrease the sales of magazines, at least from the current demographic targeted (but an absence of interest from other potential reader groups could be likely). Although women's magazines have long been derided as the cash cows of the publishing industry, blatantly exchanging editorial copy for advertising dollars, gaming magazines really have no better record. And like women's magazines, they suffer from the same charge from the wider publishing world of a lack of seriousness.

Despite these problems, however, game magazines have succeeded in several key regards: focusing on building and nurturing a key game-playing demographic niche, and shaping expectations about not only what to look for when purchasing a game but what kind of experience one should have when *playing* that game, and how to go about achieving it. Just as game magazines promote new games on the basis of graphic excellence, intricate story lines, balanced gameplay, and relations to previous games, they have also shaped how players envision the process of playing a game, how difficult that experience should be, and what types of guidance are acceptable (or not) when playing. Such information is critical, for as Espen Aarseth reminds us, games are ergodic texts, requiring "non-trivial effort" to play.[44] It is inevitable that players will experience difficulties—get stuck, confused, lost, or just stumped—when playing a game. How much time must players spend wandering fruitlessly on their own before they ask for help? What kind of help should they get? And where should they seek it? Game magazines have provided a primer that shapes how players answer these questions.

Conclusions

The first Easter egg in a videogame was a cheat as well—the game developer cheated the company by taking his paid time to do something he knew it would have forbidden. And throughout the history of games, game developers have always walked a fine line, trying to keep publishers and potential censors happy, yet at the same time trying to cheat the system by installing their own secret rooms and surprises. That the capitalist mode of production should incorporate and commodify those efforts is not even ironic anymore; it's expected.

But the businesses that rose up to teach players about these secrets and how to play games also participated in the creation of a lively paratext that has become nearly indistinguishable from the core game development industry. And these industries function in a yin-yang interdependence (as I write this, E3 is running, which is probably the largest, loudest, over-the-top paratext for games yet devised). These groups have grown together, adding elements to games that can be promoted and exploited by gamers through the proper consultation of various paratexts. To do so, the game industry had to market that information as a form of gaming capital, which the power gamer would possess and lesser players would lack. But in being so successful, two interesting contradictions arose.

First, although possessing gaming capital is supposed to be about game players' superior playing abilities and knowledge about games, it is often through the consumption of paratexts—not actual games—this knowledge can be gained. A players' knowledge of the latest graphic enhancements, secret codes, and sequel release dates is the main currency of gaming capital, and that information is drawn from the paratext rather than the primary text. Indeed, gaming capital is paratextual itself, and all of these elements have fused, becoming indistinguishable from actual game-playing ability.

Second, the mark of the power or cool gamer often means a repudiation of help in game playing. As the next chapter demonstrates, for example, strategy guide publishers have always experienced their strongest sales with segments of the market that are *not* the hard core—these players treat guides disdainfully, as for those lesser beings who actually need help. That is likely a reason for the gradual shift in focus of game magazines from extended strategy sections to news, commentary, and extended reviews and previews of games. This information does not suggest the need for help but does still (subtly) instruct the reader on what the newest enhancements are, and what they "should" expect in future "excellent" games (and what the poor games look like as well). And so again a tension emerges: keeping the paratext cool enough to convey the essential gaming capital, without making it seem too didactic or juvenile. This is probably a reason for the rise of Web sites and blogs devoted to game news and strategy; they lend that critical aura of cool to the same old content, but in a new digital wrapper.

Just as game magazines have played a critical role in the development of a support industry for the larger game industry, another segment has arisen and further fragmented this market: strategy guide publishers. That industry is examined in detail in chapter 2.

GUIDANCE GOES INDEPENDENT: THE RISE OF STRATEGY GUIDE PUBLISHERS

Game magazines still provide players with guidance for getting through games, and have been crucial in shaping expectations for what that guidance should look like. But due to their multiple demands, magazines will always be limited in meeting that goal. Magazines themselves recognize this, as they limit their strategy sections, sometimes provide supplemental cheat guides mailed separately to subscribers, and publish more detailed information on their Web sites.[1] Another type of print publication has emerged to play a more dedicated role in meeting this need: the strategy guide.

While Nintendo continues to produce its own guides, most game developers and publishers farm out that work to other companies such as Prima Publishing, BradyGames, or Sybex via their marketing department or licensing person.[2] Two of those companies, Prima and Brady, are themselves parts of much larger publishing houses (Random House and Pearson Education, respectively), which largely control this market. Although there are many small and independent sites online that publish walkthroughs and game information similar to what is found in strategy guides (GameFAQs.com being a notable example), here I limit the analysis to commercial ventures that have worked closely with the game industry. Later chapters will examine the strategic importance (and uses) of such sites.

Such consolidation mirrors the activities of the core game production industry, where publishers like Electronic Arts are worth billions of dollars, due in large part to their control over a significant percentage of each year's triple-A titles. Stephen Kline, Nick Dyer-Witheford, and Greig De Peuter argue that such developments indicate the videogame industry is an exemplar of the West's move to a post-Fordist economy, featuring the production of information rather than durable goods, in a flexible, specialized, just-in-time manner.[3] That would appear to be so, and guides are even more representative of that shift. Guides can signify, as game magazines have, the further commodification of gaming capital. Here that capital is produced through the work of a collective of writers, editors, and artists, congealed as game-playing capital (labor) that is ultimately sold to game players as easily consumable game knowledge.

This chapter extends the analysis begun in the first one, exploring how the content of print strategy guides (as well as mass-market paperbacks, VHS videos, DVD guides, and other electronic formats) has developed over the past decade. It argues that guides took up (and did best) where magazines left off, providing a wider range of player-readers access to instructions on how to play games and how to conceptualize their gameplay experience. Guides also went further in appealing to a wider audience, and extended the idea of gaming capital to those outside the hard core of the player base (who ironically rarely used retail strategy guides).

Guides solidified for many readers the various elements essential to gameplay (and game capital), and further hierarchized particular elements such as the game-consistent traveler's guide, bare-bones directions and puzzle solutions, and secret areas and items to be found. Those findings are here related back to the concept of gaming capital, and how guides played a role in its continued shaping and growth.

This chapter also presents a detailed analysis of the economics of the guide industry as it has become enmeshed with the larger game development, marketing, and retailing industries. It investigates how the business of guide production has shaped content and how guide publishers attempt to differentiate themselves in a medium that leaves little room—ironically—for creativity.

The chapter concludes by considering the more recent appearance of digital, dynamic strategy guides. Their content is examined, along with the evolving shape of the market. Finally, guides' general omission of cheat codes is explored in relation to the growing commodification of such individual elements in a profitable industry.

The chapter ultimately demonstrates that just as "peripheral" products can help shape and stabilize a larger industry, intertwining text and paratext, so too business practices shape content. Understanding how cheat codes and Easter eggs have developed value and been commodified can provide a key to further deciphering the larger game industry and, more important, players' expectations for what is part of—and not part of—the central gaming experience.

Guide Content: Walkthroughs, Screen Shots, Weapons Guides, and More

Strategy guides contain information similar to what can be found in the strategy sections of *Nintendo Power* and early issues of *Electronic Gaming Monthly*, yet in much greater detail and length. Readers now have access (depending on which guides they choose) to charts listing all the items and/or weapons available in the game, perhaps with detailed statistics and information on how much they cost or where to locate them. In addition to providing maps and explanations for how to defeat difficult bosses, contemporary guides can contain lavish amounts of art, including numerous screen shots, original game concept art, and additional graphics created for the book itself. Guides also now commonly include extra features designed to appeal to fans of particular games or game series, such as interviews with members of the development team and inside information about the production process.

Until recently, though, guides have been most successful formwise as a static entity explaining a dynamic universe. A few companies have begun to compete with the print guide publishers (as well as with online free guides) with the release of electronic guides including Digital Video Guides for *Tom Clancy's Rainbow 6* (2004) from Game Time Media, and iGuides from g-NET Media for *DRIV3R* and *Hitman: Contracts*. Before such companies appeared, the major guide publishers had tried their own versions of digital guides, and they are now currently marketing digital versions of their printed guides, but with no additional content other than updated information, which had traditionally been posted to their Web sites anyway.[4]

While publishers are worried about the free online versions of the same, so far they have dismissed electronic versions of such guides as too difficult for readers to consult while in the midst of playing a game. But if a player now has a DVD player adjacent to her Xbox, she can easily toggle back and forth between the two devices, and gain dynamic help on the fly. I will explore the details of those new guides later, but first I study the traditional printed guide.

Just as game magazines performed important work in defining what gaming capital should encompass and its importance for those interested in games, so too strategy guides have added to and refined the notion, with their very presence acting as a commodified form of gaming capital. Guides also introduced divisions into definitions of gaming capital, as game players began to self-select in their gaming practices and interests, with strategy guides as something to accept or reject as a component of the wider gaming culture.

Strategy guides, then, continue and extend the work done by early game magazines. While magazines have become more specialized and are marketed to different niches in the game-playing demographic, strategy guides have picked up some of the basic functions of early magazines: teaching players how to play games, in all the ways described previously. They also can act as a litmus test for players, as a form of gaming capital that can either enable certain experiences or destroy particular pleasures in gameplay. In that sense, they work to begin stratification of the player base, and players must construct for themselves how strategy guides fit—or don't—in their pursuit of gaming capital.

As a paratextual structure, then, this industry and its products continues the tradition of shaping core elements of the game-playing experience, and like the elements surrounding a book, contextualizes and gives better focus to the elements within: the game itself. And through greater examination of the business practices of strategy guide companies, we can see how enmeshed such industries are growing with the core and how interdependent such industries are becoming.

The Early History: From Hint Books to an Industry

Early computer games ranged from the simple to the complex, and could contain lavish (for the time) graphics or text-only screens. Although guides began to appear in the early 1990s for games such as *Sim City* and *King's Quest VII*, it wasn't until games gained popular attention that the sale of guides really took off. One of the first popular guides to lead the way was *Myst: The Official Strategy Guide*, published in 1993 by Prima, and written by Rick Barba and Rusel DeMaria. Although thin compared to later offerings, the guide supplied the new or casual computer game player with something that the game lacked: help in figuring out what to do in the beautiful world of *Myst*. By the time of the guide's second printing in 1995, over three hundred thousand copies of the original guide had already been sold, and that figure would rise to over a million copies, making it one of the best-selling guides of all time.[5]

The way that the guide went about helping players followed some of the same themes as early magazine miniguides. Strategy guides may be one of the few, if perhaps only, texts that actually beg you *not* to use them unless stuck or to rely on them too heavily. For example, the Prima guide for *The Legend of Zelda: Majora's Mask* contains a sealed secrets section that provides information about the end of the game. It must be literally broken open by the player, thus ensuring that the player actually buys the book and does not just browse for answers in the store, the secrets contained within are thought to be of great value, and the book's publisher cares enough about the gameplay experience to not let it be accidentally ruined by a careless flip of the page.[6]

Such warnings indicate the delicate positioning of paratextual elements to the text itself. While use of a paratext can help a player make clear or uncover certain elements of the text/game, overuse of the paratext strips away too much of the game experience, revealing it as an exercise or mechanical components to be manipulated. Or it may just ruin a surprise. Use of the paratext/guide is therefore shaped as "in the last instance," although what exactly that means is left to individual players to decide.

Beyond urging readers to limit their exposure to the guide, or better yet, only consult it during the second play of the game (here extending the value of the original game), the *Myst* guide also relies on several different strategies for presenting information to further organize for the reader the stages to be followed in seeking help or guidance for the game. Each stage is a further de-*Myst*-ification of the game's challenges.

The large bulk of the guide is taken up with a fictionalized account of one person's adventure in the strange world of *Myst*. The guide starts off as a narrative, with the (fictional) author explaining that while researching photography books in the library, he discovered the *Myst* journal, began to read it, and suddenly found himself transported to the island. The account then details his explorations and adventures, and his efforts to solve the mystery of *Myst*. Even before the story begins, however, the reader learns that this account will provide "an Everyman sort of narrator who chronicles his attempt to unravel the *Myst mys*tery. . . . So you can read the various sections of the *Myst* journal for hints if you don't necessarily want puzzle solutions right away. Note, however, that the journalist will always give you detailed solutions sooner or later."[7]

Following that more subtle account of how to progress through the game is the "Quick Guide" section, which is "a straightforward, no-frills 'walkthrough' that omits the narrative style and gentle approach for a practical "do this, go there" style for getting through the game."[8] To illustrate the differences, compare the explanation for the first few movements in the Channelwood Age.

In the distance I saw a twirling windmill. I worked my way to it pretty easily—all pipes and pathways seemed to lead there. I entered the structure. Explored. Saw that it was pumping water up from the surrounding body of water into a large tank. I noticed a spigot down at the base of the tank. I figured that opening it would let water flow through the pipe system below. I twisted the spigot counterclockwise. Water gurgled down the pipes behind me.[9]

1. Work your way to the windmill. Just keep heading toward it—all pipes and pathways lead to it.
2. Inside the windmill, open the spigot at the base of the water tank. (Click on it; it will turn to the left.) You should hear water flowing louder now.[10]

The information is roughly the same, but the presentation differs considerably. The first style emphasizes a narrative telling of events, encouraging the reader to envision their own progress on the same journey through the *Myst* universe. It is as if the player has stumbled on, or been given, a previous traveler's journal or diary of the same adventure, and can therefore consult that guide if problems arise. The fiction of the mythical world is maintained, and the reader is allowed to stay within the magic circle of the game.[11] In contrast, the second style breaks the illusion that the reader is part of another world and points to the constructedness of the game as it explains necessary actions—"click here"—rather than "I turned the valve." While each version offers the same basic information, the context is different—the second version draws attention to the interface and how to manipulate it, rather than keeping with the fantasy construction of the game.

Those differences in context do more than construct for the reader a particular approach to the game and its puzzles. In addition to allowing players to choose their preferred style of communication, they also subtly encourage certain uses of the text. Alongside the plainly stated request to use the text as little as possible, the arrangement of the information is also a key to how the authors wish the reader to use the text and therefore interact with the game. It is the fictionalized account that is presented first, and the plainly rendered quick guide walkthrough that follows. That ordering is intentional, and one that is repeated in other guides that offer multiple accounts. For example, the guide for *The Seventh Guest* (also written by DeMaria) offers the reader a fictionalized account of the adventure, and following that, a listing of all puzzles and how to solve them. It is notable in the *Guest* guide that in the first recounting, there are no solutions offered, just hints, and the second part offers only the puzzle solutions, rather than including a stripped-down walkthrough as well (in *Guest*, there is little doubt about where to go—only how to solve puzzles to advance the game).

That style has recurred through the years, although it works best only with certain types of games and for companies that wish to take a certain approach. The recently released successor to the *Myst* series—*Uru*—has a similar tactic in its own guides, with more travelers and journeys helping the game player along.[12] Such paratexts encourage the reader, explicitly and implicitly, to use the guides in certain ways, and therefore classify and categorize various types of information and help. As mentioned earlier, a de-*Myst*-ification is occurring, yet on several levels at once. Simultaneously with the game player gaining access to knowledge of how to progress in the game, the player is learning preferred ways for playing the game. The player is also learning how to read guides, choose among sources of information, and play games in general; even as guides can instruct, though, they cannot prescribe, and indeed, several types of instruction are offered. Some players may only need portions of the first account to move on, or perhaps more, yet may not need or want to even look at the second account. Other players might read the first account, find it of little value, and move to the more explicit version. Finally, a third set of players may skip the first account entirely and only consult the second version, when they really need or wish to do so.

In setting up such a system, however, one account is privileged over another: the fictional before the utilitarian. Help is offered in in-game (game-centric) and out-of-game (interface-centric) terms, from hints first to basic commands last. That ordering creates a hierarchical value chain of information, which players then make choices about, stemming from their own needs and interests. Yet the consistency of this design has contributed to a structure where certain types of help are preferred (or given preference, or seen as more acceptable) over others.

And just as a subtle approach is first preferred, leading next to a more explicit account, what is generally *not* offered is just as important: there are usually no cheat codes in the guides, suggesting to the reader through omission which elements are not central facets of the game experience. The use of codes, their circulation in game culture and as part of gaming capital, is dealt with in the last section of this chapter. First, though, I need to widen the scope to examine guides beyond the adventure game genre, as they are a shrinking part of the market. While they exerted tremendous influence in the early days of the industry, segments such as action and sports games now receive far more attention and sales dollars.

Multiple Game Genres: Few Guide Differences

Nintendo Power did a good job of teaching readers how to play and beat their games. It also apparently created a template for the future of guide design. For example, the recent guides for *Final Fantasy IX*, *X*, and *X-2* published by BradyGames contain at least half a dozen sections including basic contextual/pregame information, a general walkthrough for the games, bestiaries listing all known monsters and bosses with their hit points, strengths, and weaknesses detailed, the aforementioned weapons and items charts, and a separate section for side-quests and hidden areas along with items to find or unlock.

For instance, the table of contents for the *Final Fantasy X* guide lists the following elements, which appear in a carefully ordered presentation:

1. Introduction
2. RPG Basics
3. A Summoner and Her Guardians [information about the game's central characters]

4. Aeons [Yuna's summoned spirits]

5. Abilities and the Sphere Grid [advancement methods]

6. Weapons and Armor

7. Items and Key Items

8. Shops List

9. Walkthrough [the bulk of the guide]

10. Side Quests

11. Secrets

12. Blitzball

13. Bestiary

14. Interviews [with several game developers]

The ordering of the sections mirrors many early miniguides in *Nintendo Power*. The player is introduced to the game world and central characters as well as basics for the game genre. Items are described, as are places to find/acquire them. Next, a detailed walkthrough of the game commences, coupled with many screen shots and maps that help the player, yet are careful not to reveal too much. Finally, the guide includes sections on side quests and secrets. Those sections offer information about material peripheral to the game's main story line, but which add depth to the characters as well as (and probably more important for the developers) more playtime to the game. While some of this information might be found by the player through exploration or trial and error, in case it isn't, it is offered here.

Such ordering keeps intact certain preferred styles of gameplay; secrets are not exposed, and players now expect a certain amount of hidden material, but are challenged to first find it on their own.

Here again, the guide publishers have worked to keep the secrets and bonus materials slightly separate from the central quest of each game, yet they understand how important that information can be for dedicated players and fans. The material is laid out in a linear fashion to follow the narrative progression in each game, although the story elements are mostly absent from the explanation or narrative of the guide. As multiguide author Bart Farkas explains, echoing the argument that the paratext cannot impinge too far on players' experiences of the text, players of the game want to discover the story on their own and not have their experience ruined by glimpsing too far along in a guide.[13]

Some readers of the Brady guide for *Final Fantasy VII*, for example, were quite upset that the death of a central character was revealed in the guide; they felt the information should stay in the game for players to discover on their own.[14] Thus, the guide publishers walk a fine line in trying to give readers the information they need, but not enough to spoil the game. That may seem ironic, as guide readers are, according to those who would never consult such a guide, cheating. But as later chapters will demonstrate, individual players have specific views concerning the types of help that they consider appropriate or not, with those helpers often functioning dynamically—changing over time, depending on context, and reflecting specifics needs and interests for each particular game player.

More recent game guides have increased production values, but otherwise have not changed much over the years. Although some guide writers (and game players) question the necessity of having guides for particular games, and some of those guides do border on the obvious, the presence of a guide for a triple-A game has become practically a necessity (or a practical necessity) for developers and game publishers.

For example, while the multiple side quests and challenging puzzles of a role-playing or adventure game make a guide useful, guidebooks for action games such as *The Hulk* can seem fairly empty. While the book weighs in at 158 pages, in full color, the text doesn't stray far from serving as a didactic walkthrough: "Drop from the hole in the floor above into the catacombs. A text message warns that to progress, you must defeat the enemy. There is no way to escape the room until you defeat twelve Rifle Soldiers. Use the crates and area attacks to quickly snuff the threat."[15] While this guide also contains some of the optional elements that appear in other guides including concept art and interviews with the developers, here the addition props up a flimsy base, resulting in a form of padding that doesn't seem necessary and works to distract rather than enhance.

Such guides do help sell the game, even if they do not actually help players tremendously in beating the game. And with most guides, there is a common core of elements, irrelevant to the genre of the particular game. So whether one is reading the guide for *The Hulk*, *Quake*, *Halo*, *The Sims: Hot Date*, or *Primal*, common features include a section on how to use the guide, basic information about the game controls, characters, items, and weapons, a walkthrough with full-color screen shots to illustrate power-ups, secret rooms, and the like, maps of the levels, and various charts listing detailed specs for such things as weapons, monsters, spells, in-game items, job attributes, and minigames.

Probably the only difference in guides is between those for console games and those for computer games. And here, the difference is mainly cosmetic. While there are exceptions, generally guides for console games are large format (eight by eleven inches) and use full-color glossy paper, while computer game guides are smaller in size (seven by nine inches) and stick to mainly black-and-white, plain paper. Guides cost roughly the same amount (between $15.99 and $19.99) at retail, although often there are discounts offered by retailers for purchasing a guide and game together, or markdowns on selected guides after a certain period of time.

All guides stress basic knowledge about game characters, items, and controls, they feature walkthroughs, offer detailed charts and maps, and then provide variable amounts of extra materials. It is safe to say that the formula is set, the paratext has been stamped, and guide publishers might experiment with narrative style or design, but usually stick to these general parameters.

Evolving Business Concerns: Guides Grow Up

Just as a few game magazines helped shape the larger industry, so too only a handful of guide publishers were influential in continuing that progress. That development took approximately a decade for the industry to reach its current point, where only two major companies control the market. Prior to and in the beginning years of the 1990s, several one-off books appeared that concentrated on successful strategies for playing particular games, such as *Playing Ms. Pac-Man to Win* and the more broadly focused *Compute's Nintendo Tips & Tricks*, but most of these books were put out by nonspecialist publishers and the titles suggested the exploitation of a fad, rather than a systematic publishing program.[16]

Those early books were generally trade paperbacks, and featured little in the way of the lavish extras and content that is now associated with strategy guides. For example, Richard Kissel's *The Ultimate Strategy Guide to Super Mario Bros.* had no screen shots, and was a thin little paperback with a few hand drawings to illustrate actions and map markers. The guide of the book consisted of a series of chapters delineated by the world and then the level. For each level, there were three columns to read: "where to go," "what to do," and "what happens." As an example, on page 65, for world 5, level 1, the first tips included "Jump over two pipes. Go to bricks," which "releases Starman for invisibility."

Such tips, while valuable, were just that: tips. There was no attempt to "extend the experience" of the game beyond helping the player progress past an explicit point, and nothing beyond a utilitarian exchange of information. At that point in time, game magazines such as *Nintendo Power* and *Electronic Gaming Monthly* were already providing that sort of contextualized information, and for the more casual game player, who was more likely to seek information from a mass-market paperback than a specialized game publication, the basics were deemed all that was necessary to satisfy their particular needs.

Gradually, the paperbacks took on more of the magazines' characteristics, with the *Compute* book being much larger, and including some narrative explanation of games as well as trying for a style that captured the experience of gameplay: "You play Bart Simpson, nuisance extraordinaire. Using very few tools, and a little help from Maggie, Lisa, Marge and Homer, you must prevent the Space Mutants from collecting enough objects to build their weapon and destroy the Earth. Pretty cool, huh?"[17]

Further, the *Compute* book included not only basic descriptions of each game, general and specific strategies, and black-and-white screen shots, it also contained secret codes for each game that allowed the player such things as invincibility and the ability to select which stage of the game to play. While the Krissel volume mentioned the code for secret restart, the *Compute* guide went further, giving players knowledge of such codes and increasing expectations about what might be possible in gameplay as well as what might be hidden in any game attempted. Overall, however, the guides were limited, especially in the attention given to any particular game, and production values indicate the mass-market "cash in on a fad" nature of the enterprise. That would soon change.

Dedicated guide companies started operating in the early 1990s, or about ten years after the magazines began. Initially, these were primarily expanded versions of what the magazine *Nintendo Power* already offered. Early companies included Prima Publishing (1990) and BradyGames (1993), although at first the guides were more focused on generalized strategies for beating all sorts of games rather than examining a single title in depth. Other early publishers included Sybex and Sandwich Island, which are now producing a limited number of titles or have since folded.

The production process was also somewhat piecemeal, with publishers mainly hiring many freelance writers, including mostly videogame fans, some still in college, to produce their copy.[18]

Those early guides, often referred to as "hint books" or "cheat books," were not taken seriously by the game industry, if they were noticed at all. Yet with each year, the market took on a more serious cast, and the number of single-title strategy guides steadily increased. At first many of those titles were unauthorized and unlicensed, meaning that a guide publisher had no relationship with the game publisher and had just decided to create a guide for a game that was popular. Such guides often boasted of their "totally unauthorized" status, which was frequently code for a poor guide.[19]

While a few such guides still appear, the vast majority of titles have shifted over the decade to a "licensed, authorized" status. That is likely due to three reasons. First, as a majority of guides are now bought in tandem with the related game, the guide needs to be planned in advance so that it is available the day a game is released. Only a licensing deal will give a guide publisher access to a prereleased game. Game developers can also help guide publishers by providing weapon statistics, maps, and secret area information. As this information is most prevalent in role-playing games (RPGs), and RPG guides have the highest attach rate, it would be rare to see an unauthorized guide appear instantaneously with a game's release that provides all the relevant information.[20]

Second, in order to have adequate distribution of a guide, guide publishers must have stable relationships with retailers, including specialty stores such as EB Games and GameStop as well as more general retailers like Wal-Mart, Best Buy, and Toys "R" Us. Unless a guide publisher releases a significant number of titles per year and thus can guarantee a certain revenue stream, store retailers will most certainly pass on carrying their titles. For example, the now-defunct guide publisher Versus attempted to sell licensed, high-quality guides, but a failure to broaden its lineup probably led to its demise.[21] For those reasons, the game guide publishing industry has shifted from multiple-title, often unlicensed books to the more specialized single-title, authorized guides that can command a spot on the limited shelf space at Wal-Mart.

Third (but not least), many game developers and publishers have recognized the value of releasing guides alongside their games. For most publishers, it's strictly a matter of revenue—having a guide is seen as building credibility, as it lends an aura of quality to a new game release.[22]

Game publishers see the presence of a guide as a way to extend the brand and advertise in another venue. But some game publishers see guides as a way to help players have a better experience playing their game. Publishers such as Square Enix and Blizzard take great care, and give guide writers access to many elements of the game production process to ensure that the guide is a quality document, which reflects well on their larger image to the gaming public.[23] For such developers and publishers, the move to licensed guides provided more control over the product and helped enhance the value of such items not just from a business standpoint but from a gameplay perspective as well.

Along with a shift in guide publishers' relation with game publishers to one of greater collaboration and legitimacy has come an expansion in the size of the guide market. In the early 1990s, BradyGames published 30 titles a year on average, but in 2003 the company produced more than 70 guides. The industry leader, Prima Games, now regularly puts out over 100 titles a year, and in 2003 released more than 145 guide titles. Smaller publishers such as Sybex contribute a handful of titles per year, with the global guide industry producing between 220 and 240 titles annually.[24] While that number is a definite increase from a decade ago, it hides the fact that guide publishers are publishing fewer titles as a percentage of the games released, so that each title will generate more profit.[25] Currently, then, approximately half of the videogames released per year have guides, and the guide industry produces revenues between $100 million and $250 million yearly.[26]

With that rise in profitability has come the greater professionalization of the industry, and a more systematic approach to producing guides. While early guides were haphazard efforts put together by novices, today's titles are the product of marketing, licensing, and editorial teams, in addition to the actual writer of the guide. Although the larger guides do have an identifiable author, that person is generally only one in a chain of workers, putting together the guide in a style vaguely reminiscent of the assembly line. Although there are a few individuals still working who can realistically describe themselves as full-time "strategy guide writers" who make a living playing and writing about the games, far more guides are produced by writers working on a part-time, contract basis. Alongside the individuals who largely put words on paper are the graphic artists, copy editors, designers, and managing editors who ensure the production ships at the same time as the game's release. Sometimes this means that a guide writer is given five days to deliver the copy and the guide is produced in four weeks, but to miss the launch date of the game would be far worse.[27] That reflects the just-in-time nature of game guide production, as cultural workers are increasingly employed in positions where they can be quickly tapped for their labor and just as quickly set aside when the project is completed. This growing practice helps explain why the average strategy guide writer is growing younger and working on a per-title, contract basis. This is not to suggest that there was a golden age for guide writers (or guide artists) but that certain practices such as the offering of royalty payments are disappearing (or gone already) alongside a sense of individual creativity in guide production. While guides may be increasingly beautiful or dense with information, that product is increasingly systematized and stripped of excess labor.

Of course, the specialization in guide production echoes the growing compartmentalization of the game development industry. As game development does not rely on one or two dedicated individuals, neither does the guide business. Most games now have budgets in the multimillions of dollars, leading to teams that number from a dozen (considered small) to the hundreds (fairly large, but not uncommon). Although some games are still marketed as arising from the vision of a particular person such as Will Wright or Sid Meier, most games are the product of multiple decision makers and many pairs of hands, all working to try and create a product that is consistent with a design document as well as (often) a brand license or publisher expectation. Guides now follow the same route, as writers provide copy and designers produce templates that can be changed "at the blink of an eye" to suit the game publisher's needs. Game publishers themselves treat guide production in varying ways, some seeing their value and providing information vital to the guide, and others supplying next to nothing and leaving it to the writer to find his or her own way.

Along with the standardization of production processes for guides, guide publishers work in a shrinking market for games themselves. And with the growing imperative in the game industry for fewer releases that sell more units, guides are following the same trend.

Although unofficial guides do still exist, the vast majority are now the authorized (that is, licensed) versions. Sales can range from five thousand to over a million units, with attach rates ranging from 15 percent for most games to a high of 40 to 50 percent for Square Enix's line of *Final Fantasy* RPGs. Square Enix (as well as BradyGames) is also responsible for the best-selling console game guide, *Final Fantasy VII*, which still occasionally appears on retailers' "top five" charts and has sold more than a million copies.[28] Given that there is such a wide range in sales for guides and that production costs remain stable (apart from the particular license fee paid for a guide), title publishers are consciously after ways to broaden their market, gain more development partners, and concentrate on producing guides that generate the most revenue. That often means focusing more on the triple-A titles and eliminating the "B" games, which may only sell ten thousand units.

Along with these changes, the guide industry has been consolidating, as game publishers form longer-term agreements with the remaining guide companies, and as the knowledge of how to produce a guide and generate enough cash to cover the licensing fees (which can range from nothing to the high six figures) grows more scarce. As mentioned above, one industry challenger, Versus, folded in 2002, and several others have disappeared from public view. It is no accident that the publishing giant Pearson Education owns BradyGames, while Random House holds Prima. As guide publishers need access to six- and seven-figure sums for licensing fees for a single guide title, they must be able to find deep pockets—the kind of pockets that come in the form of a media conglomerate.

The creation of gaming capital has quickly become a multimillion dollar business, if it was ever anything less. Although later chapters examine player agency, and the development of independent sources for the production and circulation of such capital, dominant channels exist to direct and shape that flow. As large publishing houses and magazine groups join the transnational game publishers and developers, we see how text and paratext not only intertwine but become more tied to money and big business. Yet that flow is nothing without players to manage it, which is never a straightforward process.

Publisher Differentiation: Signature Series versus Market Research

Videogames are gaining more popular attention with each passing year, due in large part to high-profile titles such as the *Grand Theft Auto* series and franchises including *Madden NFL*, *The Lord of the Rings*, *Star Wars*, and *Harry Potter*. But even as public attention is drawn to the seemingly ever-expanding industry of game production, both game and guide publishers are competing in a shrinking market. Fewer big budget games, fewer big budget guides, and fewer companies to make them concretely affect how these two industries—text and paratext—relate to one another in order to survive and flourish.

More frequently than ever, game publishers enter into exclusive relationships with individual guide publishers, but these guide publishers must still compete to maintain their current licensees as well as seek to expand the guide market overall. The two remaining major guide publishers, Prima and Brady, take different approaches to this problem, and their strategies suggest how the guide industry may develop in the future. They also demonstrate how paratexts not only shape the contours of the game industry but also how business concerns constrain the paratext as well. Both Prima and Brady have approached the issue in slightly different ways, and in the process, they have further shaped game players' expectations surrounding help and support in relation to gameplay.

Prima is the current leader in the guide industry, with over eleven hundred titles published, and ninety million guides printed.[29] Given its large number of titles, Prima can wield influence with a retailer that a smaller publisher (such as Versus) cannot. The sheer size of Prima's list ensures that a certain percentage will be hits, and Prima also has the pockets to work with retailers to promote games and guides in a win-win scenario. In addition to its sheer bulk, Prima markets itself as a company that conducts detailed research on the guide-buying market, and carefully listens to its readers about what they like and don't like to see in guides, how to arrange materials, and other aesthetic concerns. Prima also relies on market research from groups such as NPD FunWorld, an industry analyst for the videogame and toy industry. So while guides may have a shelf life of three-to-five months, Prima can get them on that shelf, and assures game publishers that it has done their homework in how to appeal to game buyers.

Moreover, Prima works to actively expand the guide-buying market. It recognizes the potential of the casual gamers market, which currently makes up one fraction of its audience, as a larger source of future revenue. And much as early game magazines did, it positions its guides as a place for the education of newer or less experienced game players regarding what is needed to play and succeed at a game today. Prima also works with its partner Del-Ray Books to cross-promote products, and it advertises in places such as *Sports Illustrated* and *Entertainment Weekly* to expand its potential audience. Having Random House's pockets helps, but Prima sees its place in the industry as the leader, relying on research as well as dedicated to knowing its market and trying to create new segments of that market at the same time.[30]

In contrast, Brady positions itself as the quality guide producer with a feel for what actual gamers want in a guide. Although Brady produces fewer guides per year, it has a high percentage of hits and holds licensing agreements for sought-after titles including Square Enix's *Final Fantasy* line of RPGs. In 2004, the company claimed to hold 42% of total guide market share revenue, suggesting that even with fewer guides on the shelves, they continue to be a strong competitor in this market.[31] Brady also differentiates itself by making it known that its managers, writers, editors, and even the publisher all play games themselves. As with the guide writer, the insider knowledge of the games themselves is exploited, as the company argues that since its employees play games, it can develop better guides because of that knowledge. Brady thus relies more (or claims to rely more) on staff knowledge of games over formal market research, claiming the insider status to Prima's more cut-and-dried approach.[32]

Brady also distinguishes its guides in the market by its "Signature Series" line, an expanded, deluxe line of guides that feature lavish artwork, developer interviews, and posters, among other items. Furthermore, Brady has deep pockets due to its owner, and produces enough titles on a yearly basis that it can compete successfully with Prima for retail space in every venue. Both Brady and Prima work to expand the larger guide market by nudging the boundaries of the guide industry, producing titles such as Brady's *Power Up: How Japanese Video Games Gave the World an Extra Life*.[33]

Both guide publishers seek to differentiate themselves in a diminished market, and both still compete for the loyalties (and dollars) of game publishers. It is probably to the advantage of each and to the game publishers that there are at least two guide publishers in existence, as that way a certain level of quality is assured, and guide buyers are guaranteed some modicum of choice, at least in relation to print guides.

Beyond Print: E-guides, Tapes, and DVDs

Although print guides have remained the dominant format for professional guide publishers, there have always been alternative formats for game guides, hints, and tips. In 1989, two short (thirty-four and twenty-three minutes, respectively) VHS videos were released from Kodak, each explaining *How to Score More Points on Nintendo Games*. Far from being alone, other VHS tapes describing secret game tricks and tips also released that year included those by White Janssen Productions (*Secret Video Game Tricks, Codes, & Strategies*) and Studio Video Productions (*Video Game Guide*).[34]

Yet the videotape was never an ideal medium for guides, as it could not be readily searched and required additional hardware to operate. Further, as with other types of guide formats, videotapes often could not be used simultaneously while playing the game, leaving players with a less-than-ideal form of help. That doesn't mean those early tapes weren't successful (sales figures could not be found for them) but that as a long-term solution, they were not the ideal format.

Both of the major traditional publishers have been experimenting with digital variations for guide offerings, although the print guides remain (for now) the most prolific style being published. Brady and Prima have been branching out, offering readers access to online guides and e-guides, respectively, for selected games. For example, Brady offers an online handbook for *World of Warcraft* that can be continually updated and added to, depending on how players progress in the online game. Prima's guides are mainly less expensive PDF versions of print guides that can be paid for online and downloaded immediately.[35] Whether such guides catch on or not—due to their lack of portability, limited use, or other factors—is an open question.

Another (revamped) version for strategy guides has also emerged: the DVD walkthrough, with various extras. Such guides offer the viewer dynamic walkthroughs: captured video of gameplay segmented by level, with voice-over narration explaining how to progress through missions, accomplish tasks, and generally beat the game.

Companies such as g-Net and Game Time both released officially licensed versions of such guides in 2004, although by mid-2006 there were still only a handful of such titles and the companies' respective Web sites had not been updated in months. Yet whatever the bottom line is, these guides come with significant advantages as well as disadvantages, and each will be discussed in turn.

One of the earliest challenges that game magazines and strategy guides faced was how to explain key in-game movements or actions in a dynamic universe through a static system: the printed page. Those constraints led to the use of sequential screen shots to illustrate successive movements or the effects of certain movements. Such depictions are not perfect, though, and cannot entirely capture the essence of the situation. Walkthroughs that are dynamic can overcome that limitation; they not only explain what to do, they can also model the action for the player. So just as giving someone a written description of how to tie shoes, complete with screen shots of the process, can be helpful, it is not nearly as useful as a video demonstration of the procedure.

For example, the DVD guide for the Xbox game *Tom Clancy's Rainbow Six 3* allows the player access to video walkthroughs for each of the game's missions. Those walkthroughs are separate chapters on the DVD and can be accessed in any order the player chooses. Additionally, the player can pause each mission walkthrough as needed or replay as many times as necessary. Each walkthrough features a narrator running through the parameters of the mission to be completed as well as a guide to what weapons or items will be most useful to gather or practice with before beginning. Such elements echo the warm-ups of early *Nintendo Power* game guides, where the player was encouraged to learn as much about the upcoming challenge as possible.

Next, each chapter progresses with a walkthrough of the selected mission. That includes video footage of an "expert" player going through the game as well as voice-over narration. The video scenes are smooth and successful, with the on-screen game avatar succeeding in each challenge. The narrator blends a functional and stylistic approach to the material, trying to both give practical information about what to do next for the player and impart a specific mood. For example, during the "Alpine Village" mission, the narrator explains:

Move your team to the first building on the right. Check to see if there's a hostile up the hill. [Pause.] Advance straight ahead. Let your teammates deal with any stray hostiles. As you proceed, you'll encounter your first terrorist. Eliminate him and move to the top of the hill, where another terrorist will greet you. . . . Move forward and take cover behind the red fuel tank to shoot at the next tango. Regroup your team.[36]

Even a short clip like this demonstrates both elements at work. The narrative is practical in its advice—warning the player of a "hostile" up on the hill as well as offering the strategic information that hiding behind the red fuel tank will keep the player safe for at least the immediate present. Likewise, the verbal narration of such information is reinforced by the video, which shows a player actually doing such things. In that way, the narration of practical advice almost seems redundant, but does give the player vital cues as to what is coming next and reinforces such strategies.

The narration, however, also keeps the player in the world of the game, to some extent, through the careful use of language. Drawing from the world of Tom Clancy, enemies are "hostiles" and "tangos." The player is encouraged to "eliminate" such terrorists, who of course don't really "greet you" so much as attempt to shoot you on sight. The point is not about the glossing over of violence but instead the attempt at keeping consistent a player's actions and the explicit directions on the DVD, with the fantasy world of the game itself. Just as the early guide for *Myst* encouraged the player to walk around and explore, "turning spigots" and "heading west," so too do present-day DVD walkthroughs try to keep the player in the imaginary space created by the game, or at least as much as is possible. So even as the guide business expands as a paratextual element, it continues to work to preserve the integrity and space of the primary text, by extending a particular game's flavor outward, to guides and hints.

The (Non)Obvious Absence

Ironically, though, one item that game guide writers consider essential to their job is usually not included in the final product: cheat codes.[37] Especially when working on a tight deadline, guide writers, like game developers themselves, need to be able to move around a game world quickly to gather information. Help is provided in the form of developer-provided cheat codes, giving writers full life, bonus weapons, and the like. Yet those codes themselves, so helpful to the process, generally don't make it into the book that the writer produced from them. What happened?

Just as gaming skill is commodified in the guide, so too have cheat codes become commodities for game developers or publishers to deal with in relation to the peripherals industry. Sometimes promised to game magazines as an exclusive deal (in exchange for a game appearing on the cover one month), cheat codes pass through the hands of guide writers and enter into their own commodity universe. More valuable as another source of capital separate from guides, the codes can breathe continued life into aging games, encouraging players already eyeing new games to have another look at that game they bought last month, played for a while, and then discarded.

As more and more people actually finish fewer and fewer games, the opportunity to extend the life of games becomes important. Returning to magazines and the shaping of player expectations surrounding gameplay, there is now an expectation that game codes will be released shortly after a game's release, which can add value to a game and return revenue to the game publishers as well as the magazine publishers' pockets.[38] Likewise, current DVD walkthroughs follow the path of the majority of print strategy guides, which do not include cheat codes. While codes would make the game easier to play or perhaps more enjoyable, they also take the player out of the game world conceptually, focusing instead on manipulating an interface as well as a game code.

Such codes are carefully guarded by game publishers and developers, who are fearful that the growing legion of contract-only guide writers might release the codes on the Internet, perhaps ruining an exclusive deal with a game magazine for coverage of the game. Although all codes do eventually appear on the Internet—on scores of free sites, no less—the control exerted over the fate of such codes, originally created as developer tools, demonstrates the extent of commodification of the industry, and how every bit or byte can command a price.

Additionally, publishers are now going beyond the training of players in basic gameplay with their ever-expanding array of "supplemental" materials, including posters with timelines, special character attacks, and other arcane and detailed game information. These sorts of materials become almost necessary for the titles currently released, which promise upward of fifty to a hundred hours of gameplay. Such big games now mean including numerous side quests, minigames, secret areas, hidden weapons, and bonus materials. Guidebooks can help the game player *find* all of that bonus material, without perhaps adding yet another twenty hours to the game. They also aid in securing gaming capital—just as magazines do—by giving players the means to fully beat the game and talk more knowledgeably about it with other game players.

Yet even as the guide publishing industry reinforces the tradition of appealing to the core demographic, it does make efforts to reach out—ironically to the hard-core segment of gamers, which in the past has scoffed at the need for strategy guides. The industry does this by creating value-added books, which go beyond simple strategy to give readers more to focus on, such as elaborate game art, pullout posters, and specialty items like the inclusion of game music on a CD insert.

The guide publishing industry capitalized on and further commodified a segment of the game-playing market, which has grown to expect help and now likely feels (sometimes) as if it *needs* that help, as the games have grown both more expansive (needing guideposts to get through them) and more expensive (getting one's money's worth out of a game).

This segment of the industry, like the magazines, has grown and matured, and is now considered a vital segment of the larger game industry, even though some guide publishers have encountered legal challenges from game publishers in the past decade.[39] Game developers and publishers often work closely with guide publishers to create detailed and accurate books, and frequently promote these books in the (ever-shrinking) instruction manuals that come with the games. Most game publishers see this industry as another revenue source (royalties based on the game title) and also another valuable marketing tool in promoting a particular game. Critics would argue that the guide industry also shores up shoddy game production (games that are so poorly designed that players require help to get through them) and adds an invisible cost to the game (instead of paying just $50 for the game, players need to lay out another $15 for the guide).

Conclusions

This chapter has explored the establishment of commercial strategy guides in relation to the larger game industry. Just as game magazines first did, guides took over and further developed a pedagogical function, teaching players how to play games as well as helping them finish particular games, or find specific sites or items within them. Guides also established themselves as a paratextual support to games, offering players a greater chance to succeed with games that have increased with complexity over time. Just as early magazines taught readers the importance of high scores and beating bosses, so too guides further developed the significance of the fantasy world found in each game, working hard to preserve those illusions. After some early missteps and trial and error, guides now attempt to draw the player into a game world, provide multiple paths to success, and offer the potential to acquire ever-more gaming capital. Those guides are also now officially licensed and approved by game developers and publishers, and able to command valuable real estate on shelves in Wal-Marts across the United States.

Guides have also exposed splinters in the game-playing public, however, such as the split between the hard-core players who are versed in particular areas of gaming capital but would never buy a guide, and the more casual game players who see no problem with buying a guide to complete a game and gain capital along the way. Various types of players prize different sorts of knowledge, echoing the growing fragmentation of the game industry's products. So just as Brady's book on the Japanese influence on the game industry will appeal to those gamers interested in eastern RPGs, there are also younger players reading guides for how to catch all Pokémon in the latest version of the game. Likewise, fans of adventure games still likely need help solving certain puzzles, and those interested in a game tied to a movie may check a guide to be certain they've unlocked all the secret bonus movie outtakes. For each style of gameplay, there's a guide or "enhancement" to suit the player. But can the enhancements go too far? Are game companies always eager for players to learn about every way possible to beat a game?

The following chapter ends the first section of this book by going that next step, examining physical artifacts used to change the game-playing experience, including GameSharks and mod chips. While there were some early problems with strategy guide publishers over their rights to use game materials in their products, hardware was the first consistent area of trouble for the paratextual industry. As various companies sought to profit from and further develop the game-playing market, the game development (and publishing) industry fought back, determining that such modifications went too far in altering the game experience as well as the business of the market. But the overall development of chips and sharks demonstrates that even as business develops channels for "proper gameplay," each game player ultimately negotiated that concept individually.

GENIES, SHARKS, AND CHIPS: THE TECHNOLOGICAL SIDE TO CHEATING

A couple of years ago, I bought a disc at my local games store that lets me play imported videogames on my GameCube. Normally, the GameCube, like most other commercial game consoles, only allows games designated for its region to play on it—either North America, Japan/Asia, or Europe/Australia.[1] The "Free Loader" is a minidisc that temporarily rewrites some game addresses and values, fooling a region-locked game console into running games from any region. That way, I could try out the Japanese version of *Final Fantasy: Crystal Chronicles* before the North American one was released. Unfortunately, getting the Japanese game to run was easier than trying to figure out the spoken and written Japanese in a text-heavy game.

The disc was sold by Datel, which also makes the Action Replay series of "game-enhancer" devices. The name Free Loader is itself interesting, as it embodies some of the contradictions at play in the realm of technological cheat devices. While the disc allows all games to load freely on a Game-Cube, the name also alludes to people who contribute nothing, yet take their fair share or more. While consumers must pay for the Free Loader disc, the producers are indirectly referring to either someone who uses the disc to load pirated games (which have been illegally copied) or games that have not (perhaps yet) been released for a particular region. In either case, the players are freeing themselves from the rules of the game distribution industry, which are codified in the hardware of the console. The Free Loader embodies values—but values that challenge those dominant in the console business.

More commonly sold cheat devices such as the GameShark and Code Breaker units pose similar challenges to the technological restrictions.

While those discs don't allow pirated or imported games to run, they do unlock or allow access to hidden or advanced elements of supported games, and with each year more functions are added to them. Those products have been around since at least the 1980s, and they challenge us to ask not only if such devices should be legal but who should control the gameplay experience and how much control should reside in any kind of technological device.

For example, in an ad for one such product, a fascinating question is posed: "Can you still call it a game if you can NEVER LOSE?" That's the headline from a two-page ad in the February 1996 edition of *Electronic Gaming Monthly*. The ad is for the GameShark, described as "the ultimate game enhancer," that allows gamers to "Kill faster! Jump higher! Never die!" The ad tries to position the person who uses the device as somehow outside the law or not afraid to break the rules of the game (the tagline reads, "Make your own rules"). The exhortation to "make your own rules" is somewhat ironic given the troubled legal past of game-enhancement devices.

The rise of the technological enhancement industry has been more problematic than the strategy guide business, although both now largely coexist with the larger industry. This chapter examines the history of technological cheating devices, from Galoob's Game Genie to its contemporary counterparts the Action Replay, the Code Breaker, and the GameShark, to mod chips that can be installed in game consoles to allow illegally copied games as well as imported games to be played. The technologies employed present a greater challenge to the game industry, particularly console manufacturers, as they question who controls the game space—is it the game companies, players, third-party technology makers, or some combination of all three?

These products can be positioned as more invasive than other cheat methods as they temporarily or permanently alter the game or console, refiguring code to create a different gaming experience for the player. Going beyond manually entered cheat codes to the digital manipulation of extensive number/letter strings and the bypassing of certain hardware code to alter the play experience, the area of sharks, genies, and mod chips provides a fascinating space for exploring the limits of cheating and official help in the industries of digital games.

Galoob Lets the Genie out of the Bottle

The Game Genie, the first popular U.S. console game enhancer, was released in 1991 by Lewis Galoob Toys of San Francisco after an extended court battle with Nintendo.[2] The cartridge-like device could be inserted into the NES, and allowed players to enter codes into the game machine that changed aspects of the game being played such as the number of lives allowed or the availability of weapons. Thus, a player could gain infinite lives for Mario, or acquire the ability to become invisible and thus avoid all enemies.

Such alterations to a game were not permanent, as the device did not change the programming of the game; instead, it looked for certain bits of information and overwrote those with new data as the game booted up. In many ways, the practical results were no different than the information passed along by players in magazines—through such places as the "Classified Information" section supplied by Secret Agents in *Nintendo Power*, or similar sections in other magazines such as *Electronic Gaming Monthly* and *Next Generation*.

Yet the addition of a peripheral device that would read and (temporarily) rewrite code was perceived as dangerous by Nintendo executives, who argued that the Genie "not only alters Nintendo games, infringing on copyrights, but can make them less fun, too easy to play."[3] Nintendo subsequently filed for copyright infringement against the Genie's manufacturer. Galoob countered by suing Nintendo, requesting a judgment that the Genie device did not infringe, to which Nintendo responded by demanding an injunction against the Galoob company, so that no Genies could be released to the market while the case was being decided.[4]

Nintendo claimed that the device shortened the life of games, allowing players to finish the game too quickly, thus diminishing enjoyment and the overall gameplay experience. In court, the company contended that the device infringed on its copyrights by creating "derivative works" that robbed it of potential profits through the sale of similar versions of the same game.[5] Nintendo lost the case for a preliminary injunction, as the judge concluded there was no copyright infringement occurring and then ordered Nintendo to pay Galoob $15 million for lost sales. That decision cleared the way for all subsequent development and sale of such devices, and Galoob went on to sell eight hundred thousand units by February 1992.[6]

Enhancers such as the Game Genie (which was also released for Sega's consoles as well as the Game Boy and other devices) thus entered the peripherals industry on a fractious note, battling with the companies that the products worked with for their existence. Yet once the initial court battle was won, the somewhat outlaw status of the devices seemed to work for their creators, as they flaunted the devices' abilities to "break rules," and give gamers access to "forbidden" or "off-limits" game materials.

From Genies to Sharks: The Development of an Industry

While there are currently three main companies that distribute technological enhancement devices, those businesses all originated from the same source: the U.K.-based company Datel. Started in 1983, Datel developed the Action Replay line of cartridges and discs, which initially let a player save and back up games for the Commodore 64 computer—an operation not normally available for games at the time.[7] Over the years, the company added new functions to its products, including the ability to enter codes into a game machine to alter data values and the option to load precreated "save games" for supported game titles. Datel continued developing such devices for computers and then videogame consoles, including the NES, the Sega Master System, the SNES, Saturn, PlayStation, Nintendo 64, Dreamcast, PS2, Xbox, and GameCube.

In 1995, Datel began selling the same devices under the GameShark label in the United States, distributed through InterAct Accessories. Nevertheless, because of strong competition from Pelican Accessories' Code Breaker line of enhancers (developed by former Datel employees), InterAct dissolved, and the GameShark property was sold to Mad Katz Accessories in 2003 for $5 million.[8] Currently, Datel claims that its Action Replay line of devices is dominant in the United Kingdom with a 90 percent share of the "cheat product market during 2003."[9] The GameShark line is more prevalent in the United States, along with the Pelican Code Breaker series.

All of those devices still market themselves as offering players the ability to use thousands of cheat codes for a library of games, specific to a particular console. Yet with each new version of the device, new functions are added and extras are offered to players. Given that the most recent devices can now download new codes and other items directly to a player's console, the device creators need to perpetually develop new abilities and options for their product lines in order to keep selling units year after year.

That must be done even though next-generation consoles are only released every five or so years, and most players are unlikely to own all consoles in a particular generation. Another way that device makers compete is through the release of special discs sold at a low cost and devoted to a particular triple-A title, such as *PS2 Ultimate Codes: Kingdom Hearts 2*. This particular disc, produced by Datel, retails for $7.99 instead of the regular $19.99–39.99 price range of the "all-in-one" discs. Items like those help extend the brand line, but also reach out to players who might not be interested in playing many games, or have never tried such a device and are looking for a low-risk way to try one out.

In addition to more targeted sales, device makers also try to position their units as being more than just collections of cheat codes. For example, the Datel line of Action Replay devices positioned itself in 2004 as letting the player do "more than just cheat."[10] Running a series of pieces titled "It's Not Just for Cheating" on its Web site, the company tried to convince potential (or current) users of its technology of the variety of uses to which an Action Replay unit could be put. In the seven-part series, Datel explained how the unit would (in addition to offering codes and game saves) let the player access minigames hidden within games, play as alternate characters, and play any NTSC DVD movie as well as use a proprietary instant messenger and chat channel.[11] Likewise, Mad Katz promotes the GameShark brand, and Pelican Accessories its Code Breaker brand, with similar promises of thousands of cheats, quick access to codes for the latest games, and increasing options for use.

Yet while the accessories and extras might enhance each devices' potential, the central function of each unit is the same: to offer players tools to advance in games that designers may not have wanted to provide. Does that matter? Given that the legal battles have been waged, and such devices have been deemed legal, it would seem they do have a right to exist, and players have additional options open to them for gameplay. But should they?

Some designers oppose the use of codes or technological devices, as they take control of the gameplay process out of their hands and change the experience of how a particular game "should" be played. Certain players echo those beliefs, claiming that using such devices can ruin the gameplay experience or that such devices should only be used in particular circumstances, such as after a game has already been beaten or if a player cannot advance past a particular stage despite multiple attempts. Other players happily embrace such devices, though, using them to access all parts of a game they desire, in whatever order they wish. In that way, the devices can serve as a ludic piece of technology, allowing players the ability to not only play a game but play *with* a game, tweaking and remaking it in the image they wish it to have.

At one point in their development, however, the enhancers went a bit too far in letting players access such codes. In 2003, some players discovered they could cheat in online multiplayer games of *SOCOM: U.S. Navy Seals* using certain Action Replay codes found by searching the Internet. Those codes and the rampant cheating that resulted turned the online version of the game into an unplayable experience for many, and game developers have since modified such codes not to work in online games. Likewise, from that point onward, enhancement companies have not marketed their devices as allowing for cheating in online games.[12]

But even if some players see the abilities gained by using an enhancer as central to their fun, most of the larger game industry views that activity as marginal. Part of that is the smaller size of the enhancer business, and another part is likely the image that the enhancers choose to portray in order to sell their products. As devices that are boldly about cheating and unlocking access, which are often alluded to as unauthorized or wrong, the enhancer manufacturers are positioning themselves as marginal to the mainstream. That positioning has handily served the device makers, as they market the coolness of their products and try to create new demand for ever-expanding types of help in games. Such help costs more, yet simplifies the steps involved in cheating; rather than having to search and identify particular codes for specific games, the devices (cartridges and now discs) provide players with a "one-stop shop" of codes for the gamer in need.

The latest versions of the enhancement devices—the GameShark, Action Replay, and Code Breaker—offer players continued access to the secret codes as well as numerous saved games and Web sites with even more information about how to beat or unlock aspects of the latest games. Although many gamers I've interviewed scoff at such methods, others see them as ways to continue playing enjoyable games that have devolved into unbeatable bottlenecks. While the use of such codes and saves may detract from the feeling of satisfaction found in beating a game, there is little pleasure overall if a game is abandoned midstream because it became too difficult or unenjoyable to play.

Seen like that, the devices do provide a service to some players, and have continued to sell decently for at least two of the three main device companies: Mad Katz and Datel. In 2004, Mad Katz reported an increase in its net sales "primarily attributed to $10.5 million of GameShark product sales" due to its acquisition of InterAct.[13] Datel claims the vast majority of the UK market and outsold "its main competitor by a 5 to 1 unit ratio in the cheat product market" in the United States in 2003.[14]

Although the core game industry may have settled into an uneasy existence with enhancement device makers, other peripheral companies recognize the value of partnerships and affiliations. BradyGames announced a multiyear partnership with Mad Katz, and stated that it would publish the *GameShark Ultimate Codes* series, "the only printed resource that includes more than 60,000 exclusive GameShark codes for all the latest titles."[15] Similarly, some contemporary game magazines run strategy sections in the back of their issues, listing GameShark and Action Replay codes for various games, along with player strategies and secrets, and their own hints and tips for beating (or just altering) the latest games.

The development of technological approaches to cheating shows again how artifacts—here, cartridges and discs—can be used to alter the gaming experience. Such technologies were first positioned as disruptive and illegal by console manufacturers like Nintendo, which saw them as a threat to their control of the gameplay experience. When the law failed to side with Nintendo, companies such as Galoob were allowed to continue manufacturing these products, yet they have not gained much mainstream acceptance with game players, who readily see them as cheating and don't (openly) use them in great numbers. Yet even as they are legal, companies such as Datel and Mad Katz market their products by leveraging their former outlaw status, daring the consumer to break the rules along with them.

Cracking the Console, Modding the Market

In addition to temporary devices, hackers have developed more permanent technologies for cheating, such as the mod chip, which first became popular with the release of the original Sony PlayStation. Mod chips, like the Free Loader, also allow players to load and play pirated and import games, and became the main way to do so for the newer console systems (the PlayStation and PS2 as well as Xbox). With the advanced technologies of such consoles, game enhancers (with the exception of the Free Loader) were limited to giving players access to cheat codes, saved games, and other peripheral options.

Mod chips typically require more technical expertise to install than disc-based enhancers, thereby limiting their widespread use. Installing a mod chip into a console first necessitates opening the console, which automatically voids the warranty. The chip must then be soldered on to a console's motherboard, requiring precision and skill. While companies exist to install chips for users, there are still individuals who do those jobs themselves, although not nearly in the numbers that use the GameShark, Action Replay, or strategy guides.

The name mod chip appeared first in early 1996, and encompasses several types of devices. "Swap" mod chips require the operator to first load an original or specialized load disc that the console (in this example, a PS2) then "authenticates and region checks. At this point the modchip disables the eject notification feature of the PS2's DVD-ROM drive, allowing the user to swap the original disc. Once this swap has been performed, the operator can instruct the PS2 to load the code from the non-original disc. Since the PS2 does not realize the disc has been changed, the authentication code is never rechecked."[16]

Later, more advanced generations of mod chips included "no-swap" devices that "replicate the authentication signal that is normally sent by the PS2's drive hardware when an authorized game disc is present, causing the BIOS to believe that a copied disc is the original and boot it."[17] Finally, flashable mod chips for the PS2 contain more features than previous versions, including menus and configurable options, and can be upgraded from a CD-R, USB pen drive, or other devices.[18]

For the Xbox, mod chips allow a user to do even more. They can "run code, such as user-created applications or games. . . . [O]ne of the main uses in the modding community of this ability is to . . . run the Linux operating system from a DVD or the Xbox hard drive."[19] Certain types of Xbox mod chips also let the user manually turn the chip off, as their use can be flagged by Microsoft Live's gaming service, which runs automated security checks looking for evidence of just such devices. If found or even suspected, the system will ban offending (or alleged) mod chip users.

Given their invasiveness, it's no surprise that makers of mod chips have also been the subjects of legal challenges globally. While the devices and their installation are still (as of late-2006) illegal in the United States, however, they have been ruled legal in Australia and Italy, and their status is ambiguous in other countries.[20]

Mod chips go further than genies and sharks in reconfiguring game hardware, as they are most often permanent additions to consoles. They not only allow but also inscribe particular practices and uses that console manufacturers attempt to prevent. Specifically, they let individuals play duplicated games (either pirated or backup copies of licensed games), homebrewed games, and games not native to the regional encoding of the console. Installing and using a chip is a clear challenge to who controls the access to or experience of the gameplay situation. Chips *re*enable hardware to play software—a functionality that was locked out by console manufacturers. While this might present a challenge to Digital Rights Management tools and their owners, it does give users more functionality in their game machines and allows them to choose how to use those options.

In response, console manufacturers have officially positioned mod chips as dangerous and illegal technologies that threaten game markets as well as the futures of game developers, who are alleged to lose money because of the circulation of pirated games. They have vigorously pursued the makers and retailers of mod chips, many of who also install them for customers. For example, in 2004 federal government agencies raided a Washington, DC–based retailer who was allegedly "selling modded systems with games already copied onto the hard-drive," and the agencies had the "authority to seize circumvention devices, modified Xbox and Sony PlayStation 2 consoles, and copyrighted game software that was apparently being installed on 'modded' Xbox consoles."[21] Likewise, a "major mod chip vendor," David Rocci, received five months in prison in late 2003 for selling Xbox and PS2 mod chips.[22]

Pursuing such cases is often the job of the Entertainment Software Association, a trade group and lobbying arm for videogame publishing companies. The association actively promotes antipiracy legislation, legal enforcement, and criminal prosecution both domestically and globally, and in doing so works to construct the belief that piracy is bad, and that technologies such as mod chips can only be destructive or dangerous to game industries.

As an example, when Microsoft launched its Xbox Live service in Southeast Asia in 2003, it was reportedly with caution, as "software piracy is rampant" in the area, and "most shops will offer to solder a security-breaking chip into a console for under US$70, or will sell pre-modified sets."[23] Xbox owners there had to choose between turning the chips off, buying new consoles, or staying away from the online service because it would detect their modifications and ban them anyway. Yet the prevalence of the practices of modding and buying pirated discs reveals how difficult it can be for game hardware (as well as software) companies to completely dictate the terms of use of their products.

The practices of modding and the denial of service are about controlling (or challenging) the access to and flow of technologies, most often using other technologies to channel or disrupt, especially when laws or social norms prove not to be up to the challenge. In *The Control Revolution*, James Beniger writes about controlling flow, and the importance of the proper flow of products and information in a capitalist society.[24] Technology is frequently used to maintain control over as well as direct the flow of global products. It can restrict or enable, and is just as often the product to be directed as the tool that serves to channel. Companies such as Sony, Microsoft, and Nintendo create technological devices (consoles) that have the potential to play many types of software, but they then restrict access to particular types of software, for various reasons. In doing so, they attempt to dictate the proper use of a technology by allowing particular uses and disallowing others. Mod chips are a direct challenge to those restrictions. They allow the user to determine her own proper use, ironically by restoring consoles to their full (original) capabilities.

Enhancing Gameplay, Confusing Gaming Capital

Previous chapters have covered how magazines, guides, and codes have helped game players cultivate gaming capital, both in learning how to acquire it and then how to display it appropriately. While some players scoff at purchasing strategy guides, many do still read them or look for their free equivalents online at spaces like GameFAQs.com. So even as a particular form (a commercial guide produced by Prima) may be objectionable, the information gleaned is not. Technological devices that can allow a player to cheat seem to occupy a more ambiguous space in gaming culture and relative to the acquisition of gaming capital.

Enhancement devices, as I've mentioned above, seemed unpopular with the players that I've interviewed. Obviously the devices sell in large enough numbers to keep their product lines going, but they don't appear to be as widespread as other types of technologies or methods for cheating/altering gameplay. Although device-making companies see them as an integral part of gameplay, the players do not. The players I talked with never mentioned the devices of their own accord, and while admitting to knowing what they were, would not say they used them. Part of that reluctance could be simply in admitting that they used something not deemed acceptable by their circle or that they themselves felt the devices were not quite fair. Either way, enhancers do little to enhance gaming capital, at least among those I have spoken with. If anything, it seems such devices would be more likely to diminish a player's capital, if such use were discovered.

The installation and use of mod chips is quite different, and draws on a much smaller subset of game players, at least in the United States, where the selling of already-modded consoles is fairly rare (and of course, illegal). Individuals who either install the chips themselves or pay someone to do it for them are interested in a several things: playing imported games (usually Japanese), playing pirated/copied games, or playing with the console itself (usually an Xbox) to unlock more of its potential as a Linux machine and/or to run homebrew games. For whichever use, the activity draws a smaller subculture of game players, who view the activity as an acceptable pursuit. And within each community, knowledge of how to install chips, or how to overcome technological problems or creatively experiment with the capabilities unlocked in an Xbox, can create versions of gaming capital that have currency within the smaller group.

Overall, then, gaming capital as thought about in relation to technological devices is ambiguous, and depends on the particular technology and group of players being examined. Facility with the installation of technology (chips) can confer capital, yet too great a reliance on an enhancer might deduct capital. Just as technology use is contextual, and constituted and understood through use, so too gaming capital is mutable and responds to the particulars much more than the general situation.

Paratext Meets Technology

The technologies discussed here help to extend the gameplay experience in particular ways. Those ways have, from their beginning, been contested by the core game industry, which has challenged the legality of enhancers (and lost) and mod chips (and won, at least in certain countries). The industry and its delegates continue to take action against those using any technologies, or modifying technologies, in ways they do not approve. Technological approaches to cheating (or game enhancement) therefore point to the boundaries of acceptability currently operating in the core industry.

The core, it seems, has agreed to work with enhancement makers to a certain degree, licensing their brands to allow Datel, Pelican, and Mad Katz to advertise their products linked with the appropriate console names. Yet they don't do much more, and the enhancement companies reengineer the cheat codes on their own as well as gather other needed game data. They remain, likely by choice, decentered in relation to the game and console makers, even as they help to define—and occasionally challenge—the uses of that software and hardware.

Even further along the periphery lie the chip makers and installers, who work in a shifting legal environment, depending on location. In the United States they are illegal, and have increasingly been tracked, prosecuted, fined, and imprisoned. The core industry would probably say that such individuals and companies aren't part of the game industry at all, but their products and services also help define boundaries and construct technologies as systems of power and control. Chips rewrite console functionality, adding value where it had previously been locked out.

As parts of the paratext, then, device and chip makers show us the current edges of acceptability for the rest of the industry. They are the points where expansion can happen and legal challenges still occur. Technology is harnessed to reroute or reengineer other technology. In the process players gain more options, and core industry players see their norms and business practices confronted. But even as they seek to limit that, they cannot ultimately stop it, and the paratext continues to modify the rest of the text/industry. So as at present we see enhancers letting us unlock regionally protected DVDs, we should also keep an eye out for future practices, where the Free Loader might also work for the Xbox 360, for example.

Technologies, Access, and Player Experiences

As I've discussed earlier, the manufacturers of technological cheat devices as well as those opposed to their use have worked to position those artifacts in specific ways in order to achieve particular results. Although genies and sharks were ruled legal, they are still positioned to some degree as outside the bounds of the rules of regular gameplay. The marketing for enhancers suggests that the player can use them to achieve great things and be a rebel in doing so.

In contrast, mod chips are illegal in many places, and their "dangerous" status contains a greater threat. In addition to being hard to find and difficult to install, they can damage a user's console or restrict offending users from participating in online gaming services. The Entertainment Software Association continues to position mod chips as equal to piracy and then argue that piracy costs the industry billions of dollars a year. By working with government agencies and helping to pass specific laws (or sue individuals), the association also constructs mod chips as contraband and unworthy of the risks associated with such merchandise.

Yet such discursive positioning doesn't tell the entire story about technological cheat devices. While their use is definitely not as widespread as individual cheat codes or commercially published strategy guides, some players do use them for a variety of reasons, and those reasons also help position and define the technologies. For example, when players use Code Breaker to access any level of a game they wish at once, they challenge the "preferred reading" of the game encoded by developers.[25] In doing so, they redefine who is allowed to control the game experience, and its parameters and boundaries. They also disturb notions of sequential play progression, as there is no need to go through successive levels or challenges in order to "earn" better weapons or special items.

I use the word earn consciously here, as it's a term that many gamers I talked with used when discussing cheating and what it means. For players who chose not to cheat—whatever that meant for them—it was often about earning their way to achievement in a game. They wanted (or felt the need) to put in the time and effort, develop skill, and master a game on their own terms. Winning or beating a game, or even just advancing through it, was an activity that brought them rewards for their own sake and was greatly tied to effort. By contrast, they would define cheaters as those who did not feel the need to earn their achievements, either through mastery or time involvement. For them, the cheater was the freeloader, much like the product of the same name.

For both types of players, however, cheating technologies don't seem to relate much to gaming capital. Such devices as GameSharks and Action Replays seem to occupy a marginal position in wider gaming culture, as they appear to imply a lack of expertise rather than a surplus of it. Chip users are likely positioned differently, as skill is involved in the installation process and the dangers involved in their use can be currency within particular gaming subcultures.

Nevertheless, there is a continual struggle between console manufacturers and chip users in the meanings over such uses. The major publishers are served well by reinforcing general fears about playing with technology or cracking open a computer case to experiment with the insides of a machine. For Sony, proper technology use for its consumers must be simplified and commodified, opaque and delimited. It involves not cracking open machines, playing only properly purchases discs, and buying a new generation of machine every five or so years.

For those installing their own mod chips, technology is mutable and accessible. Technologies can be mixed and redefined, with the user reclaiming lost abilities and pushing at artificially imposed boundaries. Yet such activities are constructed as dangerous or illegal, and they aren't that common. If players do use a mod chip, it is most likely installed for them by a third party. So while mod chips challenge the proper use, this particular technological activity is also commodified, just by a different seller.

To a limited extent, GameSharks and more so mod chips point to fault lines in the game industry. They expose a system of choices and decisions points, made to encode or direct a particular flow of capital and distribution. Chips render encoding systems inoperative. On a metalevel, the hardware cannot "see" the foreignness of the pirated or internationally purchased disc. Technology works to fool technology. Who decides on the proper uses of technologies? Cheat devices not only let players decide, they make the question visible, where previously it was defined out of existence.

As Michel Foucault would argue, power is inscribed in everyday practices, and here we see power embodied in the consoles that encode particular types of use to the exclusion of others. So even if an Xbox is really a

PC with an operating system hidden within it, Microsoft attempts to limit that functionality through code. Yet just as power is expressed, it always meets resistance, a counterforce. Here, that counterforce is the hackers who figured out that by loading a special save game file for the *MechAssault* title, they could force the system to allow the loading of unauthorized files from a DVD drive or USB storage device, and turn the Xbox into a desktop computer running Linux.

Such pressure and counterpressure ensure a productive system—one that keeps all (or most) attempts at monopolizing control at bay—and also ensures that new activities, new options, and new technologies are produced. The system needs the hackers and chip makers to push the boundaries of the allowable as well as to lay bare the limits that have been carefully shrouded over by dominant interests. Power is expressed as a give-and-take, with it being a perpetual cat-and-mouse game between the dominant and oppositional positions.

Adding the enhancement device makers into the context of the game industry does demonstrate that the industry is not a monolithic entity, working together seamlessly to produce games and supplemental products for players to purchase and use. Still, items such as the GameShark do show how the overall industry is promoting ways for players to alter their gaming experiences, to perhaps play games in ways not everyone agrees with. While that trend began with magazines and strategy guides (through their inclusion of secret codes and fun tricks), those actions became more embedded in the context of the industry with the development of Genies and chips. While players may use Sharks and chips without raising such questions, they are important to ask and consider. Cheat technologies, much more than single codes or guides, expose how technologies shape practices and how competing technologies can expand the boundaries of what is possible—not just to do but simply to envision.

Part II

Game Players

GAINING ADVANTAGE: HOW VIDEOGAME PLAYERS DEFINE AND NEGOTIATE CHEATING

It is all about suspense; it is like someone telling you how an action movie ends. So what is the point in seeing it if you already know how the movie ends?
—*Jake, age twenty-two*

If a game is good and I am enjoying it, it becomes almost part of my life—I will think about it on the bus home, wake up in the mornings thinking, "Aha! I wonder if I could do that?" And [I] close my eyes at night to find flashes of the game rushing around inside my head.
—*Hope, age thirty*

How do game players play games, and does the experience of gameplay extend beyond direct interaction with the game itself? Beyond thinking about what games do *to* players, there is still a comparatively small amount of research concerning how players themselves organize their gameplay time and space(s), how they make choices about which games to play and why, and what else might be involved in their gameplay experiences, beyond a console, a controller, and a comfy seat.[1] Some researchers have explored how women enjoy games.[2] Others have analyzed the communication and community practices of FPS players.[3] Likewise, T. L. Taylor and Mikael Jakobsson have looked at player dynamics in *EverQuest*, studying how power gamers play the game in ways quite different from more casual gamers, even if they put in the same amount of time.[4]

Still, comparatively little is known about game players' experiences, especially when compared to a field such as television studies, where the audience is still presumed to be more passive than a game player. As players actively engage with games, they don't do so in a vacuum. Players have various ideas and information about games before they begin playing, and they gain further knowledge as they progress. Key components of that information flow include knowledge about supplemental materials such as walkthroughs, strategy guides, and the employment of cheat codes.

One way to contextualize such new knowledge is by thinking about player activities through the lens of gaming capital. As previous chapters have demonstrated, the paratextual industries associated with games, including magazines and enhancement devices, have helped define how players should play games, in addition to how they might evaluate and think about them. Yet such industries can't dictate the terms of use; individuals are active in how they choose to use (or not) such items as well as how they view such things relative to the games they play. Neither side (the player or the industries) has total control, but power differentials do exist. The construction of such industries and elements helps set the terms for debate as well as frames what is debated. And even as paratextual industries have helped to create a thriving system of gaming capital that individual gamers may draw from or contribute to, that very system of capital is sometimes at odds with some of the means of achieving capital.

As we seek greater knowledge about the cultural impacts of videogames, the experiences of players themselves demand attention. This chapter addresses one part of the larger question "How do people play games?" by examining players' uses of supplemental items during gameplay, how they define what is and is not cheating in reference to those items, and then, what actions they ultimately take in accordance with their beliefs and reasoning. In doing so, this chapter offers a more detailed exploration of how gameplay is experienced by a selection of players, and what is involved in that gameplay in terms of the use or rejection of a growing paratextual industry.

Cheating in Games: Breaking Unseen Rules or Violating the Spirit of the Game

First, what does it mean to cheat in a videogame? How can one cheat? Asking such questions forces us to consider the issue of just where the rules of a videogame can be found, and then determine how they could be secretly broken or bent for personal gain. Where are the rules? One easy answer is in the instruction manual that comes with a game. The manual often explains the objective of the game, the background of the characters and the situations, how to use the interface (controller) correctly, and what the player needs to do to win the game. It can give pointers for advancing through the game and serves as a (more or less useful) reference to consult during gameplay. But even if instruction manuals describe an objective and detail what characters can do in the game, they don't truly give the player the rules. And many players don't even read the manual and seem to get through the game just fine.

The rules of a videogame are contained within the game itself, in the game code. The game engine contains the rules that state what characters (and thus players) can and cannot do: they can go through certain doors, but not others; they can't walk through walls or step over a boulder (except maybe a special one); they can kill their enemies, but not their friends; and they must engage in certain activities to trigger the advancement of the story and the game. All of these things are structured into the code of the game itself, and thus the game embodies the rules, *is* the rules, that the player must confront.

Lawrence Lessig writes about the code of the Internet, but his observations also apply to games. He believes that code regulates, and "as the world is now, code writers are increasingly lawmakers."[5] He also maintains that at least in reference to the Internet, our rhetoric about its "essence" hides the truth that this space is constructed, and that real choices have been made about what processes or activities are privileged or discouraged. Although he is correct in assessing current beliefs about the Internet, something different has occurred with games. Here, too, code is law and constructs the rules of the game. But for game players, this rule of law is not a hidden construction, and is also, for some, open to question and even alteration.

There have always been attempts to go beyond the rules in videogames. If we state at the outset that a player must abide by the coded rules in a videogame, what might cheating include? For some, it means going beyond the instruction manual to friends, strategy guides, and gaming magazines for hints or walkthroughs explaining how best to advance through a certain area. Help like this has been around since at least *Nintendo Power* magazine, which as discussed earlier, provided players with extensive guidance to help them play games and find all of the hidden secrets in a game. Cheating might also include the use of cheat codes that when entered into a controller or keyboard, produce a certain (beneficial) effect, such as a complete restoration of health, unlimited ammunition, or more powerful weapons. Cheating might extend to the use of a GameShark, which enters codes electronically to a game system to unlock other features. Cheating might involve altering the code of the game itself, secretly, to gain advantage in multiplayer games. It might also include paying real money for game currency or items, through such sites as the independent International Game Exchange or Sony's Station Exchange. Those aren't the only ways to cheat, and some players would definitely not label them all cheating, but this is at least an idea of what could constitute an advantage for a player.

But how prevalent are certain constructions of cheating? Do all players see cheating in the same way? How do individual game players define cheating for themselves? This chapter investigates those questions, and offers a variety of views and insights into why the definitions vary, and what this can mean for individuals as well as groups of players.

Gamers, Game Players, Gamegrrls, and Gamegeeks

As part of this project, I conducted in-depth interviews with twenty-four self-identified game players ranging in age from fourteen to forty-one. Of that group, eleven were girls and women. Two interview methods were employed: half the sample was interviewed face-to-face, with each interview being audiotaped and then transcribed; and the second half of the interviews were conducted over e-mail, with questions initially e-mailed to participants recruited from several sources, and then follow-up e-mail(s) sent for clarification and expansion of certain answers. I also conducted an open-ended survey of fifty game players ranging in age from nineteen to thirty-two who were part of a college-level course on digital games and culture. All subjects from both samples were active game players (with variation in the types of games played, the hours played, and experience levels). Interviewees were recruited through a snowball sampling method, identifying more game players from those first interviewed (initial interviews were with university students who responded to a call for gamers, and others were recruited through Web sites such as womengamers.com and joystick101.org). All interviewees and survey respondents have been assigned pseudonyms, or chose one for themselves, for identification purposes in the study. Interviews and surveys were conducted between May 2001 and May 2004.

This chapter explores several issues, including how respondents chose to define cheating in their own terms, both as an abstract concept and related to game playing; if respondents cheated or not in actual gameplay and why; how this reconciled with their definition(s) of cheating; and what actual material and social elements they used, including such items as walkthroughs, strategy guides, GameSharks, hacks, cheat codes, online sites, help from friends, and any other artifact or source mentioned.

Players' Definitions of Cheating

This section looks at how peoples' definitions of cheating vary and what the differences could mean to us, and does not take into account subsequent player actions. Here, my interest is in how people define the actions they will or won't take, rather than which they actually choose. The way players talk about cheating appears to fall into three categories, with one overarching theme. It's important to note that players' answers sometimes spanned categories, but when they did, there was always a logical progression in how they did so.

Overarching: Cheating Gives You an Unfair Advantage

Running throughout all the definitions was the feeling that cheating creates an unfair advantage for the cheater. Although many times this advantage was in relation to another player in a multiplayer game, it was also mentioned in regard to single-player games as just an unfair advantage in general. And it was mentioned as well by players who thought walkthroughs "were" and "weren't" cheating, and those who felt you could "certainly" or "never" cheat in a single-player game. The common thread appeared to be that cheating was more than just *breaking* a rule or law; it was also those instances of bending or reinterpreting rules to the players' advantage. Players actively made ethical judgments about gameplay that extended beyond the coded rules of the game.

Even as digital games can code in rules for players to follow, there are also "soft rules" that are negotiated. Those rules can be broken more easily than the game code or "hard rules," but to many players they are still important in understanding the bounds of acceptable gameplay and how far one can push those boundaries before an accusation of cheating is made.

The three categories that follow all draw from the unfair advantage conceptualization, but begin to draw distinctions between certain actions and items that when used, can constitute cheating. These categories actually might better be thought of not as separate but as lying on a continuum. That allows for players' more fluid practices to be taken into account as well as to see linkages between concepts.

"Anything Other Than Getting through the Game All on Your Own"

At one end of the continuum or spectrum would be the purist. This player would take the position highlighted above—believing that anything other than a solo effort in completing a game is cheating. Players here define cheating quite broadly, such as "when you use external sources to complete a game" (Tina, twenty-eight). Yet this position quickly becomes qualified, or is a bit of a straw person, as players in this group usually modify their statement along the lines of "anything other than getting through a game all on your own, with the exception of having a friend in the room helping you figure things out" (Mona, thirty-two). Even the most hard-core purists admitted to asking a relative, spouse, or friend, when they got stuck in a game. And for this group, the "ask a friend" lifeline seemed acceptable, but was couched in terms of "but only if you're really stuck," meaning that you had already tried to figure out the situation on your own first.

Along those lines, this group sees commercially published strategy guides, Web site walkthroughs, cheat codes, real-money trade, and everything "beyond" that as all being cheating. For example, one player states that cheating is "using information acquired outside of the game and your head to get items, find shortcuts, etc., that you wouldn't otherwise, while playing earnestly" (Jessica, twenty-five). Likewise, another player explained that "using information from a site, purchased guide, or telephone hotline in order to get around a problem, kill an enemy, solve a riddle, gain a skill, or something like that—without having at least tried to solve the issue yourself—is cheating" (Hope, thirty). While this group sees the use of items like walkthroughs and strategy guides as cheating, even they generally maintain that the use of such things is "acceptable," but in specific situations only—such as when the player has already tried repeatedly to solve the puzzle or kill the boss (or so on), but can't and is thus stuck. At that point, the player might stop playing the game out of sheer frustration and a real inability to progress further. It appears that even if it is labeled as cheating in that instance, it is considered OK.

Likewise, if a player has already beaten or completed a game, and wants to play again to explore new areas or try new things, the use of guides and other items becomes acceptable. A forum on the game magazine *Electronic Gaming Monthly*'s Web site that asked the question "Do you use cheat codes?" was answered by numerous players, the majority of whom responded that the use of such codes and other items was fine, once they had completed the game and were on at least the second round of play.[6]

It's important to keep in mind that the players defining cheating in this grouping are all referring to single-player games. These are not games where a person is opposed to another player—only to the machine (multi-player cheating is discussed in the third theme). While there is much talk of "only cheating yourself," which may not be serious, these players do still see cheating in games where the player is not competing against anyone but oneself as well as in games that are multiplayer. How can that be, when cheating is normally defined as gaining an unfair advantage over another player?

This particular formulation of cheating can be better understood by referring to Johan Huizinga's concept of the magic circle as well as Espen Aarseth's discussion of aporias and epiphanies in adventure games.[7] For Huizinga, play can only occur in a magic circle that sets the boundaries for the game to played, where "inside the play-ground an absolute and peculiar order reigns . . . it creates order, is order."[8] What bounds the circle are the rules of the game.

As discussed before, the rules of a digital game are contained within the programming of the game itself. Yet players also acknowledge certain soft rules in defining for themselves how far one could perhaps venture outside the circle for help. This is certainly not the breaking of rules such as the cracking or hacking of codes that form other definitions of cheating but is instead a more complex negotiation of cultural systems of support in gaming culture. How far will players move into that support system? At some point, players must make individual decisions about what they will and won't read, who to ask and for how much information, and so on, in playing a game.

For this group, gameplay is a bounded experience, and the use of almost any external item or resource could be considered cheating. Acceptable gameplay, then, is limited to interacting solely within the game world and cannot include other elements. The more interesting question is what are the implications of doing so? If we can see the benefit of such support (getting past a point where one is hopelessly stuck), is there a drawback as well? If one is only cheating oneself, why would a player be concerned with seeing guides and walkthroughs as wrong in any way?

Just as the magic circle defines the rules of the game, Aarseth's formulation of gaming's aporia-epiphany structure lends clues to this puzzle. Aarseth explains that in digital games such as adventure games, there often arise aporias or gaps that are "local and tangible, usually . . . concrete, localized puzzle[s] whose solution eludes us."[9] We must search for a solution to a puzzle, or the correct strategy to defeat an enemy, to move past the aporia and continue on with the game. The moment when we grasp the logic of the puzzle or determine what attack to employ is our epiphany. "This is the sudden revelation that replaces the aporia, a seeming detail with an unexpected, salvaging effect: the link out."[10]

While Aarseth does not speculate further on the instance of the epiphany for the player, it seems that it is frequently an emotional "aha!" moment, when the player either realizes that she overlooked an important clue or she has painstakingly solved a difficult problem. The greater the struggle is, the more satisfying or bigger the epiphanic moment. Taking this back to the use of guides and walkthroughs, such items will either reduce or eliminate the satisfaction derived from having an epiphany. The player is, essentially, looking up the epiphany in a book. While players themselves admit that such use is acceptable to salvage a failing game or in a second play, they reject the overuse of such items in the first round as cheating. Perhaps they are objecting to being cheated out of the epiphany or the emotional gratification of the epiphany. While they are not breaking any rules, an essential aspect of the gameplay—excitement and satisfaction—is reduced further and further with each glance back through the guide.[11]

Code Is Law: Breaking the Rules of the Game

Midway across the continuum is a group that doesn't see the use of items like walkthroughs and guides as cheating but draws the line at items such as cheat codes, unlockables, and alterations of the game code itself. Here again, people accept the possibility of cheating in single-player games (as well as in multiplayer games), where the manipulation of code *for its own sake* can be enough to qualify.

For example, one player talks about cheating as "altering the framework that has been set forth, either something like what I understand is done in some online games where the code is actually altered to assist a certain player or using a cheat code" (Roy, twenty-six). Likewise, another player believes that "cheating is when you unfairly take advantage of 'quirks' in the game to further the development of your character in the game or your progress in the game itself" (Sally, twenty-four).

Players make distinctions between using codes that have been created by game developers, and those that players design to hack or alter the game code. Yet for this group, the use of both amounts to the same thing: cheating. There is an echo here of the danger of "epiphany loss" mentioned with the first group; one player said that the use of codes to win a fighting game would be a "hollow win" (Sally). But for this group, there appeared to be a distinction between, on the one hand, asking friends and consulting guides, and on the other, using code to win. The difference here was in the level of interference with the game—a player would have to actively alter the game rules, break the rules, in order to gain the (unfair) advantage.

For this group, as for Lessig, code is law. Players acknowledge that items such as cheat codes are readily available and accepted in some quarters, but the reconfiguration of game code is the central key to what constitutes cheating for them. Here the bending of rules is shifted—lines are drawn more closely around the game itself and further from "outside" elements like walkthroughs, which this group sees as acceptable. While actively hacking the game code is a clear rule breakage, the use of codes to unlock items or benefits not earned through gameplay becomes the bending that is deemed unacceptable. The magic circle bounding play contracts; to push or bend the boundaries involves the use of code, rather than using outside information or items. At this location along the continuum, cheating can involve other players, but can still be a single-player issue.

You Can't Cheat a GameCube, You Can Only Cheat Another Player

Finally, a third group of players defined cheating as only existing in relation to another player. These players more closely aligned with J. Barton Bowyer, who characterizes cheating as a social activity: "to cheat, not to play the game that reflected the norm, indicated that there was another world, the world of deception, in which people did not play the game, your game, but their own."[12]

One person described cheating as involving "wrongdoing. Someone has to be worse off because someone else took unfair advantage. . . . You can only cheat another person" (Ralph, twenty-four). Similarly, other players talk about cheating as "breaking the rules or finding a loophole (like a bug in the code) to gain an advantage against someone else who is playing by the rules" (Niles, age not given). It is also implied here that cheaters are using hacks or other enhancements that other players are not—they are hiding their advantage. This should be distinguished from groups of players that, for example, all agree to play a game where player killing (PK) is allowed; in that situation, killing a fellow character would not be cheating, yet playing on a server where it is banned would be.

For this group, cheating is necessarily social (or antisocial), involving others. The use of items such as walkthroughs or code devices in a single-player game is acceptable because, by definition, one cannot cheat a machine or oneself. Those items may further progress, but they do not make another player worse off. Cheating means the introduction of deception and possible chaos into the game world, which is shared with other players. Since players are unaware of who may be cheating, uncertainty and distrust increase, especially as players move from multiplayer games at home with friends and relatives to online games that can feature thousands of unknown colleagues and opponents. Eventually, cheating (or its rumor) can lead to the breakdown of games—such as the problems that have occurred with *Diablo* and *Speed Devils Online Racing*.[13] While some correctives can be attempted (such as the creation of the company Even Balance and its PunkBuster product to stop cheating in online games, discussed in chapter 6), at other times game worlds are simply abandoned due to the rampant cheating.

For this group, the magic circle admits many players, yet the "game" being played differs by player. While deceiving others is the key to cheating, that can include hacking or altering code, exploiting systems, or socially exploiting other players. To cheat is to deceive others, but to make it appear that you are not doing so. The bounds of the magic circle have been cracked in some way, yet only the cheater can perceive the change.

Do What I Say, Not What I Do: Cheating as a Daily Practice

Although players have definite ideas about what does and does not consti-tute cheating, most of them engage in the practice on a regular basis:

I've cheated in games before because sometimes it is fun to not play by the rules or get that "god mode" feeling. (Abe, twenty-two)

Yes, I find some games far too difficult, and due to my lack of patience I will find a code to make me invulnerable or allow me to skip levels. (Noel, twenty)

Yes, I have cheated, but no one was taking the game seriously anyway! I mean, *everyone* was cheating! We all knew. It was funny. So, my cheating was OK because the rules were redefined. (Cathy, twenty-one)

I have *definitely* cheated in games. I cheated in *Diablo II* online and I had to agree not to cheat before I started playing. . . . I like to have any possible ad-vantage against people who do not necessarily want to play fair with me. (Pete, twenty-two)

As these excerpts demonstrate, players who may define particular actions as cheating have few qualms about actually using that information or resource, at least in specific circumstances. They usually feel the need to justify their actions, however, given the generally negative connotations associated with the term cheating. Notice even in the above examples that players talked of "everyone else cheating" or other players who don't want to play fair to begin with. Likewise, even in single-player games, the activity of cheating is justified—games are too difficult or there is fun in playing god.

When players do decide to cheat, what is it they are using or doing? Most often, it's the benign activities that players engage in—asking friends for help with solving puzzles, going online to consult a Web site or walk-through with tips on how to beat a specific opponent, or the steps neces-sary to gain a particular weapon. Clearly the Internet has been a boon to game players, as the availability of what is likely gigabytes of free informa-tion makes playing games more fun, more communal, and easier to do.

Almost all players utilize free sources of information—asking friends and family in person and strangers online, and consulting informational sources on the Internet. Next in line are print sources such as strategy guides. Many players do not admit to using such sources or at least to purchasing them on their own. At that stage money is involved, and a greater need must be identified than one simple problem (or the player must have a larger investment in a game, such as being a fan of the series) in gameplay. Following guides would be (legal) technological devices such as the Action Replay and GameShark. While those products are more versatile than a single title guide (being able to hold codes for many games), they also carry with them a greater stigma of cheating and offer one central type of cheating—the entering of codes—that does not appeal to all players.

Finally, coming in last are real-money trade and tip lines. None of the players who I talked with admitted to using real money to buy in-game currency, items, or accounts. That is probably due to the stigma that the practice still carries for many players as well as its violation of most games' terms of service agreements. I'll discuss such dedicated cheaters more in the next chapter, and will offer a more detailed account of real-money trade in chapter 7. I also couldn't find any players who admitted to calling a game tip line for information, although a couple of individuals did mention that someone they knew (a "friend?") had done so. Tip lines seemed to offer the least utility, and especially with the prevalence of information on the Internet, tip lines were seen as a waste of money, and it is questionable how many still exist.

Yet beyond the constraints of money and convenience, which certainly play a certain role in individuals' cheating and noncheating behaviors, why did people cheat? They cheated for different reasons, each of which is discussed in detail next.

To Cheat or Not to Cheat: What Made Me Do It?

There is no one single reason why people will cheat (or "enhance their gameplay experience") in games. After talking with interviewees, game developers, those working in peripheral industries, and monitoring discussion boards for many games over a period of several years, it is apparent there are multiple reasons for player cheating that are not mutually exclusive. Further, these reasons can change for individual players in different situations, on different days, and in different games. Perhaps the only constant is the lack of a constant factor.

That's because cheating isn't just about subverting the (game) system; it's also about augmenting the system. It's a way for individuals to keep playing through:

- boredom
- difficulty
- limited scenarios
- rough patches or just bad games

Cheating, or however such activities might be differently defined, constitutes players asserting agency, taking control of their game experience. It is players going beyond the "expected activity" in the game. Knowledge of how, when, and why people cheat (or refuse to) can help to better understand the gameplay experience.

Because I Was Stuck

It may seem obvious, but individuals want to play games and succeed in some way at them.[14] While learning can come from making mistakes and failing, too much of such negative "learning" destroys the pleasure in playing and may ultimately end the game. The most cited reason that players offer for cheating in games is *getting stuck* and being unable to progress any further. That failure happens because either the player or the game does not measure up in some way relative to the other.

Although researchers have begun to investigate the differences between play styles and the interests of men and women (and boys and girls), there is little information concerning the actual skill levels of different players across different types of games. It would probably even be difficult to determine what skills to measure and how to measure them—either in a game, over time, across game playing, or by any other yardstick. Even without such information, however, we can guess that player skill varies enormously, and the challenges that various games offer also differ, along with design competencies. And even among the best players, gameplay difficulties can occur, such as when a highly skilled 2D platform gamer moves to 3D FPS games for the first time. Different screen-reading tactics, methods for controlling the interface, and recognition of iconic elements all come together to create an experience that can be exciting and fresh, but also confusing and potentially discouraging.

Those situations occur with great frequency, especially as we move away from considering the abilities of the hard-core or power gamers to the more casual (and much larger) game-playing audience. Individual players run up against roadblocks to their game playing in many instances, including but not limited to:

- a puzzle they cannot solve
- an enemy who cannot be beaten
- a level with no obvious end point
- an unclear objective
- bugs that inhibit certain actions

Virtually every player I have talked with will use some form of help or cheat to get unstuck in the above situations, whether they define it as cheating or not. Such actions are perfectly rational, as without the help, it is unlikely that gameplay can even continue—the game is put aside in frustration and anger. Yet even as players know that they are trying to salvage some fun out of the game and have no intentions of further cheating, they still often try to justify their actions. For example, Mona explains that

If I'm stuck on a level and just cannot figure out what to do next, I'll look at the walkthrough for just that part, but not for the whole game. In that way, I can get on with the game, but I haven't spoiled all of it.

Likewise, another player argues that guides:

help me get through certain points where I just need to get to the next point and I'm not *seeing* what I need to see. It's probably 'cause I haven't had enough sleep and I've been overeating in front of the TV for the last few days, but it's a, uh, that's what I use them for, more than anything else. And before I buy a guide I'll call my brother-in-law, Ray, and say "Ray! You've played this game, haven't you? What do I do? Here?" (Harmony, twenty-eight)

Even if players do not see these activities as cheating, they still justify the actions as legitimate in some way:

If I am stuck I will use walkthroughs. I also employ friends' help. I don't consider that cheating because you can justify it in odd ways. That is, using a walkthrough can be like a character's gut reaction. (George, nineteen)

I only use the help as a last resort. In the past when I didn't, I would not finish games when I got frustrated. (Ely, thirty)

Why would players try to legitimize an activity they don't see as cheating? In part, perhaps because cheating has a negative connotation to it and players are aware of such meanings. Many players have also stressed the importance of playing and winning a game "on one's own," and therefore, without outside help. The pleasure of a game often comes from achievements, and as players relate, when achievements come from consulting a guide or using a code—rather than the players' own ingenuity, creativity, or skill—the pleasure is hollow.

Such explanations can also tie back to gaming capital. Although guides and magazines can give players essential knowledge, and thus capital, overreliance (or perhaps any reliance, depending on the player) comes at a cost: admitting to an initial lack of gaming capital, at least in that particular situation.

While gaming capital has evolved, it has done so in interesting ways. Although industries have arisen to help players increase their enjoyment of gameplay, there is a striking contradiction at work. Players are not supposed to need help. If a person claims a certain amount of gaming capital, that capital bespeaks a certain level of expertise, which the player should possess. And so, the use of enhancement devices becomes furtive, in order to save face. Gamers in the know are not supposed to need such things—yet they do. So they may talk of only using them "when stuck" or "when a game is already beaten." Of course, not all players see gaming capital as limiting their options, but the coolness and "elite gamer" attitude fostered by such industries can work against as well as for their efforts.

These justifications, for whatever reasons, suggest that when players cheat to get unstuck, they are performing an *instrumental* action relative to gameplay. Codes, walkthroughs and hints are tools that players employ to restart a game that they cannot play—either because their skill level does not equal the games' imagined audience or because of faulty game design. It is not about extending or enhancing the game but about reentering it. Here, cheats are the "key" that allows players back into the game world and gives back the opportunity to re-create lost pleasure.

Finally, it should be noted that players themselves see these cheats for getting unstuck as "a last resort" and something that does have the ability to diminish their enjoyment. That could be due to either the concern that the use of outside information may destroy the pleasure of the epiphany or a fear of others' discovery of a player's lack of gaming capital. Yet players are willing to sacrifice some pleasure or admit to a lack of gaming skill if it means they can continue to play the game.

For the Pleasure of the Experience: It's Fun to Play God

I have cheated on certain occasions in some off-line shooter-type games, simply to make the game more enjoyable and long lasting (so I didn't have to start over again and again. (Drew, twenty-seven)

Sometimes it's good, at the end of a long, frustrating day, to put on the god cheat in *Quake III* and just mow opponents down left and right. . . . It can be very cathartic for me. (Mona)

Although less frequently mentioned, many other players also report cheating for the pleasures it can bring. For the most part, this group referred specifically to playing either single-player games this way, or in situations with friends where cheating was openly acknowledged and condoned by the group. Cheating for pleasure in multiplayer games is discussed in the last section of this part of the chapter, as there appear to be different reasons for that sort of cheating.

Here, contrary to the player using a cheat to get back into the game, a cheat is used to bring even more pleasure to an already-pleasurable experience. The player may have already completed and beaten the game once, or is curious about secrets or alternative options within the game. In such situations, the paratext surrounding games comes into play—players have read or heard about secrets within games, including things like side quests for powerful weapons, or ways to get the Golden Chocobo in *Final Fantasy IX* or the bicycle in *Crazy Taxi*. The information might have come from friends, Internet sites, or a strategy guide. Whatever the case, players are often invested in getting a complete gameplay experience, and so for many of them, that includes doing everything possible in a game.

In such situations, players may or may not see such activities as cheating. For those who do, they are careful to stress that they only do such things after they have beaten the game once already. Tom (twenty-one), for example, explains that

the help that I use is usually unlimited weapons; no damage; sniper-fire for all guns. I cheat so I can go back and have fun [but] . . . only when I have already beaten the game and started over with codes.

Relatedly, some players don't explicitly mention pleasure or fun as a reason to cheat but instead talk about wanting to "obtain everything," "uncover secrets," or "explore the game freely and more easily," or doing it "for the novelty." Here, enjoyment is tied to completion or a deeper knowledge of a particular game. Gamers are aware of all the extras now built into games, and are intent on experiencing as much of that content as they can. In that regard, the paratextual industry has succeeded in creating high expectations for game players about what *should* be part of regular gameplay and "how much" content they should be getting.

Cheating, in this instance, is not the instrumental action that it is when a player is stuck—it's more ludic in form. Cheats here are a playful expression for the player, intent on staying within a certain frame of mind, whether or not that action actually constitutes cheating or not. For those who do consider it cheating, it seems that certain instrumental obligations must be met first—such as finishing the game once or justifying the purchase through reference to spending a lot of money. At that point, the player can turn to (or see as justified) such actions. For those who don't consider it cheating, it is pure pleasure.

Time Compression: Hitting Fast-forward

As Julian Kücklich explains, some cheats allow players to speed up the narrative of games and thus involve a "condensation of space."[15] Such cheats can take different forms, depending on the type of game being played—adventure gamers may consult a walkthrough to learn how to solve a puzzle more quickly, while FPS gamers might obtain a code to give them unlimited ammo and therefore clear levels at a faster rate. Importantly, though, the player is moving through the game at a presumably higher speed than they would "on their own."

Kücklich doesn't explore specific reasons for players choosing (or not choosing) such cheats, and although conceptually they may go together fairly well (the walkthrough hint and the unlimited ammo code), often players do see distinctions between them. As mentioned before, players tend to draw lines based on how "conceptually close" the cheat is to the game. For some players, walkthrough hints are OK, but codes are too similar to altering the structure of the game itself. Although both might achieve a similar end (that is, fast-forward), they do remain distinct for some players.

And yet, different players do employ such cheats. Players specifically mentioned using codes or walkthroughs to "get through a game as quickly as possible" to achieve some sort of completion. If a game had a particularly involved story, the story was frequently cited as a catalyst for the action:

I could have figured it out, but I was in a hurry to get to the end. I wanted to see what was going on, what was coming next. (Harmony)

I am more interested in the advancement of the game's story than the value I place on the game's ability to challenge me. (Steve, twenty-one)

Players can become involved in a particular story line, and want to see the conclusion without investing the required time to accomplish all the game-given tasks. And as many RPGs can require fifty-plus hours to complete, it's really no surprise that some players would want to arrive at the ending without spending the equivalent of more than an entire week of paid work to get there.

Such practices by game players do speak to the desire of some players for still-engrossing but less-lengthy games. Codes and hints can be fruitfully employed by the savvy gamer to tailor the gaming experience to their own time frame, but other players (or potential players) may be put off by the required time investments and not even attempt such games.

In counterpoint to wanting to witness story resolution, other players simply felt the need for closure with the game and wanted to hurry to the end point.

Just to get a game over with. (Kris, twenty-four)

When I give up on the game, so I don't want to invest the time to finish it, but I still want to see how it ends. I paid for it. I might as well see the ending. (Tim, thirty-two)

Here, the instrumental use of cheats returns, as they help players achieve a goal that is not entirely in line with the developers' original intent. The story isn't mentioned as a driving force for finishing the game, leaving us to speculate that players may also desire a certain amount of closure for its own sake—either being able to say that one has finished a game or the self-knowledge of completion. Some players also suggest that more interesting parts may be coming, and they wish to get past the "crap" and hopefully find more engrossing subject matter.

The instrumental nature of the cheat is in evidence, as it allows the gamer to move on to different games or activities that offer more promise of pleasure. In the case of those wishing to complete a story, the cheat may also allow pleasure in the knowledge of the story ending, if not in the actual gameplay.

Being an Ass: Multiplayer Cheating

Finally, there's the person most of us think about when we envision the cheater. Playing against others, either online or in person, the cheater is the player who everyone else loves to hate.

Sometimes I just feel like being a jerk online and will use cheat programs online. (Tim)

I think I cheated (multiplayer) because I was an ass, and/or I wanted revenge against another player. (Victor, twenty-one)

I have *definitely* cheated in games. I cheated in *Diablo II* online and I had to agree not to cheat before I started playing. . . . I like to have any possible advantage when playing a game online against people who do not necessarily want to play fair with me. (Pete)

Multiplayer cheaters were the definite minority of the players I interviewed. Players offered multiple reasons for such behavior, and most acknowledged that it was wrong or at least illegal to cheat in those ways. Several players admitted to doing such things as using aimbots and hacking the game code for the fun of causing distress and anger in other players. Others pointed to an already cheat-filled situation, and claimed that their own cheating was only to level the playing field. And one player mentioned his prowess in gaming, declaring that superior players had earned the right to cheat. By contrast, he felt that those without elite gaming skills were the ones not deserving of the greater abilities to be gained by cheating.

That last informant was illustrative of the "game the system" type of cheater who others have written about.[16] They tend to see themselves as elite gamers who have already surpassed the normal challenges offered by a game and so turn to gaming the game itself for exploits. In keeping with that approach, it would make sense for such players to express disdain for lesser-skilled players who attempt the same hacks. As Derek (twenty-one) explains,

If a person knows how to play the videogame, if they've proven time and time again that there aren't many games that can keep them like, you know, that they can't beat, then I have no problem with cheating. It's the people who don't know videogames and then they decide they want to cheat so they can run off and play people who are way bigger than them and kill them. 'Cause that's just not, I don't know, I mean [if] you don't have any actual ability within the game, you shouldn't in a way be privy to that knowledge of how to soup your guy up.

Yet in addition to the act of earning the right to cheat, players such as Derek and others also engage in the activity as a way to cause trouble or disturb other players. Cheating in order to "be a jerk" or "an ass" focuses on the reactions of other players, and may not necessarily be tied to actual self-advancement in the game. While players may be breaking or bending rules to do so, they aren't necessarily better off at the end of the session. Such types of behavior tend to be categorized as what Chek Yang Foo and others have termed "grief play."[17]

Much like hackers, such cheaters are using the logics of code to demonstrate superiority over certain other players. For some this may be less directly confrontational, such as achieving great wealth by the careful deception of others (as a scam on Eve Online reveals), or it may be through actively defeating others in gameplay, by illegally (or unethically) acquired skills or items.[18]

I'll explore this concept and important exceptions to it in the next chapter. Yet it is fairly safe to say that the vast majority of game players consider the cheater as beyond the bounds of fair play—and often the cheaters acknowledge this themselves. Mostly, however, where the line between the full-on cheater ends and other activities begin to appear is a blurred one, which most players dynamically negotiate.

Conclusions

This chapter has investigated how players define and enact game-playing practices that could fall into the category of cheating. All players define cheating in a game as an activity that confers unfair advantage to the player. Yet that's where the consensus begins to break down. In their operational definitions, players identified different items and activities as cheating or not. From the purist to the purely social, cheating ranged from anything outside "one's own thoughts" in a single-player game to activities that had to make other players worse off. What can such a range of definitions tell us?

First, it reminds us of the diversity of play styles and practices that players bring to their games. Although it can be tempting to think only of the *Counter-Strike* hacker or the gold-buying player subscribed to an MMO, cheating, as defined by players themselves, can encompass a wide variety of actions. Second, that diversity points out the different ways that players make distinctions. For some players, the game world is defined quite narrowly—it is the game's code itself and the player—and all else is conceptualized as ideally out-of-bounds. That player wants to experience the game on its own terms, believing the game world to be cohesive enough to provide all the clues and skill builders necessary to complete it. Of course many games (or players) fall short of that expectation, at least occasionally. But that is how the purist approaches the game and sets about playing.

Next is the player who defines the game situation more broadly: the game world admits the game as well as help from other people, walk-throughs, and guides. Here, the line becomes the code of the game itself; altering it is the boundary line that players do not wish to cross—or at least during the first pass on a game. The physical code is the limit, yet the player allows other items and help into the game world.

Finally, there's the social player who only sees unfair advantage as something that can be expressed with other players present. Items and activities that are freely available to all are by definition not cheats; only secret activities used to best or gain advantage over others can "count." The game world in this instance must contain other players in order for cheating to potentially exist. And it must result in gain for the player.

If that's the range of how players define cheating, how do their actions measure up? It would be easy to argue that player definitions are based on ideal situations and their actions reflect actual playing difficulties, but while this is true to some extent, that explanation misses some key elements of cheating behaviors.

As mentioned, getting stuck is a major reason for cheating, and while making better games might diminish that problem, it will never be eliminated. Players have widely different skill levels as well as patience thresholds for different games, on different days, in different situations. Game developers will always be limited by deadlines and budgets to finish products, perhaps before they are all truly "done." There will always be times when players get stuck, or do not have ninety-plus hours to spend finding every secret item and location in a game. Likewise, even a twenty-hour game may be too long for some players, who would prefer to spend ten hours playing, see the ending, feel a sense of completion, and move on to another game. For all such reasons, people will cheat or use items others consider cheating.

Yet beyond instrumental reasons to cheat, there are purely ludic ones as well. Being playful—running around with ninety-nine lives or a bobble head—can be immensely satisfying for its own sake. It may have nothing to do with advancing the game or gaining skill. The player is gaining more enjoyment from the game, in a variety of ways.

The instrumental and the ludic, moreover, come together in social spaces, when the cheater enters the game. To be about more than grief play—which implies a solely ludic approach—the cheater incorporates instrumentality into his activities. The cheater gains the advantage and has fun in doing so. The enjoyment might differ from the form described above, as it often comes at the expense of other players (to be an ass), yet it is still about pleasure in the game.

To conclude, what does such knowledge tell us? Paratextual industries have created products and practices that play a contested role in players' experiences. They may contribute to the acquisition of gaming capital, but for some players signal its lack. Players carefully negotiate the use of such items in their gameplay, and there is a diversity of approaches in that use. Players are active and thoughtful, accepting and resisting various forms of guidance, help and cheats. Their activity indicates the complexity of the gameplay experience, which this chapter has only begun to explore. That investigation continues in the next chapter, which examines the cheater in greater depth. It asks who such players are, and how the cheater performs a critical role in the world of multiplayer games.

| 5 |

THE CHEATERS

In the past few years we've seen a surge in interest in multiplayer games, with the development of online capabilities for console systems, most notably the success of Microsoft's Xbox Live service. Likewise, there's been tremendous growth in the MMO genre with games like *World of Warcraft* and *Lineage 2* drawing millions of players, and casual games such as *Neopets* and *Yohoho! Puzzle Pirates* demonstrating the reach of digital games beyond the traditional player demographics. So it's natural to think of cheating in relation to such games and consider the consequences for such spaces when contested practices invariably emerge.

As the last chapter showed, there are a variety of reasons that many players cheat when they play games, but the vast majority of that activity is limited to single-player games. Those who decide to gain an unfair advantage in multiplayer games are relatively few and far between, yet their actions have implications that go deeper than their individual preferences. Their conduct has effects on other players, virtual worlds, and the economics of the wider games industry. I'll concentrate here on those individuals and activities, as they are a focal point for understanding both what good and bad gameplay mean, and how we define boundary points or lines between the two. Likewise, I'll bring in how multiplayer cheating relates to gaming capital, and ways to understand such types of cheating in relation to the concepts of performance and play.

The information in this chapter is based on interviews I've conducted with game players, game developers, and specialized game security personnel (working at both development studios and game security firms), material taken from published sources on game security, and lectures and roundtables about cheating in games at the four Game Developer Conferences held from 2003 to 2006.

According to those sources, the majority of players engaging in multiplayer cheating are male, with one important exception. The players I interviewed who fell into this category were also relatively young, ranging in age from nineteen to thirty-two. Similarly, executives from firms such as Even Balance (the maker of PunkBuster) confirm that the majority of online multiplayer cheaters they have encountered are young males.[1] Of the women I interviewed who admitted to cheating, only a couple said they cheated in multiplayer situations, and as Cathy explains, "It was only because everyone was cheating. We all knew."

Yet while conducting this research, I discovered further activities that challenged the predominant assumption that it's mainly males who cheat online. As I'll discuss later in this chapter, in virtual worlds where a majority of players are girls, cheating by girls is just as common as cheating by boys.

The majority of players who use hacks or other cheats that alter the game code do not develop the cheat they use. As Jeff Morris of Epic Games notes, in his experiences going after those who employ such cheats, 90 percent of cheaters in *Unreal Tournament* are individuals who find and download a preexisting cheat online.[2] Those players generally surf the Web looking for easy places to find cheats, and can thus also be stopped by drying up the distribution sources—Web sites that offer or advertise cheats and hacks.

According to Morris, there are two other types of players who are much more troublesome for game developers, and demand more time and resources, if indeed the developer wishes to go after cheaters at all.[3] They include the (approximately) 1 percent of players who write an original cheat, distribute it, and develop a following, and another 9 percent or so who "want to take your game down," feel rewarded when developers pay attention to them, and actually "don't think they're doing anything wrong." That's because they position themselves as customers, and the developer as someone who promised them the ability to modify and customize their gaming experience.[4] The 1 percent who write cheats themselves are the most difficult to catch, according to Morris, yet the most valuable to find, as they are the supply source for the majority of those who wish to cheat.

Individuals who have admitted to cheating in multiplayer games say they enjoyed the activity quite a bit, or at least reflected that they did, if they cheated in the past. Cheating was a ludic activity, playful in intent, although a component of this effect was gained at the expense of others. For example, Neal (twenty-two) defined the act of cheating itself as "breaking the fundamental rules of the game, *and thereby ruining the enjoyment of others*, or utterly destroying the challenge of the game" (emphasis added). For him, cheating was not merely instrumental but by definition also relational. Neal may be close to the griefer in gameplay style, but he still needed two elements for his activity: cheating was gaining advantage as well as playful in some way.

While for the rule-abiding player a cheat might be ludic in that it allows greater freedom or options within a game, that particular cheat is limited to strictly benefiting the player, with no other players involved. It is not a zero-sum game—no one else has to be worse off for that player to gain. Yet for the cheater, the ludic experience is gained in part through someone else's disadvantage.

The cheater needs to be distinguished from the griefer, who plays mainly to cause distress in other players. While the griefer is using cheats ludically, that individual is doing so with one central goal in mind: the reactions of others. By contrast, the cheater gains pleasure from using cheats, but does so for another reason: to gain advantage and progress further (or win) in the game. Perhaps for some cheaters there is no ludic sense involved; cheats are solely instrumental to getting ahead and winning. Nevertheless, of the players I talked with who admitted to cheating in such fashion, most felt that pleasure played a part in their activities. And many of these players drew little or no distinction between the activities of the griefer and those of the cheater—both activities were wrong, and were conceptualized as cheating. While that might seem to conflict with the overarching definition of cheating as gaining an unfair advantage—the griefer gains no real advantage from his activities—it might be that the griefer is seen by players as acting unethically, or is cheating other players out of the acquisition of gaming capital or at the least an enjoyable gameplay experience.

Where They Are: The Worlds of the Cheater

Cheaters can be found almost anywhere there's a game being played. While some players I interviewed mentioned cheating in off-line multiplayer games, the greatest popular attention has been paid to online games, where opportunities to cheat multiply, and the risks of being caught and damaging a reputation decrease. Yet cheating in off-line games is also significant and worthy of investigation, especially as it prefigures many actions found online. To gain a better picture of the many places in which cheating occurs, I want to explore the constraints and affordances offered by different gaming locations, and how each can encourage as well as discourage particular types of cheating behaviors.

Off-line Play, Many Players

Individuals have cheated at games long before the existence of videogames. The cardsharp or card counter, the shell game, the gambler with weighted dice, and the self-serving *Monopoly* banker have all contributed to what we know about cheating. Some cheats are perpetrated without conferring advantage, such as the parent who cheats to end the (endless) game of *Candyland* and allow his child to win the round. What I want to focus on here, however, are cheats that do confer advantage in some particular way. In off-line games, played face-to-face, there are still opportunities to cheat in videogames as well as players who take advantage of that opening. What can vary are the nature of the cheat along with its seriousness in infringing on gameplay and others' reactions to it.

Individuals are aware of many opportunities to cheat in videogames and often will take steps to eliminate situations where the temptation to cheat might be too great for (almost) any player to ignore. To do so, players frequently negotiate rules before play starts (and many times as play progresses), much like players of nonelectronic games, in order to limit accusations of as well as temptations for cheating. While players cannot cover every contingency nor know of every possible action other players might take that might be considered cheating, individuals often negotiate in good faith before gameplay begins. Such actions are a reminder of the many ways that gameplay is alterable outside the actual code of games.

In off-line gameplay, players frequently know one another, and the game space is bounded to one physical locale, which gives players greater control over how that space and game are utilized. So, for example, players can negotiate beforehand if one player (or more) is allowed a handicap in a golf game. While the self-conferral of advantage might result in cries of cheating, working out and modifying the rules in advance limits such problems. Likewise, in games such as the FPS *Goldeneye*, which uses a split-screen view for each player, some competitors have chosen to prevent the temptation to cheat by taping a barrier down the middle of the television screen to keep each other from ascertaining a rival's location in game.[5]

Activities like these suggest the dynamic nature of cheating—it is not always the easily definable activity we would like it to be, such as the file-hacking player who uses code to see through walls or perfectly aim his weapons. Instead, it can also include players who "peek" while their counterparts are lining up plays in the latest *Madden* or are checking another player's location in one of the iterations of *Army Men*. Player-improvised negotiations and modifications can help prevent the tempting cheat from being plucked as well as limit the activities of known overzealous players. Yet even in the same game, if there are different players involved, checking out a rival's position might be considered shrewd game strategy and allowable. The key is in the negotiations that take place either before play begins or as it proceeds, as players work out what they consider unfair advantage as well as skillful gameplay. Once such negotiations have been made, though, the opportunities to cheat have been named and those who cheat can be punished accordingly.

In physical spaces, the opportunities to cheat are not only limited technologically but socially as well. As J. Barton Bowyer has written, it's easier to cheat in anonymous situations, as a player's reputation does not precede him in that case. In face-to-face gameplay, the cheater may occasionally succeed, but if her cheating is uncovered, the subsequent damage to the cheater's reputation often prevents her from participating in future opportunities to gain advantage.[6] When identity and behavior can be physically associated and gameplay is also a physically bounded activity, cheating cannot be easily dismissed nor confused. The cheater, once uncovered, can be more easily removed from future gameplay situations or have his gameplay discounted. Yet when the cheater goes online, a new world opens up, and cheating becomes magnified in terms of both lowered risk and the types of cheats attempted.

Online: Play the World

Early researchers of cyberspace remarked on the anonymity and freedom from bodily constraints to be found online.[7] Users could experiment with different aspects of their identities, creating (or expressing) entirely differ-ent selves online.[8] Participants in text-based multiuser dungeon (MUD) games were especially interesting to study, as players might explore the ex-pression of different genders, or create new virtual societies with elaborate rules and punishments. Richard Bartle, who created the first MUD in Britain in the late 1970s, has written some of the earliest work examining player types, but textual spaces never gained widespread popularity or at-tention.[9] One of the earliest graphical online games was *Habitat*, released in 1987 on an Internet service to become America Online, which further revealed the varied nature of player approaches to online games, with chal-lenges like duping and PK appearing early in the game's run.[10] Similar actions in the larger world of *Ultima Online* demonstrated that cheating could exist quite easily in online as well as off-line game spaces.

That isn't to say that cheating in online spaces is the same thing as cheating off-line, however. Although later researchers have revised ideas about anonymity online, there can still remain a certain degree of it, espe-cially as game worlds or servers become bigger and reach global popula-tions. And with large spaces unmoored from more traditional identity markers (a physical body or a legal name), repercussions for poor behavior, including cheating, become more difficult to make stick. As Bowyer argues, not only does anonymity make punishment more difficult to apply to the violator it can also increase an individual's propensity to cheat.[11] So as it becomes easier to get away with, it becomes even more alluring to try. Individuals who would never cheat in a face-to-face game might readily do so in online situations. Without the tieback to a more physical sense of identity and its constraints, some players happily push the boundaries of acceptable behavior.

Yet while online spaces may make it easier to contemplate cheating or escape its aftermath, it can also be more difficult to accomplish. The off-line cheater may only need a quick glance at another player's location onscreen to gain advantage, while the online cheater has greater technical constraints to manage. Depending on the level of the cheater (that is, someone who creates hacks versus someone else who downloads them from a popular site), greater or lesser amounts of technical skill are involved. As mentioned before, gaming capital can be involved in the realm of online cheating, as cheaters strive to impress other cheaters with their hacks, bots, and "social engineering" misdeeds. So social ostracism can result for the online cheater, in different ways. Both the elite hacker can be embarrassed as well as the more "pedestrian" bot user who is black-listed by more ordinary players.

Not all online cheaters need technological skill to succeed, though; one of the easiest ways to cheat is to simply pull the Internet plug when one is losing an online game and disconnect before the loss is official. Likewise, other cheaters prefer more sociological methods to gain advantage, such as Evangeline in *The Sims Online*, who simply through talking conned new players out of their money.[12] Whatever the cheater's preference—techno-logical or social—either method can be turned into a cheat online.

There are many different ways to cheat in a videogame, and methods can differ depending on where the game is played—online or off-line. While both are digital spaces, each resulting location brings with it differ-ent types of player relations as well as opportunities and constraints on cheating behavior. Some players cannot cheat others when physically next to them, needing the cover of anonymity to press the advantage. Others might only utilize the "easier" cheats of off-line play, rather than engage in more sophisticated technological or psychological engineering to get ahead in a game. Anonymity might be a spur to cheat for some players, while for others it is only those nearby that would do. Cheating can come in various forms, which I explore next, but those forms are delimited (or allowed) by the space in which the cheater chooses to operate.

What They Do, from Aimbots to Zeny Buying

What do players do when they cheat in multiplayer games? The answers are varied and imaginative. In this section, I want to discuss the different types of cheats that players engage in during multiplayer games, and how those do or do not relate back to the typology of cheating developed in the last chapter. I can't hope to list and explain all of the types of cheats that players can employ (new ones are certainly being developed as I write this, and as the reader later reads this), but I will cover major types of cheats, suggesting the ways that such cheats operate as well as how and why cheaters might choose those particular methods. The cheats are divided into the following four categories: taking advantage of glitches, taking ad-vantage of people, taking advantage of code, and taking advantage of third-party systems.

Taking Advantage of a Glitch: Exploits and Duping

Depending on your point of view, an exploit might or might not be a cheat, yet its very contestedness places it on this list. Exploits don't involve a player actively changing code in a game or deceiving other players; instead, they are "found" actions or items that accelerate or improve a player's skills, actions, or abilities in some way that the designer did not originally intend, yet in a manner that does not actively change code or involve deceiving others. One of the earliest examples of such an exploit was found in *Habitat*. In that game, the designers relate, players discovered at one point a vending machine that sold items for a certain price, and a pawnshop that bought that same item back for an even higher price. As Chip Morningstar and Randall Farmer explain,

Naturally, a couple of people discovered this. One night they took all their money, walked to the Doll Vendroid, bought as many Dolls as they could, then took them across town and pawned them. . . . The final result was at least three Avatars with hundreds of thousands of Tokens each. We only discovered this the next morning when our daily database status report said that the money supply had quintupled overnight. . . . We were puzzled that no bug report had been submitted. By poking around a bit we discovered that a few people had suddenly acquired enormous bank balances. We sent *Habitat* mail to the two richest, inquiring as to where they had gotten all that money overnight. Their reply was, "We got it fair and square! And we're not going to tell you how!" After much abject pleading on our part they eventually did tell us, and we fixed the erroneous pricing.[13]

A more recent example wasn't even an actual exploit but the rumor of a duping (or item duplication) exploit found after an update to *World of Warcraft* in July 2005. Players debated its existence on forums, and Blizzard responded to allegations regarding the exploit by saying it took such problems seriously, as "the potential damage a duping exploit can bring to a game can be devastating." Author Miguel Lopez of *Gamespy* reported on the alleged problem, explaining the temptation behind using such exploits and the challenges that MMO developers face:

Just like people do in real life MMO players covet expensive things. And likewise, anyone who can make a quick buck, even if the methods involved are just a little bit illegal, will attempt to do so. Like many of the elements that make up these games, it's all about risk-versus-reward; i.e., is it worth risking your account to make tons of gold? You can be damn sure that 99 percent of players would perform some kind of exploit if they had zero chance of getting caught.[14]

Neither the *Habitat* nor *World of Warcraft* exploits (real or imagined) involved hacking code or the deception of others, yet both resulted in gameplay not intended by the designer. Cheaters can also use exploits to escape death as well as increase their chances of killing opponents. For example, in the PC version of *Halo* there is an exploit known as "lag jumping": "With this exploit, when the cheater is threatened (that is, fired on or about to be run over by a vehicle) they deliberately cause themselves to lag. As a result, their on-screen avatar will blink in-and-out of the game world and appear to teleport several feet, making them difficult to hit."[15]

Not all players see exploits as cheats, for a couple of reasons. First, they are available to all players shortly after they are figured out, and can sometimes become an acceptable part of gameplay, at least in particular games. They thus function as another aid for gameplay, much like strategy tips or maps made available to any player dedicated enough to search for them and then practice their use. Likewise, most of these exploits require no alteration of the game code—another practice that signals cheating to players. Many players reason that because it is not specifically prohibited by the developer's code, it might not be a cheat.[16] Some exploits are more readily agreed on as cheats by players, however, such as the "lag kill cheat" in *Halo 2*:

This is an XBox Live modem exploit that allows a cheater to cause all other players to go into standby mode while the cheater remains active within the game. As a result, everyone else in the game world is frozen in place (with their televisions displaying a loading screen), while the cheater is free to run around killing players or stealing their flags. Bungie has addressed this exploit and threatened to terminate the accounts of any players who utilize it. Fortunately, it is extremely obvious when it is used.[17]

Such exploits stretch the notion of "allowable" so far that most players deem them cheats and disallow their use in gameplay. Such cheats also go beyond increasing the abilities or advantages of one player to actively hurting other players, thereby making it more likely that most players would see such activities as cheating.

The discovery of bugs that allow players to dupe items or currency in games is also usually defined as cheating by both players and developers.[18] Duping problems were particularly troublesome in *Diablo* and *Diablo II*, with some players making multiple copies of high-value items, which then entered into general circulation. In attempts to curb the duping, Blizzard worsened the situation for players who had unknowingly purchased a duped item, which subsequently disappeared when the game was "fixed."[19] Those duping cheats were also widely known about, and the player response was often strong opposition to those practices.

Some players went so far as to create elaborate warnings for other players, such as those found on the Diabloii.net site, which has extensive information about duping, hacks, cheats, PK, and other cheating and antisocial behaviors that can be found in *Diablo II*, in addition to general game information and strategy. The site also takes the developer, Blizzard, to task for not cracking down on cheats seriously enough:

Instead of having and enforcing clear rules about hacking, Blizzard does nothing but issue never-enforced warnings, and has their support team fix hacks/cheats once they are discovered. Since there isn't any punishment for hacking, hackers of course try to find new methods constantly, and as soon as Blizzard fixes one, others appear. This means that Blizzard's tech support is forever chasing around, trying to figure how new exploits are being done, and then figuring ways to stop them, and the hackers are always at least one step ahead.[20]

Depending on who is asked, developers take actions against cheating that are either too aggressive or not nearly good enough. Keeping cheaters at bay has become a full-time job for developers, and online games now have a variety of staff dedicated to eradicating as well as preventing various forms of cheating, as I'll talk about in the following chapter. But Blizzard was an early entrant in this category and learned things the hard way. After working on various methods to disable and prevent duping and cheats, Blizzard eventually turned to a more direct approach to rid the game of the worst offenders. In 2002, it banned 8,500 players from the game, and in 2003, closed more than 131,000 accounts and banned thousands of CD keys.[21]

To sum up, the cheats in this first category are variable to a degree, with players viewing activities like exploits and duping as contested. Most often the definition depends on the extremity of the action, and the amount of advantage or disadvantage gained as well as its impact on other players. Yet here, game laws have not been broken, just carefully bent.

Taking Advantage of People: Social Engineering

Rather than seek out glitches in game code, certain players use the social nature of multiplayer games to their advantage. Social engineering can take many forms, but mainly involves players who "game the player" rather than the system, searching for ways to trick other players into giving them what they want. That might include asking to "borrow" items from others to use temporarily and then keeping them, taking advantage of a friendship to borrow access to an account and then selling off valuable equipment, or tricking players into traveling to dangerous areas in order to kill them and steal their loot. The central element that's involved is the exploitation of player trust.

In such scenarios, cheaters know (or learn) how to exploit the relative anonymity of game spaces as well as player expectations for other players' and game administrators' behavior. The cheater might create multiple personas that can't be tracked down easily, in order to trick other players into giving them what they want. For example, an experienced player might pose as a new player, and ask others for money and items to get started in the game. Players of *Final Fantasy XI*, for instance, regularly complain on game boards about players who engage in such deceptive (and annoying) activities. Such actions are designed to take advantage of other players' generosity and willingness to help those just beginning. While players do alert each other if such begging by a character becomes widespread, cheaters often simply start a new character and begin again, with an untarnished reputation.[22]

In other situations, players may collude to artificially raise the price or value of certain items in order to gain a profit. For example, in *Whyville* two players can enter a public Trading Post and make a big deal about trading a certain item for a large amount of clams, the in-game currency. Other players watching will get excited, thinking the item is worth a high value. "But it's either one kid with two accounts or a kid with a friend" who have just raised the price on a particular item in order to sell more of them later for inflated sums.[23]

One of the best-known examples of such a scam was the one (allegedly) perpetrated by "Nightfreeze" on the MMO *Eve Online*. After encountering players who Nightfreeze felt did not play fair, Nightfreeze decided to get even with them as well as the game itself. He worked out systems to amass great amounts of wealth, and then engineered an elaborate scam that bilked several players out of all their (considerable amounts of) money. This scam included help from an in-game friend, the creation of multiple fake accounts to promote the scam, and the use of a library telephone number so that a suspicious player could be appeased. What is noteworthy about the scam, in addition to Nightfreeze's highly entertaining narration of it, is its reliance on fooling others as its central strategy. As Nightfreeze narrates,

This is a story of deception, intrigue, and double crossing. It is a story of liars, bandits, and greed. It is a story of the worst of the human condition, and how the motive for profit will drive a normally nice guy to the deepest depths of evil and betrayal. This is the story of my life in *Eve Online*. *Eve Online* is a space-based MMORPG with a level of depth and breadth that blows games like *Shadowbane* and *City of Heroes* out of the water. It is also a beautiful game, with glaring suns, shining stars, and exorbitant ship detail. Beneath its gilded beauty, though, there lies a poorly designed game which rewards the greedy and violent, and punishes the hardworking and honest; and if you think about it, that's a good representation of capitalism.[24]

Nightfreeze goes on to relate personal experiences in the game, how other players were equally unsavory, and his ultimate actions. While definitely extreme, the story does point to how cheaters can gain advantage over others without having to know anything about code or hacks. Rather, they need to be experts in human behavior and self-interest.

In addition to deceiving other players through actions purported to come from other players, cheaters can also attempt to impersonate game administrators and obtain passwords from other players in order to gain access to their accounts. Such activities are not exclusive to games, of course, and occur in just about any online activity involving a password. Cheaters can also play off real or imagined friendships with others, gain access to their accounts, and sell or give away valuable items. In those cases, it is the alleged "reality" of the relationship that works for the cheater, who would rather have game benefits than player trust.

In sum, players can cheat without having any technological expertise at all. Rather, some cheaters play off the varied assumptions, goodwill, and shortcomings of other players to gain what they want.

Taking Advantage of Code: Hacks, Bots, and Packet Sniffers

One of the best-known forms of multiplayer cheating involves altering the code of the game. It can be accomplished in a variety of ways, and is constantly evolving due to increasing security efforts by game developers as well as the creativity of the cheaters. Cheats based on code can include aimbots, which allow a player to aim automatically at opposing players with unnatural speed and accuracy, and wall hacks, which let players see through walls and therefore find opponents who are hiding nearby. Code-based cheats also include the alteration of the messages sent to the game's central server in order to send more favorable information as well as cheats that give players increased speed, better ways of spotting opponents in a game (such as by painting them with fluorescent skins), and ways to lag the system for other players. The focus in all of these cases is on cracking or hacking the code of the game in some way favorable to the cheater. Even among those who employ these tactics, however, there are some who do not see their actions as cheating but instead as modifying or customizing their gaming experience.

Because the majority of players who use hacks or other cheats that alter game code do not develop the cheats they use, they generally surf the Web looking for cheats, and such players will look almost anywhere. For example, several of my personal blog posts have dealt with cheating in *Final Fantasy XI*, and at least one of my threads (which discussed the use of fish bots and their banning by Square Enix) unexpectedly turned into a debate among players about bot use, where to find bot macros, and whether this type of cheat is wrong.[25] Without my prompting (or even initial awareness), various players began posting to my blog, to ask the question directly:

How do u get a fishing bot. (Sagi)
How do u bot? (nightskater)

I wanya free bot. (Orane)

I was wondering if anyone could tell me on where/how to get a fishing bot. (Lupin)

In addition to the direct demands for bots, or information on where and how to find them, some individuals also asked, but with some sort of justification first:

This game is nearly impossible to make gil in, I've lost over 160k in goldsmithing and I'm a crippled level black mage [i.e., poorly equipped or leveled black mage], how am I suppose to keep playing this game? I'd really appreciate it if you could tell me how to bot fish in this game. I really need the gil and equipment. (Kanstar)

Another player, who seemed to make some distinctions between types of bots used, remarked on the various uses for bots, and what was the "correct" and "incorrect" use:

Fish bot. Ok this is a little different. It's not an aimbot like in a first person shooter so it doesn't directly affect other people. I think the fish bot is fine as long as the person sits at their computer. It's not fair if they fire the bot up and then go to their job and come home and have a stringer of black eel. They're 7000 gil a stack by the way. That's not fair. (gilMakah)

Despite their approaches, all of those seeking a fish bot could be included in Morris's 90 percent of cheaters—not willing or able to create their own cheat but amenable to using one found online, for reasons that were articulated to various degrees.

It's the 1 percent that Morris refers to who write cheats who are the most valuable to find, and include such individuals as "Joolz," who wrote cheats for *Counter Strike* in his free time (during the day, Joolz worked as a corporate software engineer). Cheats such as his "Lookaim" have been downloaded by more than fifty thousand people, which allows a player to spin around and shoot an opponent behind him if the opponent looks at the player. An article about Joolz and cheating reinforces the idea that cheaters like Joolz form the top of a pyramid of cheaters, who are revered for their skill: "He gets fanmail. It's given him a name and a Wild West notoriety. When Joolz walks into certain online chatrooms, a reverent quiet falls."[26]

Yet even the elite cheaters disdain the more run-of-the-mill individuals who download the cheats they themselves have created. As Joolz states, "I've sat there for hours on end, writing the thing. They've just downloaded it from a website." Joolz also built a "backdoor" into the cheat, which lets him spot when others are using his cheat, and allows him to disable it. "I don't like being beaten by people using my cheat," explains Joolz.[27] Cheats can be multilayered, designed to not only work to the advantage of the cheater but also be responsive to the original designer's intentions. It may allow a player to bypass or alter certain game code, but can also be a marker revealing the cheat-in-use, allowing the creator to "see through the walls" of the cheat, in addition to letting the user see through the game walls.

Taking Advantage of Third-Party Programs: Mods and Ends

Finally, some players cheat by relying on specialized programs or tools that they (or usually others) create. These tools are more than a bot, a macro, or a hack, in that they have an executable code that can run either separately from or in tandem with game code. Some of the earliest examples of such programs were UO Macros and its successor for *EverQuest*, ShowEQ, which "passively monitors network traffic for *EverQuest* data and displays it on screen in an easily readable format," giving the player access to "EVERY mob position in the zone, its level/class/race, items it is HOLDING which affects the way it looks" and more.[28] The creators of the program made it an open source project, and encouraged users (who had to run it on a separate computer, in Linux) to use it in "good" rather than "evil" ways. By that, they meant that "ShowEQ makes it fairly easy to farm rare spawns. It also makes it easy to find and kill rare spawns that others might have already been after for hours. This is NOT what ShowEQ was intended to do. Farming for EBAY is another of the bad uses. While the developers can't stop anyone from doing this, they ask that you don't."[29]

Whichever way the developers intended the tool to be used, Sony obviously felt the program was a cheat, and those found using it could have their accounts suspended or banned. The requirement of a second computer and the ability to run (and understand) Linux, however, likely limited the widespread use of ShowEQ.

More recent third-party programs for online games have proliferated and include programs that enable players to play a game in Windowed mode (if the game does not usually allow it), and more easily level and farm individual characters. One such program is the WoW Glider, designed for players of *World of Warcraft* who wish to automate certain aspects of gameplay. As its creators explain, "WoW Glider is a tool that plays your *World of Warcraft* character for you, the way you want it. It grinds, it loots, it skins, it heals, it even farms soul shards . . . **without you**."[30]

The program, once installed, will run a player's character and keep it traveling on a preset path through a certain area, killing all the enemies it encounters as well as gathering items and experience points. Yet here as well, the makers of the program admit that it violates the game's terms of service, but insist that Glider isn't a cheat. Instead, "Glider is intended for people who want to quickly level up an alternate character or glide through the last few levels to 60."[31] They believe that players who want to quickly get a new character to level 60 should not rely on Glider or other third-party programs, as the players would be missing out on the fun of the game. Their program, it seems, is a way to fast-forward through the undesirable elements of gameplay. While they can try to encourage its use in particular ways, like the creators of *Habitat*, they can never fully control that.

Why They Do It: Expertise, Power, and Play

Players cheat in multiplayer games for a variety of reasons, many of which are similar to why players cheat in single-player games. Players may find a game too difficult or time-consuming, and so wish to find a bot or a hack that makes gameplay easier or lets them acquire in-game resources in less time than the developers likely planned. They can thus fast-forward through tedious content, areas, or gameplay. Players may also wish to acquire status or prestige in a particular game or game world, and use specific techniques or programs to gain that wealth and power more quickly than they would if they didn't cheat.

But in addition to looking at cheating in multiplayer games as instrumental (time-saving or problem solving) and ludic, how else can the activity be conceptualized or theorized in order to better understand it? While I've used the concept of gaming capital to explain the rise of para-textual game industries, it can also be tied to cheating behaviors. Players who are considered elite by other players are thought to possess large amounts (as well as particular types) of gaming capital. Such players may excel at playing particular types of games, or be quite knowledgeable about gaming hardware or the latest releases. They are aware of multiple options available in games, and can probably provide help or advice to other players. Such is the ideal gamer. Having such gaming capital confers a certain degree of power within gaming circles, whether that is a group of high school or college friends, an MMO guild, or a chat site devoted to a particular game.

Game players possessed of the proper kinds of gaming capital—for their own gaming circle—are powerful in the sense that they can often dispense advice with confidence, are looked to as experts in some way, and can, through their behavior in game, enhance or reduce opportunities for others. For example, a high-level player in an MMO might be asked for advice on the best equipment for particular levels or strategies to use on certain monsters. Likewise, a dedicated player on that same MMO might not have a high-level character but instead have much more experience in crafting. That player might be asked to craft specific items or be looked to as the expert in that area for their guild. Each of those players has a certain kind of power or expertise, which they can use productively or destructively.

Relating back to the topic at hand, cheating can also confer certain kinds of power and gaming capital, depending on the audience sought as well as the particular situation. In addition to having fun, saving time, or solving problems that are too difficult, players also can cheat as a way of gaining gaming capital. While for most players multiplayer cheating would destroy gaming capital for them, in the world of multiplayer cheaters, a subculture of cheaters can subscribe to its own beliefs about skilled gameplay and the clever exploitation of game resources. Thus, players such as Nightfreeze and Joolz can gain a following, and be revered for actions that most other players despise. So even as game companies look to stop cheaters and their hacks from working, companies like Even Balance are also interested in destroying the reputations of famous hackers in order to wipe out their gaming capital, which is potentially even more damaging than eliminating one piece of code.

Cheating and Gender: Rethinking Assumptions

Initially I had conceived of multiplayer cheating as a predominantly masculine activity, yet after learning of the many scams perpetrated by young
girls in *Whyville*, I began to reconsider that assumption. While statistically
the majority of players who cheat in online multiplayer games are still
male, I believe it would be overly simplistic to ascribe this behavior or
practice to a particular gender or gendered construction of gameplay. As
T. L. Taylor and Nick Yee have written, many of the practices, behaviors,
and interests that we initially ascribed to women or girl gamers have
changed as they gained more experience playing games, or changed as researchers moved from studying girls to adult women. Sometimes, it seems,
scholars conflate what girls and women want and do with what are actually
newbie player practices and interests.[32]

Given that, it seems logical to suggest that certain player activities
may be reflective not just of individual player interests but also of the
larger context in which those activities occur. In spaces that are either
actually or assumedly disproportionately weighted toward a particular
gender (or race, or class, and so on), we cannot ignore the effect that un-
balancing will probably have. For instance, research has shown that
women who major in math and science fields in small liberal arts colleges
as well as women-only colleges are more likely to finish their programs
and go on to graduate study in those areas.[33] Likewise, online researchers
have found that in online spaces where rules are not explicitly set or
women are not the primary users, women tend to participate less frequently and let men dominate conversations, tend to drop out of or ignore
arguments, and are supportive rather than assertive in their communica-
tive styles.[34]

That's not to say that such differences are negative but that they do
exist. And in game spaces that are predominantly male or masculine, it is
likely that some girls and women will adjust their behaviors to either not
draw attention to themselves or fit in with particular norms. But when in
game spaces where gender imbalances disappear, interesting things start to
happen. Such evolving practices can be found in the online game *Whyville*,
an educational game that has received almost no popular attention from
the media. The game has over a million registered users, mainly preteens,
with a majority of the players being girls.

The game space consists of a series of minigames based on math and science problems, which allow players to earn salaries (clams) that they use to buy "face parts" to decorate their avatars. Players can amass wealth from salaries, but more likely from successfully designing and selling face parts to other players. A small minority of players owns most of the wealth in the game, with the richest player currently holding about twelve million clams.[35] As with any game, some players wish to take shortcuts to acquire as many clams as possible, either for the prestige of having wealth and great face parts, the power of having money, or perhaps the enjoyment of scamming the system and other players. The difference here is that many of those cheaters are girls.

Jennifer Sun, president of the company that runs *Whyville*, estimates that of the approximately twenty thousand players per day who log on to the game, there are "tens of such incidents" of cheating scams that occur. Those scams can range from the "relatively stupid" where a player will send another player an internal game e-mail stating it is from a game administrator asking for an account password, to more clever attempts such as when players send e-mails saying "you've won the Why lottery. Send us your password to verify who you are." Such practices use greed to hook someone and potentially cheat a player out of her clams.

Players also engage in other social engineering practices, which can get quite elaborate, as well as putting up external Web sites explaining either how to cheat at the *Whyville* minigames, easy ways to solve the problems, or outside sites that pretend to be clubs for *Whyville* and need a player's password to send them valuable gifts or information. While the administrators of *Whyville* do stop cheating as they find it occurring, and will take away improperly acquired items or clams from scammers, they take a relatively permissive stance, maintaining that "we rarely banish people because they are still playing the game. We only ban for seriously inappropriate behavior on the site."[36]

So if girls are just as likely to cheat in situations where they are equally represented in games, what can be said about cheating in addition to arguments about power and prestige? Sun believes that the girls who cheat are equally, if not more, represented in the social engineering cheats, but the company doesn't keep track of infraction by gender, so it is difficult to make conclusions about particular types of cheating that may appeal to different genders. Yet one can conclude that girls and women, just like boys and men, are interested in gaining power and prestige in games, occasionally through improper or illegal means. One of the first scams in *Whyville* involved a girl named "Flower" going around tricking other players into giving her their account password, whereupon she'd clean out their accounts. So girls too are willing and able to cheat others, simply to be able to do so.

Such stories suggest that as more gender-balanced game worlds appear, there will also be a range of play styles that are both positive and negative emerging from both male and female players. Advancement, power, and prestige matter to all players (although in varying combinations, to be sure), and all players have various challenges to confront when in game spaces, including gameplay difficulties, boredom, and dissatisfaction with developer-presented options. What this preliminary exploration of girls cheating online suggests is that one needs to be careful to consider how virtual spaces shape expectations, consciously or not, and how players may react to those spaces in unexpected ways. Just as paratextual industries like game magazines have helped to shape what gamers see as a good videogame, so too virtual spaces can shape behaviors, and the makeup of those spaces is critical to keep in mind when analysis begins.

Conclusions

In this chapter, I've explored some of the contested practices that individuals and groups engage in while playing multiplayer games. Although I've called many of the activities cheating, it's important to remember that at least some of them are still debated over and argued about, whether they should be conceptually defined as belonging to either the cheating or skillful gameplay category. Exploits can easily reside in either location, depending on the particular trick and the player community. Social engineering varies and can also be thought of as a skilled variant of playing the game (or the gamer), rather than doing something unethical. Yet the use of technological code—hacks, bots, or third-party programs—seems to raise more of a red flag for those wishing to demarcate lines between cheating and fair play. Such tools confer advantage in ways that other players might find difficult to replicate. Additionally, the tools are generally explicitly against a game's terms of service, and so their construction as a cheat is all but assured.

Players who use such advantages often (but not always) do so for the same reasons that players cheat in single-player games—except by using them against other players, rather than simply matching wits with a computer program. But because the stakes are higher, this form of gameplay needs more careful consideration. It's where the boundary lies for acceptable and unacceptable play, and it's here where the debates rage as new territory is contested, staked out, and then perhaps fought over once again.

Cheating: Activity or Identity?

One of the questions that this chapter (and book) raises concerns how to think about cheating by individuals in a broader sense. Succinctly put, is a person who cheats someone engaged in an activity or have they taken on a particular identity? Or does that distinction make a difference? As with gender and cheating, it might be premature or incorrect to ascribe too much intentionality to identity or at least the core identity of individuals. I believe it is more helpful to instead examine cheating as a practice, particularly one that is ludic, situated, and iterative in its expression.

As players themselves explain, cheating can be enjoyable and playful, both in the act of getting ahead as well as perhaps in the knowledge of besting other players in some way. Many such players see digital games as a space apart from "real-life" consequences, and so cheating is divorced from the fallout of what would happen if the person cheated in some way in daily life. Even players who may not draw such distinctions see cheating as enjoyable in some way or as part of the game they wished to play.

If cheating is situated, it can only come into being through active engagement with a game and other players, which suggests players are constantly being confronted with more and less meaningful choices regarding how to play a game. Exploits, for example, demonstrate how players must either decide as a group or individuals how to see such abilities in games—as cheats or clever advantages. Generally the group norm is the default for gameplay, with those not wishing to abide by general definitions then accepting the consequences for their actions, if caught.

And finally, cheating is iterative in nature—with each decision made in a game, a player "plays" at a game and a particular play style. Sometimes we play earnestly, sometimes we play carelessly, and at other times we may stay up all night, ignoring the phone, our families, sleep, and food in order to play a game. We might ask others for help or sit there alone, desperately trying to figure out what to do next. In all of those situations, we are faced with questions about how to play.

As an example, players in *World of Warcraft* may sometimes, often, or never ask questions of themselves such as "Should I try again to camp that rare and difficult monster that someone else always seems to claim? Should I instead go to the International Game Exchange and buy some game gold? Will I only do it this one time?" With each question and each answer (as well as even the refusal to entertain such questions), the player is making choices about his or her preferred form of gameplay. Each act, each play session, "performs" the resulting avatar identity as well as shapes a player's attitude toward a game and his or her own understanding of what it means to play. Each decision may not logically "fit" with the others—we are not consistent creatures—but each decision does have meaningful implications. Are we iterating a playful performance, a cheating performance, something else, or some mixture of actions?

Such questions have no easy answers, and only reside in the actions of players. So we can certainly ask how and why individuals cheat as well as look at what happens when people do cheat, but to ascribe such actions to core identities or individuals seems misguided. Practices are situated, and game spaces have contexts, histories, and practical limitations. We need to see cheating as an important part of those practices and spaces, but not as a static "thing" or core trait. Besides, that would be impossible, for just as games and gameplay practices change, what we consider cheating and how we respond to it have changed over time as well.

The next chapter examines some responses to cheating, both by game companies and the newly forming "anticheating industry" that take a variety of approaches to how cheating is defined, and most importantly punished, in online multiplayer games. Companies like Even Balance and NCsoft have a range of techniques they employ, each of which helps to codify what we see as cheating in contemporary games. Their particular, practical implementations are crucial to examine and discuss, as they are codifying and delimiting what we know of as cheating, and acceptable responses to it from game developers, publishers, and occasionally even game players.

BUSTING PUNKS AND POLICING PLAYERS:
THE ANTICHEATING INDUSTRY

Most of the game industry has little concern for players who cheat in off-line games, unless a mod chip is being employed to play pirated copies. Yet when games move online and become multiplayer, cheating becomes an issue. It can be seen as both a security and a public relations issue. Cheating exposes how code can be corrupted or altered by those not intended to access it; it can also ruin the play experiences of noncheaters, and potentially kill a game's longevity or even initial sales. Thus, an increasing number of game companies that have some kind of online component in their games are thinking about cheating and its implications for their game's success.

Many companies work on the problem internally, developing their own security measures, both technological and social, to combat the problem. Programmers work to limit access to particular types of data, either through encryption, better protection of the data stream or game assets, or other methods. MMOs like *Lineage 1* and *2* (managed by publisher NCsoft) have a team of community managers who watch and intervene in gameplay on a regular basis. However, MMOs have a monthly revenue stream to help support such efforts. Many other online games—those that do not have a persistent world or charge a recurring subscription fee—have less to rely on in terms of continuing support for such issues.

While game developers have and will continue to implement their own systems to counter cheaters, a specialized industry has also sprung up in the past six years to develop anticheating technologies. Companies such as Even Balance, IT GlobalSecure, and the now-defunct United Admins have developed software tools and ongoing service support to prevent cheating in online games.

This chapter examines those businesses and their approaches, which differ considerably in their understandings of and approaches to stopping cheating. In many ways, their different constructions echo the discussions brought up at the end of the last chapter, which explored cheating as both an identity and an activity. As such, their strategies serve to (re)construct and reinforce particular ways of seeing cheating and those who cheat.

Likewise, the growth of such companies signals another development in the larger digital games industry: the emergence of another subindustry that works to support and shape the core. Just as publishers of magazines and strategy guides helped focus what players believed to be acceptable help in a game (among other things), so too the anticheat industry (as I'll call it here) attempts to place bounds on the other side of player activity. Players can explore games and use external elements to enhance their gameplay, but only to a point.

When player activity exceeds certain bounds, the anticheat industry will step in and take action. What that action is, though, depends on the particular approach taken. Carefully defined limits for acceptable and unacceptable play activities are now being formulated. Another paratextual element of the larger industry is coalescing, exerting pressure on the industry and players. This element is multifaceted, as individual companies have come from very different places. They arise from player communities, development studios, and the federal government. As such, they represent or at least echo the concerns of different constituencies, and their approaches mirror that diversity.

Additionally, how both the core industry and players respond to such new elements of the digital games industry is important, as there are variable levels of buy in that players and developers must support in order for these companies to succeed. While many, if not most, players say they are opposed to cheating in online multiplayer games, just what they mean by that quickly gets muddied when they are asked more detailed questions. Although there is a large player community that supports such anticheat measures and plays on, for example, PunkBuster-enabled servers, there are also players who are either neutral toward cheating or openly welcoming of it. As Nick Yee noted in relation to gold buying in *World of Warcraft*, for instance, many players report they have bought gold for various (often well thought-out) reasons, and do not see it as a big problem for the game or other players.[1]

Yet even as internal and external groups work to combat cheating, most concede it is a perpetual cat-and-mouse game. Cheating, and the ready availability of cheat codes and programs, can be reduced and made harder to use, but the activity can never be entirely eliminated. Early game developers Chip Morningstar and Randall Farmer worked to rid their game of exploits, yet they determined that ultimately "it was clear that we were not in control. The more people we involved in something, the less in control we were."[2] More recently, security development engineer Dave Weinstein argued that "unless you can control all software running on the machine, all machines in the game, and the network that links them, it is impossible to prevent cheating."[3]

Perhaps in recognition of that difficulty, game developers have also worked with their player communities to self-police games for cheaters. The developers of *Habbo Hotel*, for example, have created a system of player police officers. Players who discover improper behaviors are empowered not only to report the activities but to punish the offending players as well. Such activities point to novel approaches to controlling cheating in games, where players are envisioned as allies in the battle rather than being painted with the broad brush of being potential cheaters themselves.

Finally, in addition to examining the practices and perspectives of each business, this chapter reads such practices through Foucault's theorization of discourses of power.[4] Game code can be thought of as an expression of power—it creates the possibilities for player actions in a game, yet at the same time sets bounds for that expression. It is in the "play" that individuals enact with code where the game is performed. Some players, however, refuse to accept such limits, and instead seek to exercise their own power over code. For them, game code has limitations to be overcome, and power is found not just in exploring the limits of code but in breaking and reconfiguring it to the specifications of the player. Anticheat companies seek to reinscribe those boundaries through reinforcement of game code.

Likewise, through active collaborations with players, game companies seek to redress power imbalances in their games, redistributing power to "honest" players in an attempt to control those who have wrested advantage away through cheating. Relationships of power can then be thought of as being constituted through code, both the code of a game and that of anticheating software.

Before going into specifics about approaches, however, I should briefly explain how online games operate and the options for cheating that are present. For instance, when a player gets the latest version of *America's Army*, she loads it on to her PC. The player then connects to the Internet and searches for a game server to connect to. Games make that process fairly easy, as there is usually a connection and server search option built into game interfaces. From there, the player can view a variety of servers, which likely have different requirements (or perhaps none at all) to join them. Some servers may require the PunkBuster software that came loaded with the game to be enabled, for example. The player then connects her computer (known as the client) to that particular server, which will then link a group of players together. Those players can then team up and play the game as long as they desire. The server runs the game, and both receives and sends information about the game to each player's client computer.

Cheaters have several ways to cheat in that setup. They may try to intercept game data that is being passed along from the server to each player or from the player's own computer back to the server. So if the player has tried to use a wallhack cheat, she will have altered code on her own machine in order to see through the walls that the game has constructed. Similarly, a player may try to send out false data to other players, making her avatar move faster than it should be able to or be a better shot with a gun. As Weinstein has contended, because of the multiple places and ways that cheaters can attempt to alter data, it is impossible to stop every instance of cheating. We can certainly reduce cheating, but we can never stop it.

It's about Shoring up the Code

Steven Davis, Cheryl Campbell, and Bill Snyder launched the information technology firm IT GlobalSecure in 2000, with headquarters in Washington, DC. In addition to general business security technology, IT GlobalSecure's SecurePlay Division "is dedicated to game security product development and license sales."[5] The chief product in this division, SecurePlay Software, is a "secure game state engine" that lets developers break down their game code in particular ways, and then encrypt it to make it safe for traveling between a game server and various client machines. Games can be created using a variety of platforms (C++, Java, Flash, and so forth), and the engine helps the developer integrate their gameplay mechanics into different types of "transactions," which are then securely encrypted.

Those transactions are at the heart of the product and are defined in relation to different types of gameplay. Transactions send messages to all of the people/machines involved in a particular game instance via a communication channel. Each message contains a header and a message body, although it is only the body that is encrypted. Each action taken within a game is classified as some type of transaction and is separately encrypted. For example, a "blast transaction" is a message that is sent to all players simultaneously. That might include a move a player makes in a poker game to play a particular card, because each person as well as the "house" must see what card is being played. By contrast, a "secret transaction" goes only to the players who need the information, and no others. Thus, if players are competing in teams at a card game, secret transactions are passed only between the players who are teamed up with each other.[6]

The encryption works at the "protocol" level of information, meaning that even if a cheater was able to decrypt some game information and change it, she could almost never successfully reencrypt it to send it back to the game server and other clients, and have it be accepted by them. The changed information would be rejected, and attempts to cheat would be thwarted. As IT GlobalSecure states, "Total knowledge of the software has given him [the cheater] no advantage. Even if he alters or reverse-engineers the software, the worst that he can achieve is ending the communication."[7]

In marketing their software, the developers have come up with a pricing structure that attempts to attract as diverse a body of clients as possible. Developers are conceptualized as small business indie firms, regular developers, and commercial licensors. Licenses range in price, depending on the size of the developer, the use of the product (it can be purchased for use, evaluation, and testing while a game is in development as well as for distribution with a finished game), and the expected sales of the game. Fees extend from $60 (for free downloadable games, up to a hundred thousand downloads) to more than $10,000 (the minimum, which is negotiable, for high-volume games), with the option of either flat pricing or a smaller up-front fee with additional royalties charged.

Just like the code it produces, the pricing structure at IT GlobalSecure is flexible, and adapts to the particular situation or developer at hand. The company has a core set of products that can be adapted to suit almost any game developer need, big or small. Based on initial beliefs that it was mainly online gambling that would require secure transactions, the company has transferred or widened its focus to digital games generally quite well.[8]

IT GlobalSecure's system of encrypted transactions is designed to prevent cheating rather than finding cheats or identifying particular cheaters. As its promotional literature touts, "We have developed the first anti-cheating solution that stops cheating before it starts."[9] So rather than going after individuals who create or distribute cheats, or develop ever-increasingly sophisticated software to monitor games for cheat use, IT GlobalSecure tries to prevent such activities from happening at all.

The approach taken by this firm relies on encryption technology to do the work promised—code protects code from improper access or manipulation. In this instance, the value is placed on protecting game code before it is intercepted and altered. Code is defended, shielded from attacks on its integrity. Cheaters are (if the encryption holds) unable to alter messages in the data stream of a game, even if they can access them. Cheaters also cannot fool game servers into accepting their own substituted code in place of the original version, as it will not be encrypted and therefore vouched for by the game security.

Such an approach takes no stance on the rightness or wrongness of such behaviors, nor does it attempt to seek out cheaters or cheat codes and expose them, much less punish them. Cheaters (or those trying to cheat) are simply frustrated in their efforts, which will ultimately fail. Cheaters remain anonymous, and cheat codes or other executable files introduced into the data stream or game memory will simply not work.

The approach makes sense given the backgrounds of the companies' founders. In the company information, the founders explain that "we bring our experience in advanced government and commercial security problems to the games industry. Our adversaries were not individual hackers or software pirates, but highly motivated foes with substantial resources and motivation. We understand that the 'bad guy' only has to win once to have a devastating impact."[10] Viewed in that light, it's easier to see why the actual person cheating, or any punishment they might suffer, doesn't really matter.

Bad guys, in governmental terms, don't need identities, as they are continually present and active. Governmental security concerns are ongoing, never-ending challenges. To leave systems relatively open to attack, and then try to identify and catch those breaking in, would be ludicrous at best and criminal at worst. For this company and this approach, the identity of the cheater does not matter, as there will always be another cheater in line behind the one currently trying to break into the system. And with each cheat that is developed, and then found and disabled, there will be another cheat coming out. Better to prevent problems before they begin by developing encryption to seal game code away from the prying eyes and keyboards of the cheating public.

It's about What's Being Done

Although it stopped updating its software in late 2004 and was declared officially dead in early 2006, the program Cheating-Death originally developed by United Admins took a different approach from IT GlobalSecure in trying to stop cheating in online multiplayer games. The program, created by a nonprofit group, tried "to make cheats less effective, and to prevent cheats from getting information. In most cases this leads to cheats simply not working."[11]

United Admins originally formed in 2002 as a group dedicated to making anticheat software that ran with the popular FPS *Half-Life* and its many mods, played on countless servers across the globe. At first United Admins billed itself as nonprofit and loosely organized, but in 2005 the group incorporated and began to seek funding from outside sources in order to better support its activities. That included employing a full-time programmer and supporting a group of software projects in addition to the Cheating-Death project, for which the group remains the most well-known.

Rather than a system of encryption for all game-based transactions, Cheating-Death worked by "wedging itself in between the [game] engine and the cheat. . . . It does not run as a separate program outside of the game, but is actually loaded into the game."[12] Already the Cheating-Death software is distinguishable from the SecurePlay approach, as Cheating-Death assumes the presence of a cheat that can operate in tandem with the game. Cheating-Death is designed, however, to counter the presence of the cheat and "cheat it" of its attempts to gain advantage.

Once installed and operative, the Cheating-Death program would do several things. If it detected that "you" could not see an opponent in the game (because, say, there was a wall blocking your view of that player), the program would "move" the player's location behind you, at least as far as your monitor view was concerned. So while it could not actually move the other player's avatar, if you were using a wallhack to see through walls, you would not be able to see your opponent as your screen was telling you that the opponent was behind you. Thus, wallhacks, while still potentially enabled by cheaters, would become ineffective in practical use.

The program would also monitor "places commonly used by cheats to intercept data from the engine," and if it noticed that one of those locations had been changed, it would disconnect the player.[13] By doing that, the system would deprive cheat programs of the information they needed to function. So if a player was trying to determine the location of other players, or trying to change values relative to his own gameplay, he would simply be booted off-line.

The makers of Cheating-Death also explained that such disconnections had no stigma attached to them. No record was made of what happened to disconnect the player, or any account kept to see if it happened frequently or not. Server administrators would not hear why someone had disconnected—it might have just been a laggy Internet connection or a server overload. Such disconnects were represented by Cheating-Death developers as simply a matter for players to consider, and determine whether or not they wished to keep trying at such an obviously futile activity.

Cheating-Death was designed to run on both servers and clients, and could function either in optional mode, which would allow all players to join a Cheating-Death-enabled server but would check each player to see if the Cheating-Death program was running on his machine, and rename those not running the software, or servers could be configured to allow only those players running the most updated Cheating-Death client software. The software in all cases was a free download, and available for both Windows and Linux users. Initially, the developers claimed to frequently update the software in order to stop cheats that got past the code, with the "average time between cheat release and C-D release . . . currently 72 hours, but may vary depending on the cheat."[14]

The final version release number for the Cheating-Death client is listed as 4.33.4 (with the server software update at 4.29.4), indicating that the product was updated regularly for a period of time. The site lists the current version as last updated on Sunday, November 28, 2004, however, suggesting that the software would not be optimal to defend against the majority of cheats developed in the past several years. A posting not mentioned on the site's main page but instead hidden in the forums by a site administrator confirms that, stating, "As you may be aware, Cheating-Death has not been actively developed for over a year now. As a result, we can't provide the security players and admins should have against current cheats on the Internet so we have now discontinued the C-D project. We hope Cheating-Death will be a platform to start other anti-cheat projects and make them even better as Cheating-Death was [sic]."[15]

While the project ultimately did not meet with commercial success, the organization helped spur the anticheating industry forward in several ways. First, it provided a space for administrators of *Half-Life* servers to come together and share information about optimizing gameplay for the majority of players. It also gave those administrators tools to deal with practical issues, and most notably, it offered the development and then free download of the Cheating-Death program.

In addition to providing a space for game administrators to come together, the site and the project helped to develop (along with Even Balance) the nascent anticheat industry as well. It highlighted the problems caused by cheating in online multiplayer games, and offered one solution to easing them. It helped set the boundaries for the debate, offering a point of view about what was acceptable behavior online and what was not. It also drew the attention of journalists, who were looking to tell stories about cheating in online games.[16] In that way, it helped set the bounds of the debate about cheating, as popularly conceived.

Finally, United Admins, with its specific program, Cheating-Death, made a particular statement about what mattered when it came to stopping cheating in online games. For United Admins, cheating was an activity to be engaged in that could be made less effective, thus hopefully encouraging those engaged in the activity to quit. But what mattered least of all was the naming of those doing the cheating or their outing in the wider community. Those values are coded into Cheating-Death as well as embodied in the discourse of how the software works, as explained by the developers.

United Admins attempted to prevent cheating as well as make enabled cheats less effective. For United Admins, cheating was constructed as an optional activity engaged in by anonymous players. Those players might cheat all of the time, some of the time, or be trying out a cheat for the first time on a whim. That group of anonymous players would also encompass the individuals who developed the cheats (the small minority), and those who found and used them (the great majority). Yet rather than lump those various groups together as generic cheaters, United Admins made no distinctions as to player character, morality, or ethics. No matter the cheat employed, by whatever type of individual, United Admins simply desired to make cheats inoperative. If a player stopped using cheats, that was great. If a player did not learn and migrated to non-Cheating-Death-enabled servers, that was fine too.

Unmoored from identity, cheating became an undesirable activity to be managed, rather than the expression of an undesirable aspect of personality or behavior. The person who cheats is not a cheater but instead someone engaged in a futile activity. And in this model, anticheat code is conceptualized as something that can help maintain the integrity of the original game code. But rather than protectively envelop game code, the Cheating-Death program's code acts as a parallel defender, making the original game code "smarter" and more vigilant against outside attack. The power to stop cheats is added to the game system, and cheating codes are drained of their power to reformulate or manipulate a game.

It's about Who You Are, Punk

The last business that I wish to discuss was started in 2000 in Texas, also in response to the cheating in *Half-Life* and its mods. Even Balance was formed in order to "restore the FUN stolen by the selfish Punks who cheat at online multiplayer games."[17] From the beginning, Even Balance took a decidedly antagonistic stance toward those who cheated in online games. Labeling them punks and calling its central product PunkBuster, the company aimed to restore balance to online gameplay through the detection of cheating, the banning of the activity, and more important, the banning of the players engaged in those actions.

Even Balance's initial experimental system was announced and started in 2000, and in 2001 the company officially incorporated, and Even Balance began working with commercial game developers to integrate its PunkBuster technology directly into online games. Over the past six years, the company has worked with many games, including *America's Army*, *Wolfenstein: Enemy Territory*, *Rainbow Six 3: Raven Shield*, *Battlefield 1942*, *Call of Duty*, *Splinter Cell: Pandora Tomorrow*, *Battlefield: Vietnam*, *Doom 3*, *Quake 4*, and *Rainbow Six Lockdown*, among others.[18]

Like Cheating-Death, PunkBuster use is optional for the player, and free to download and use as well. As Even Balance is a for-profit company, it works with game developers to integrate the PunkBuster system into the online component of games through dedicated servers. Players choose to enable PunkBuster or not, and then play on a PunkBuster-enabled server or one not affiliated with PunkBuster. Of the three organizations, PunkBuster is perhaps the most active and invasive in terms of the player in its efforts to stop cheating.

The PunkBuster program acts much like antivirus software does, by scanning the memory of a player's computer in order to find well-known hacks and cheats. After an initial check on joining a server, the software will validate each client's computer against further modifications approximately two to three times each minute. If certain discrepancies are found at any time during gameplay, the account is flagged, and the player is automatically removed from a game. Likewise, a server administrator can perform random checks on player settings, and manually remove a player for a specified time period or permanently ban him, if so desired. All other players are notified of these actions, and that notification is designed as a central part of the system. Lists of banned players are posted to the official game boards for other players to scan in order to identify well-known cheaters.

For example, the site PunksBusted.com worked with Even Balance to develop the Auto Master Ban List, or Auto-MBL, which is a "fully automated, secure, real time spooling of the Punk Buster logs" directly from individual servers to a master database, maintained by the site.[19] The feature, which works across more than a dozen games, allows a master list of cheaters "caught in the act" to be assembled and circulated for players as well as server administrators to inspect.

Even Balance also allows server administrators to give suspension powers to trusted players, through their "Player Power" function. This system gives administrators the ability to "deputize" certain players, who can then deal out points against players they suspect of cheating or other antisocial activities. When an offending player has accumulated a set number of points (the number is set by the server administrator), that player is kicked out of the game for a certain period of time. If no official deputies are on the server, and the server is enabled for Power Points, any player can use their allotted store of points against one (and only one) player. Thus, in addition to using software to actively scan for cheats, the system allows for human intervention, through administrators, deputies, and even regular players.

In 2004, Even Balance further upped the stakes against the most dedicated cheaters through the addition of hardware globally unique identifier (GUID) tracking. Normally, if players were caught cheating, their CD key was banned and their unique player IDs were added to a public list of known cheaters. After a 2004 update, those caught trying to hack into the PunkBuster program itself had the GUIDs from their gaming hardware added to the permanently banned list, meaning that various pieces of hardware on the cheaters' computer were now "marked." In practical terms that meant the computer itself, not just the person using it, was banned from all PunkBuster-enabled servers, for all games supported by PunkBuster.[20] So even if multiple people used a computer to play different online games, if one of them used the machine to try to hack PunkBuster and was caught, everyone would be locked out of PunkBuster-enabled servers, at least until a new machine was purchased. Now it wasn't just individuals who had the label of cheater attached to them; their hardware was similarly branded cheater as well.

Even Balance's approach obviously differs from the other two quite a bit, taking the most punitive stance toward those who cheat in online games. The system is designed to identify who cheats and then ban them from protected servers. The name of the product is itself instructive—PunkBuster—as it names those who it is also trying to stop. Rather than preventing anonymous cheaters before they can access code or make the cheating of anonymous individuals less effective, this approach puts the infringing individual at the center.

And if a person is banned from a PunkBuster-enabled server, that ban is permanent. There is no returning, no case to be made for leniency. While minor infractions can get a player booted for a specified period of time, cheating comes with one punishment: banning. That doesn't mean that the player can never play the game again, only that he cannot play on PunkBuster servers. Yet for players wishing to team with and challenge honest players, that may be enough.

As with United Admins, Even Balance's business has been about more than simply creating a product. It has helped to define a segment of the industry, create awareness about an issue of significance, and perhaps most critically, worked to define more specifically what cheating is and how it should be dealt with. Even Balance's success in gaining attention for itself and the problem of cheating in online games has helped to legitimize another support industry for game developers and publishers.[21] The company has successfully defined a need or lack, and created a service to fill that gap. In doing so, PunkBuster becomes something potentially needed by all developers and publishers with an online game to sell. If an anticheat technology isn't being used, why is that? If the company has its own security, that may be fine, but if not, then a game is potentially at risk, without the security and support that products like PunkBuster can bring.

And most important, Even Balance has worked to set the standards for what we consider cheating in online, multiplayer, FPS games. In creating typologies of cheats, and then banning players who use those cheats, a set of practices has been marked, permanently, as undesirable or illegal activities. The PunkBuster program learns to see particular activities as cheating, and so that is what those activities become. And through the distribution and circulation of ban logs, game players then also see those activities as cheating and the players engaging in them as cheaters. A practice has been defined and identities confirmed through the growing use of an anticheat technology.

Internal Approaches: Community Managers and Security Specialists

Another force that deals with cheating on a regular basis is often internal to either large game development studios or their publishers. This can include a customer service team for MMOs, small groups of informal staff that might respond to player issues, or programmers and software engineers who design security protocols to attempt to thwart cheating preemptively. These groups can work with greater or lesser degrees of independence in dealing with cheating and how to control it. Yet in their official and unofficial actions they also help to define what cheating is, and what is proper behavior.

Contemporary MMOs have variable amounts of staff that deal with their community of players on a regular basis, in part to combat cheating as well as monitor other activities and assist players with technical issues. A large company such as Sony can have sixty customer support staff members who each spend "an average of one hour out of an eight-hour shift dealing with grief-related play," which could include cheating.[22] Publishers such as NCsoft will employ dedicated teams to deal with rule violations in their MMOs, which include *Lineage 1* and *2*, *City of Heroes*, *Guild Wars*, *Auto Assault*, and *Tabula Rasa*. Team members will focus on a subset of those games, and are kept busy "making sure that the decisions we make as a team stick with company and game policy."[23]

Team managers act as intermediaries between "frontline Game Masters and those who have the final decision on the product as a whole."[24] Such managers, along with the Game Masters, have come to see variations on certain basic themes in relation to cheating over time, yet must continually work to determine what legitimate and illegitimate player activity looks like. For example, bot use in *Lineage 2* is rampant, keeping team members constantly alert for the latest versions of such cheats.[25] Bots in the game can be simple programs that yell "'WTS (want to sell) dragon blade 100k PST (please send tell),' or they can be entire game client replacements that allow you to completely automate nine accounts to work in unison."[26]

Additionally, team members must watch for other types of cheating, including hacks, exploits, and social cheating. Game Masters handle all incoming calls from players about gameplay except for billing and technical support, which are dealt with separately. Those calls include questions and concerns about gameplay, recovery, and violations. The company knows the importance of such positions, and for some players Game Masters are "the police, a counselor, the referee, the judge, the mechanic, and sometimes even god."[27]

Game Masters have the authority to punish players for rule violations, and depending on the past history of the player and the severity of the issue, Game Masters can do such things as issue written warnings, give a seventy-two-hour suspension, or close an account completely.

In addition to responding to individual players who may be cheating, customer service team members also perform regular checks on the number of items on servers, for example, to make sure that fluctuations are tracked and potentially investigated before they become major incidents.

They can also get involved in legal issues such as cease-and-desist orders for posting illegal information as well as people hosting files or illegally selling copies of their games.[28]

Such teams take a mixture of approaches, being both reactive and proactive in limiting things like bot use, and trying to stop individuals as well as third-party programs from working within their games. They see cheating as something that players do as well as the cheater as someone to be stopped or banned from a game world. These workers are called on to "play god," and determine the guilt or innocence of particular players as well as what does and does not constitute cheating. And while something like bot use may seem straightforward, instances such as social cheating may not be so easy to define.

For example, in the Numedeon online game *Whyville*, players will go to a Trading Post either individually (where one person plays two separate accounts) or in teams and collude to publicly bid up the cost for a certain item in order to falsely increase its value, and sell that item at a profit later.[29] Designers may ask whether that is cheating or simply a clever use of a legal game system. But a decision must be made, and along with it, an appropriate punishment must be doled out. With each decision, what counts as cheating solidifies, and further defines what proper and improper gameplay each look like.

Perhaps in reaction to that power and defining role, players have responded in a variety of ways. So while Game Masters and their team leaders must work within well-defined parameters and rules, players tend to ascribe great powers to them and the propensity to act in capricious ways. Discussions about Game Master activities are commonplace on game discussion boards, in game guilds, and elsewhere. As a testament to their impact, one *Final Fantasy XI* player created a blog, Bannable Offenses, ostensibly written by "[GM] Dave."[30] The blog parodies the life of a hard-drinking, antisocial, ban-happy Game Master and his interactions with players. For instance, in the post "Law and Order," [GM] Dave writes,

Do you remember when you were installing the game? Do you remember accepting the Terms of Service (ToS)? . . . If you act in anyway that we (read: I) deem inappropriate, I have every right to burn your character to the ground. It doesn't matter who you are or where you're from. I have supreme power over the future (or lack thereof) of your character. Imagine me as Fate, only with a shorter temper and whisky breath.[31]

Additionally, [GM] Dave often parodies the many calls that players make to Game Masters, including those regarding seeing potential bots, cheating, and rude behavior. While the blog is fiction, it does express some unspoken truths: players can get frustrated with the rules of gameplay as well as the unethical and potentially illegal actions of others. And even as they might try to report those behaviors to game officials, they often feel their voices are unheard or unheeded. Bannable Offenses points to situations where players desire to have more control over their game world, even if that means greater punishments are meted out. In [GM] Dave's version of *Final Fantasy XI*, real-money traders, botters, and the socially challenged are always fed to a dragon, after being thrown in jail and perhaps also having their account banned for good measure.

In addition to Game Masters, developers as well as one anticheat company also employ players in helping to patrol games. As I mentioned previously, the Finnish game *Habbo Hotel* employs players as police officers to help patrol the game for adults who try to impersonate kids as well as other illegal behavior. Likewise, Even Balance's Player Power system lets players with enough points apply them against another player and possibly get that player kicked out of a game.

Such systems enable players to take partial control of a game space and become responsible for upholding norms for community behavior. While there's always the potential for abuse, there is also the opportunity to let players feel they are part of shaping the space they play within. Researchers who have studied player behavior in experiments concerning cheating have found that when players are allowed to punish others for cheating, they have a greater investment in the game. And when players believe cheating goes unpunished in a game, their participation drops off.[32]

It seems important to give players some type of voice or role to play in helping to define community standards regarding cheating. Even when not actively allowed to take part in the process, players will default to devising their own systems, as we've seen through the creation of blacklists and in-game chastisements. Integrating them into official processes can create a more cohesive group, as earlier accounts of MUDs and community formation have shown.[33]

In sum, developers and publishers have some established methods for dealing with cheating, in addition to hiring outside firms. MMOs in particular have large staffs to police game worlds and uphold the laws of the land. Some spaces also deputize players, giving them some control over who is punished and why. Yet all such practices keep the focus on individual players, much like the PunkBuster approach.

Conclusions

Perhaps calling several companies (one now defunct) a mini-industry is being too generous, but it is useful to think about the impact of such firms as well as internal efforts at game development studios and publishing houses regarding security and anticheating. Such efforts force definitions of cheating to be codified, for better or worse. Efforts to secure game code have grown more elaborate over the past twenty years, and likely will become even more sophisticated, if we move to online distribution as a more central form of commerce for games. But in doing so, we need to keep in mind the choices being made, and who is doing the choosing.

Just as with Digital Rights Management, the encrypting of game code or data closes off access to the functioning of games. Developers may leave in certain ways for players to tweak or alter that code, or they may not. Such actions will likely prevent security breaches and cheating problems, but they also might keep experimentation and exploration in check. It also becomes a greater challenge to those skilled in hacking data. The system is designed to work against the faceless enemy, and is devoid of intentionality in trying to understand why someone might wish to cheat. It doesn't matter—someone always will, and they must always be stopped.

Code can also be used to make cheating less effective, yet keep the perpetrators anonymous. It can trick a cheater's computer into believing something that isn't true, just as the cheater had intended to do to the game server or the opponent's machines. Cheating here is an activity to be managed and lessened. The person engaging in such activities is either discouraged, frustrated, or sees the light and perhaps reforms. The activity is not irrevocably tied to who the cheater is; it's more akin to a bad habit or a momentary curiosity.

Programs and services can be marshaled to weed out, identify, and punish those who cheat. Punishment is swift and (relatively) harsh: permanent banishment and the branding of the identity of punk. Certain behaviors will never be acceptable, and those who engage in them can only clear their name if they purchase new game software and start over fresh, chastened and reformed.

Finally, teams of specialized personnel can work to identify cheating as well as especially troublesome individuals in their games, and mete out variable punishments based on the severity of the offense and the company's stance toward cheating.

Cheating in each case is potentially stopped. An individual might or might not be linked with the activity. Yet in each case, cheating is further defined. Wallhacks *are* cheating. Accessing the data stream in a particular place *is* cheating. Trying to decrypt game code *is* cheating. There is no alternative—the discourse and the code have defined the activity in that particular way. At first this might seem obvious. Of course wallhacks are cheats. Who would argue that they aren't, except for someone who might use one?

Still, the categories of what cheating is and is not demand continual updating and refinement, as those intent on hacking software refine their approaches and as new games are released. With new opportunities for play come new opportunities to play with the game code, which can subsequently be defined as cheating. Even Balance has a list of categories of cheating activities that will get a player banned. It includes aimbots, wallhacks, multihacks, gamehacks, speedhacks, autofire, "cheat" video drivers, and others.[34] How many more activities will the company need to define in the next five or ten years? With each decision a value judgment is made about what is fair and unfair advantage, and what is acceptable and unacceptable behavior.

Of course, there is always the option of playing on private servers or those not employing anticheat programs. But the larger issue remains the same: that particular activities have been codified in ways with which everyone might not agree, even if they are a small minority. As prior chapters have discussed, most of the time cheating is contextual and dynamic. There is only a limited set of situations or activities that are consistently labeled cheating. And different sets of individuals and groups have varying stakes in solidifying those labels.

So what of the players involved? There is the opportunity for a limited degree of player input in some games. Initial systems have allowed players to participate in circumscribed ways, which have been carefully delimited and are controlled by others. The ability to act is constrained by predefined notions of what cheating is and what appropriate punishments should be. So players can vote to kick others off a server, but not to ban them. Likewise, players can only boot someone for a prespecified amount of time. Players don't set agendas concerning what cheats are or aren't, and they can't interfere with the banning of another player. Thus, players are invited along if they play by the rules and do not seek to challenge them. Perhaps further iterations of such systems can incorporate more feedback or decision-making authority to players, without ceding too much control over game spaces from designers.

In these instances, code is being used to define particular activities as cheating as well as draw attention to those engaging in such practices. Code is largely repressive, disallowing specific actions and enforcing certain norms of behavior. Player input on this process is limited. That's not necessarily a bad thing but it is definitely one-sided. Players may choose not to play on such servers, but that option has its limits. It encompasses an all-or-nothing approach—either you play by our rules or you must find your own way.

While dealing with the topic of cheating and how to curtail it, this framework also relates back to issues of gameplay, and what players, developers, and others believe are correct and incorrect ways to play a game. In addition to highlighting certain social norms for behavior, cheating also lets us see what we consider the correct way to play a game to be, and how that conceptualization has changed over time and become better defined. So by using only the tools that the developer has provided and not seeking to alter game rules in any way, a player correctly plays a game. Players also must try to beat a game on their own before using codes and when playing against other individuals, but must never seek unfair advantage, unless everyone else is already doing so.

Seen in that light, cheating becomes a bellwether defining what good just as much as what bad gameplay looks like. It also helps us to recognize the cheater from the good player as well as gradations in levels of cheating behavior. Moreover, gaming capital can be usefully considered, as differential sorts of capital for cheating and not cheating can accrue to individuals, depending on their social circles. Paratextual industries and companies such as Even Balance and the customer service teams at NCsoft work to define what they believe is acceptable gameplay as well as the right type of player with the correct form of gaming capital. That player knows the right way to play a game and the correct stance to take against those who don't play the same way. That force is not entirely successful (cheaters still exist) but it is strong enough that players can then decide on the fly what cheating must look like and their stance on any new issue that arises, which might be considered cheating. In that way, cheating is produced and cheaters are created through an evolving system.

While this chapter has closely examined how an anticheating industry has begun to evolve, it has taken a broader look at the gameplay activities that led to such development. In the next chapter, I take a deeper look at one game in particular, *Final Fantasy XI*, and how in one game definitions of cheating have evolved, how cheating is contextual, and how players actively take part in not only shaping those definitions but in responding to cheaters and cheats, even in the absence of official developer help.

A MAGE'S CHRONICLE: CHEATING AND LIFE IN VANA'DIEL

After playing *Final Fantasy VII*, *VIII*, *IX*, *X*, and *X-2*, I took the plunge and subscribed to Square Enix's first online version of its popular series: *Final Fantasy XI*. In the game, the mythical world of Vana'diel offers players the opportunity to group with other players and slay many legendary *Final Fantasy* monsters (as well as many new ones), go on dangerous quests, and make friends while doing so—with players from Japan, North America, Europe, Australia, and New Zealand.

I've had an enjoyable time learning the intricate strategies involved in playing in a game arena with thousands of other people, never-ending missions and quests, and a thriving economy. Being a newbie to MMOs, once I started playing the game I quickly checked out various Web sites that had information about how to better play the game, chatted with friends about strategy, checked out some discussion boards, and have bought the most recent expansion pack (Treasures of Aht Urhgan), even though I'm still exploring much of the original content. I've settled on the boards at Allakhazam.com as my primary base for game-related information, where I have followed with interest various discussions about the selling of gil (the currency in *Final Fantasy XI*) and player accounts in online spaces.

Virtual economies can be just as tough to make a living in as real ones, provided you are opposed to cheating. Living the life of an honest mage (magic user) on a server in Vana'diel requires a fair amount of time and drudgery, as is the case in most MMOs and, frankly, the "real world." Many players prefer the route of hard work and helpful tips from friends and fellow adventurers to get by, but to get ahead others turn to computer programs, online real-to-virtual money exchanges, and other methods probably not yet reported. And that's just to gain advantage in the game. Players also can cheat for the sheer pleasure of doing so or to further their game, by any means necessary. When I first began talking with game developers in 2001 about cheating, none mentioned cheating as a way to make real money from playing a game. But now, there are many ways to convert virtual capital into real-world cash, and vice versa.

In this chapter, I want to explore cheating and its place in one MMORPG: *Final Fantasy XI*. The game, released first in Japan in 2002, and then in North America and Europe, has met with great success. Square Enix claims more than six hundred thousand subscribers, making *Final Fantasy XI* one of the larger MMOs currently running, and Square Enix appears committed to updating the content and keeping the world spinning for as long as there are paying customers.[1] Yet just as other virtual-world creators have discovered, cheating in many forms is something that many players enjoy, and keeping the cheaters from ruining the game experience for others can be a serious challenge to maintaining a viable world. Another virtual-world developer, Blizzard, should know; its ongoing efforts to police the rampant cheating in its online hack-and-slash game *Diablo II* are legendary, and led to its more rapid and punitive stance toward cheating (a violation of its end user license agreement [EULA]) in the 2004 MMO *World of Warcraft*. Such actions by developers remind us that as carefully as a game can be designed to limit certain activities, gameplay is ultimately in the hands of players rather than developers. And even in a virtual world, a few bad eggs can ruin the fun for everybody else.

This chapter is based on an in-depth participant observation of one server in *Final Fantasy XI*, including more than five hundred real-time hours of logged gameplay. It also takes into account the paratexts surrounding the game, including the official strategy guide, and Web sites run by fans and professionals, including several highly trafficked sites that cater to players of many MMOs, such as Allakhazam.com and ffxi-atlas .com.

The analysis revealed that while cheating is present and a concern for many players, a debate exists about the definition of cheating and whether it actually hurts other players. Furthermore, players themselves see little common ground in what constitutes cheating, and are actively and continually engaged in working through these definitions for themselves.

MMO Research: Power Gamers, EULAs, and Addiction

Early attention to cheating in online games has mostly been in the form of popular press accounts and some player discussions. It was likely the cheating in *Ultima Online* in the late 1990s that received the earliest popular press.[2] As Brad King and Rich Borland explain, the translation of the *Ultima* world from single player to multiplayer, and a relative openness in what was allowable behavior, quickly led to a situation where some players felt that an emerging play style known as PK was an unwelcome addition to their game world. PK (also known as "ganking") involved more advanced players attacking lesser-advanced ones (through their respective avatars), killing them, and then looting their corpses. The early *Ultima Online* was designed to allow players to fight one another, but the designers had not foreseen the extent to which some players would go in order to gain advantage in the game.[3] Such actions resulted in some players quitting the game and others staging a naked sit-in at designer Richard Garriott's virtual castle, which started developers on the road toward managing different play styles that were bound to clash.

Following *Ultima Online*, the exploits in *Diablo I* and *II* gained popular attention.[4] Although *Diablo* was not a persistent online game world, the ability to play with other people in a system that allowed for player-versus-player (PvP) combat quickly led to trouble. Additionally, some players figured out ways to "dupe" items, or illegally duplicate them, creating an unfair and illegal way to gain wealth in the game.[5]

Although some fans have been quite vocal in their complaints that Blizzard did not do enough to address such problems, the developer did finally announce that it would be banning thousands of accounts at a time in an effort to control such practices. But the practices continue, and Blizzard has been forced to look at more sophisticated ways to prevent cheating rather than simply punishing those it can find. Such tactics are even more strongly in evidence with Blizzard's *World of Warcraft*.

Systematic researcher inquiry into cheating has developed only more recently and in a limited fashion, as scholars have studied games such as *EverQuest* and *Lineage*, exploring how different play styles can be viewed as cheating or not by particular players as well as how grief play is becoming a central component of virtual-world gameplay.[6] On a similar note, some researchers have begun to pay attention to player-created walk-throughs for games, and have also examined the exchange of game-playing information ("tips") for its role in building good player relations.[7]

More recently, researchers examining MMOs have studied such related questions as the legal rights of avatars, the buying and selling of player accounts and merchandise, and issues of copyright law. Ren Reynolds looks at the ethical frameworks of cheating in all digital games, asking what belief systems are operative and if competing systems of beliefs can be reconciled in massively multiplayer systems. For the time being, he leaves that an open question.[8] Legal scholars such as Gregory F. Lastowka and Dan Hunter have investigated how copyright and property law precedents are changing (or not) as a result of challenges from virtual-world players.[9] Finally, economists such as Edward Castronova have scrutinized the economies of virtual worlds as well as the economic systems of sites such as Player Auctions, and how avatars on the market come to be differently valued, depending on their gender.[10]

As the MMO Turns: Daily Life in Vana'diel

Most fantasy-based MMOs have surface resemblances, often featuring similar races (orcs, dwarves, and elves), job types (mages, fighters, and healers), advancement requirements (levels and experience points), and other in-game activities (crafting, fishing, quests, and socializing). Although quite a few of those gameplay elements are indeed similar, however, each MMO is bound by a set of design decisions that make it distinct from the others, and make gameplay a different experience in each game world. In this section, I explore some of the design decisions that Square Enix made for Final Fantasy XI, and the consequences of those choices for its players.

Me and My Avatar

One of the earliest decisions a player makes when starting to play an MMO is choosing an avatar along with its specific characteristics and traits. The choices and nonchoices built into avatar creation have a significant effect on gameplay, and so deserve to be carefully scrutinized.[11] In *Final Fantasy XI*, players are allowed to choose a race for their avatar (Hume, Elvaan, Tarutaru, Mithra, or Galka), a gender (although Galkas can only be male, and Mithras can only be female), faces and hair color, a body size (small, medium, or large), a starting job (Warrior, Monk, Thief, Black Mage, White Mage, or Red Mage), and a home nation (Bastok, San D'Oria, or Windurst). The player is allowed only one character per "Content ID" (one is given with the registration cost), and additional IDs for more characters cost $1 per month.

As with most fantasy RPG-type games, in *Final Fantasy XI* each character race and job class has a set of modifying statistics that make certain race/job combinations either strategic or unlikely. But aside from race, perhaps the only difference that might truly matter in the game is job selection. So playing as an offensive magic user (in the job of Black Mage) will provide a different experience than choosing the job of Samurai, which deals in fast physical attacks. Yet in *Final Fantasy XI*, players are allowed to change jobs without having to create new avatars—an ability that is rare in the world of MMOs.

In other games, such as *EverQuest*, once an avatar's job is set, it cannot be changed. In that game, as in more recent games such as *World of Warcraft*, it's quite common for players to have multiple characters, partly in order to be able to try out different jobs.[12] One consequence of such a system, however, is the relative anonymity that results—players are known by a range of different avatars, with different names, jobs, and races that can be spread across various servers. The reputation for a particular avatar may hold, but not necessarily across avatars. While players can and frequently do tell others about their main and alternate characters, that kind of linking most often occurs within the formal collectives of linkshells (or "guilds," as they are known in most other MMOs) or among friends. In the wider server world, those associations may not be so well-known. Square Enix has also made the linking easier for friends within a game. When a player "befriends" another player (and the other player agrees), each player then has access to a special screen, listing whether any friends are online, their in-game locations, and which characters they are currently playing. Thus, as part of the game's coding, "alts" become known to friends. Outside of friendship and shell circles, though, a reputation may be harder to link.

It is quite common (if not the norm) for players to level their avatars through many different jobs, allowing them to change their play style and level of advancement as they wish. Because Square Enix only permits one character ID per monthly fee—and as noted above, additional characters cost another $1 per month—such alt characters are less plentiful, and more often seem to function as "mules" that store and transport items for advanced players, rather than chances to experience gameplay differently.

The result of these systems for gameplay is a relatively straightforward persistence of identity. My avatar, Leiya, started the game as a Warrior, but I quickly found the job boring and soon switched to White Mage, a job that uses magic to heal and protect other group members. I later began playing the job of Black Mage (a damage-dealing magic user), which has now become my main job. For each job attempted, the avatar starts at level 1, and the player must advance each job class from scratch, although with the same name, gender, race, and reputation from previous jobs.

Such design choices can be limiting for players wishing to change their race or gender (for that they must start an entirely new avatar), but they allow those willing to stick with the same avatar a more persistent reputation in the game world. If you are known as a bad player (either incompetent or evil), your reputation will spread based on your name, and that can be quite hard to get past.

Likewise, your linkshell members will all be familiar with your name, and the ability of each player to move among various job combinations can make gameplay more variable and potentially more valuable. For example, it is difficult to gain the maximum experience points when fighting monsters in a party if the levels between the avatars in the party are too great (such as a level 5 Warrior and a level 25 Blue Mage). If a player has difficulty finding a party for her character in one job or wishes to play with friends of a different level, she can fairly easily change jobs, if that job is in the target range. Thus, the player's avatar is more versatile, as it allows players to keep building a reputation as their interests may change—either day-to-day or over time.[13]

Settling Down: Servers as Home

Just as the design of the game allows players to easily change their jobs, the activities of an individual avatar are restricted to one server—the server assigned on initial avatar creation.[14] There is a way that players can join a server that their friends are on, but in doing so, they must create new avatars, and those avatars start at level 1 and cannot be moved to any other server. Thus, players cannot easily move among servers, again establishing a certain persistence of identity and reputation. Players exploit that limitation on message boards, where they regularly post server blacklists of known disreputable or troublesome players/avatars as well as white lists of helpful players.

In addition to restricting the easy migration of players, Square Enix also designed servers to host global populations—hence Japanese, North American, and European players all play on mixed servers. An auto-translate feature has been included in the game interface to allow players speaking different languages to be able to group together and communicate, if only in a rudimentary way. But the translator remains for translation between Japanese and English only, and players often feel the system is limited at best.[15] With each population in different time zones, there is some overlap, but player self-segregation (that is, it's common to see English-only and Japanese-only parties and linkshells) does still occur.

PvP: Ballista

Although some of the earliest problems with virtual worlds and accusations of cheating seemed to arise from PvP-style combat, many MMOs have retained the system as a more or less central feature. Some games offer dedicated PvP servers, where as part of the normal gameplay, players know that other players can attack them. Many players opt for player-versus-environment (PvE) servers, where such activities are outlawed or limited, if not specifically coded out of possibility. *EverQuest* uses such a system, as does *World of Warcraft*. Other virtual worlds such as *City of Heroes* have not featured any PvP combat, but *City of Heroes* added that function with the release of *City of Villains*. Square Enix has increasingly included PvP elements in *Final Fantasy XI* to appeal to players desiring such experiences, but have kept it (at least through mid-2006) to a strictly segregated activity: Ballista.

The game of Ballista involves teams on a quest to find buried objects (stones called "Petras") and then score points by shooting the stones into "a castle-like construction known as a Rook," but individual players must also fight and defeat opponents from the rival team before being able to shoot the stones.[16] There are Ballista games on set days, for certain nations and players of specific levels (upper-level players can join in, but they must be handicapped with a level cap). This design limitation has worked well to keep players wishing to attack unsuspecting others from being able to do so, leading to an environment where combat is strictly controlled.

Square Enix has also fleshed out Ballista with Ballista Royale, where winning teams from each server then competed across servers, culminating in a finale held at the sold-out *Final Fantasy XI* Fan Festival in March 2006 in California. The last match was also broadcast live on Square Enix's playonline.com Web site, so that those not attending could watch. Such activities give players additional avenues for competitiveness, within strict limits. Those who wish to attack others off the Ballista field are required to seek other means to achieve their ends. Monster-player killing (MPK) is one controversial result, as players "train mobs" on other players.[17]

Summing Up

I have not discussed all the elements of *Final Fantasy XI* that are important to it as an MMO and that distinguish it from other MMOs, yet the preceding description should help to shed light on some of the game's key design elements. We should also remember that game developers are constantly updating the game, not only with new content and areas, but also by tweaking various elements to balance gameplay and eliminate bugs or problems as they arise. As I have been writing this chapter and book, the game has continually changed: for example, the designers have changed the fishing system to eliminate bot use, and have altered monster path tracking to reduce the possibilities for MPK, among other revisions. Such changes remind us that just like physical worlds, virtual ones are dynamic spaces, where design can shape, but never entirely predict or control, resulting player behaviors and expectations.

Cheating in Vana'diel

Cheating is a moving target of a topic, especially in virtual worlds, where code and players both evolve and change. From the earliest online games, designers have struggled with (and against) players to set the bounds of acceptable gameplay styles. Designers such as Richard Garriott learned that when launching *Ultima Online*, the game "wasn't his anymore, and it wasn't right for him to try to control its population. . . . Here the players had free will; they had control over their own environment and destiny. The puppets had cut their strings and taken over their world."[18] But even as players have free will, as we've seen, designers can make choices that encourage or discourage particular types of playing. Even within those parameters, though, there are generally hard and soft forms of playing outside the rules with which designers (and other players) must contend.

The first set of practices is simple enough to think about; when a practice is objectively defined as cheating by a developer, it is also usually made illegal, and if possible coded out of existence. For example, in earlier MMOs such as *Diablo II*, kill stealing could occur, where players could wait until another player had almost completely killed a difficult monster, and then come in, take the final blow, and loot the corpse. This form of cheating has been removed (coded out of possibility) from *Final Fantasy XI*, as drops from a defeated monster can only be distributed to either a person soloing a monster or among party members involved in the kill. Random players cannot even attack monsters engaged by others, unless the player or group specifically "calls for help" using a certain command.

Likewise (and as I will explore in more detail shortly), when players discovered in *Final Fantasy XI* that they could easily automate the task of fishing using a basic command script, Square Enix reminded players that such modifications were not just cheating but were also illegal according to the EULA, and subsequently changed the entire fishing system to solve the problem. Thus, problematic practices that developers define as cheating are usually rendered illegal, impossible to enact, or both.

What is more interesting are the practices that are contested and evolving within the game world. These include activities that developers cannot fully prevent or control (much as they would like to), and those that do not depend on exploiting hardware or software but instead can include a creative manipulation of other players or the world itself. It is those practices that this section explores, including the activities and, more important, player responses to the results as well as how discourse can shape outcomes.

Power Leveling: Rent-a-White-Mage

One of the design decisions that Square Enix made in order to prevent certain player shortcuts to gaining in-game experience and ability has resulted in the practice of power leveling, which some players feel is lazy and borderline cheating. I want to distinguish this player-provided practice from commercial-service providers of power leveling who advertise their business on Web sites such as Player Auctions and International Game Exchange. For a significant fee ($250 in early 2006), they will advance a character you create and name to a specified level, or through a range of levels, such as one to sixty. Those activities are so obviously cheating that the businesses themselves promote their activities by touting their ethical practices while leveling and assuring players that they will "never talk to random players in game," lest their practices be revealed.[19]

Because of the game mechanics of *Final Fantasy XI*, when players group or party together, the experience points each receives when killing monsters is largely determined by the highest-leveled character, relative to the monster killed. Players of lower level have their experience points adjusted according to that number, so that, for example, if a level 20 Red Mage is grouped with a level 50 Warrior to fight a Tremor Ram (a monster of approximately the same level as the Red Mage), the Red Mage will receive no experience points, even though on her own, she would have received about a hundred points—a significant amount.

That design restriction was enacted to prevent lower-level players from grouping with extremely high-level characters to easily gain experience points and level up quickly, without putting in long periods of time as part of a "grind." Yet the inability to level quickly has led to the practice of power leveling, both of individuals and entire parties. Although many power levels are now free (in the past, some players charged for them), there is a large disagreement in the player community about whether such activities constitute cheating.

Power leveling involves a (relatively) high-level White Mage watching over a group (or an individual) while it fights monsters, usually at a fast rate, which are often too difficult for the group to fight unassisted. The White Mage isn't part of the actual party, because if she were, she would negate the experience points earned, due to her high level. Her job during the party ranges, depending on individual preference (the range is described next), but the White Mage mainly serves to keep curing the party and thus keeps it alive as it fights various monsters.

Players who have argued that power- leveling is cheating believe that the experience actually shortchanges players getting the power level, as they spend less time at each level, learning how to play their jobs. For instance, players posting to Allakhazam.com have noted how groups being power leveled never learn about proper "hate control" while fighting monsters. So rather than learning how to focus the monster's attention on only one party member and carefully mete out damage dealt to the monster by the group, the group concentrates instead on "chain killing" monsters as quickly as possible, as an outsider keeps everyone alive. Likewise, parties fail to learn to pace themselves, as they don't have to worry about their own party's White Mage taking time to rest in order to regain the "magic points" that the White Mage needs to cast her healing spells, as the higher-leveled power leveler will always have plenty of magic points available to use.

Advocates of the power level explain that the high-level White Mage serves merely as a safety net, keeping the party alive at times when everyone is still learning their job. Additionally, the game mechanics of *Final Fantasy XI* almost force players to begin grouping when they reach level 10, and then continue throughout the rest of the game, to level 75. That most often means finding a party (or "pickup group") comprising six people, all within two-to-three levels of one another, and with an appropriate mix of job types (such as a healer, a person to hold the attention of the monster, and a person adept at drawing monsters to the party as well as general damage dealers and melee fighters). Sometimes players can seek or look for a party for hours or days, especially if they have an unpopular job. Thus, some players desire to maximize their experience point gain from a party through power leveling.

Because the majority of power levels are found in early leveling areas, such attitudes seem reasonable. Yet other players point out the increasing presence of power levels in advanced areas and maintain that the inability to learn how to play a job properly at any level is wrong and something to be avoided. Nevertheless, other than the claim that power levels make some players lazy and the practice devalues the experience of those players who leveled up "the hard way," why might such an activity be labeled cheating?

Part of that lies with an earlier definition of cheating, coming from the purist, who believed that playing a game should be done on one's own as much as possible and without outside help. Although MMOs can be played solo, the experience is generally a social one, and players must rely on others for help. Yet many players maintain that there are correct ways to play the game that involve not taking shortcuts that the designers likely did not intend. So in that way, such MMO players see power leveling as cheating, in that players who do so are cheating themselves out of the experience of the game. And by association those opposed to the practice are frequently implicated, as they often are involved in such parties themselves.

Furthermore, some players argue against power leveling for its de-skilling of players. In addition to an avatar's job level, each job has an accompanying skill set that must be leveled up through active use. So, for example, a White Mage must also cast her "Cure 2" spell numerous times in gameplay in order for her "healing" statistic to rise, which makes her cures most potent (that is, they will restore a greater number of lost hit points). Players who have been power leveled have not usually fully developed their job's skill sets, because they are not using their abilities that frequently or long enough to raise those statistics. Players thus advance, yet are "gimped" in some ways by power levels. Here, the fast-forwarding element again is brought into play, and players maintain that such fast-forwarding actually devalues a character, as they do not gain the requisite skill levels to correspond with their job level.

What all of these assertions suggest, however, is that power leveling is a contested practice. While some players see little wrong with the activity, the fact that it is often practiced in a group setting, where all players may not agree to the practice, makes it an issue for the larger player community to debate.

Botting with the Botters

One of the few ways that *Final Fantasy XI* players use code in order to cheat is through the use of bots. Limited to the PC version of the game, bots have been created to perform repetitive actions continuously, with the user not physically present. Players have deployed bots for fishing, mining, and "provoking," a player action that attempts to claim a particular monster before other players can do so. Square Enix takes a strong stand against bots, and regularly updates the game to eliminate possibilities for bot use. Players have differing opinions, but many do regard it as a form of cheating.

Two of the many ways to make money in the game are fishing and mining. Fishing is a skill that can be improved through repetition, and higher skill allows the player to catch more valuable fish. Mining isn't skill based, but players can improve their chances somewhat by wearing special "mining clothes."

Fishing, as first implemented in the game, was a fairly straightforward—if boring—activity. Players equipped a rod and bait or lure, cast their line into a body of water, and waited for a strike. Depending on skill level and the rod and bait/lure used, the player could land a fish, lose it, break a rod, or catch nothing. Fishing was better at twilight and at night, and fish varied by location.

Many MMOs (and RPGs) have such fishing systems in place. Because of some popular quests and food dishes that require fish as an ingredient, fishing could be a fairly reliable, if unexciting, way to make money. But fishing soon became a magnet for fish botters and later gil sellers.

Botters developed a small program that could let a player's character fish, equip new bait, and continue, unaided by the player. Periodically, the player would then buy more bait and sell the accumulated fish. Players could allegedly start the bot before going to sleep, have it work overnight, and wake up to an inventory waiting to be sold. Other players, upset at the practice, complained loudly to Square Enix.

At first Square Enix deployed its customer support staff (that is, Game Masters) to investigate potential botters—having them question whoever was controlling the avatar to see if there was an actual player present. If none answered, the account holder could be punished (which usually meant a brief suspension at first). Next, botters allegedly developed further programs that could answer simple questions automatically, playing off the perception that botters were all "Chinese gil sellers." Following that, Square Enix went back to the drawing board, and in a major game update, completely changed the fishing system. Now when a fish nibbles a line, the player has to actively engage it (much like engaging a monster in battle), wearing down its strength using various controller movements, before being able to finally reel it in. That system circumvented bot use, putting an end to that form of cheating.

While some players may have the technological expertise to create their own bots, many more players who wish to use them rely on the skills of others, and on luck to find them, as they do not have the programming skills needed. As already discussed in chapter 5, such division creates a hierarchy of sorts, classifying players along a continuum of technical skills, from the basic user to the elite programmer.

Real-Money Trade and Gaming Capital: A Clash of Currencies

Perhaps the most contentious issue in *Final Fantasy XI*, as in many MMOs, is that of gil buying and selling, or real-money trade. There are frequent and never-ending discussions of the practice on game discussion boards, and some linkshells have gone so far as to condemn the practice and promise to boot any linkshell member known to engage in either activity— buying or selling. Although few players publicly admit, either in game or on chat boards, to either practice, the trade continues and flourishes on Web sites like International Game Exchange, Player Auctions, and BuyGameCurrency.com.[20]

Why do players buy or sell gil? And why are so many players vehemently opposed to the practice? Although it is difficult to find players who admit to buying gil, some do reveal themselves in various forums, and other players regularly speculate about why the practice occurs. And while specific reasons may vary, it seems the fundamental reason for real-money trade is similar to the fast-forwarding action discussed in chapter 4.[21] For many players, there isn't enough time in their schedules to play as much as they'd like, or they are in a hurry to acquire items or skill levels as soon as possible—sooner than normal gameplay allows. The player wants to speed through what is seen as less exciting or interesting gameplay, to get to the "better stuff." Just like the player of a single-play game who wants the Corvette right away or that Vulcan Staff as soon as he can equip it, this player operates with an internal clock tied to his own sense of game progression, rather than the designer's or other player's sense of the same. Nick Yee's analysis of MMO players backs that finding as well. In his study of gold buying, he found that 22 percent of players admitted to buying currency at some point in their online gameplay. In the comments section following the report, those who do admit to such practices overwhelmingly agree that time is the chief concern, as they do not have (or wish to invest) the time required to achieve increasingly expensive game items.[22]

Yet while the fast-forward has no repercussions in single-player games, things change with the move to multiplay. Here there exists a game economy, and the actions of one or more gil buyers and sellers impact others, often with troubling results. It might not be that bad if only a few players bought items or currency, particularly if other regular players supplied that need. But with the demand for such things has arisen the dedicated gil seller. Rumors and speculation abound, but on *Final Fantasy XI* chat boards there is regular debate concerning the professional— particularly Chinese—gil sellers who are alleged to inhabit the game world.

The player buying currency likely has no desire to spend weeks mining, crafting, or farming to earn currency for the desired gear in game. Yet to the gil seller, that is gameplay—or rather, finding the most efficient way to make in-game currency. While that includes the activities just mentioned, it also includes "camping" Notorious Monsters that drop rare items, such as Huu Mjuu the Torrent, which drops a staff that sells for about two million gil. Players regularly complain about certain monsters being impossible to claim because of the presence of groups of gil sellers monopolizing the areas and occasionally even harassing other players.

Players likewise assert that the process is circular and damaging—only gil sellers can acquire rare items, which they then can set prices for at in-game Auction Houses. Players desiring those items have no choice other than to pay the asking price, as it is nearly impossible for them to claim the monster that actually drops the item. At least some players can't or won't pay the high prices through their own efforts, so they turn to buying in-game currency, which is what pays the gil sellers, creating more demand for their product, and the cycle continues.

Players have varying responses to this scenario, and many have theorized solutions that Square Enix could attempt. And the developers have made continual efforts to limit the success of gil sellers, such as changing the fishing system (which eliminated the use of fishing bots) and altering the properties of items obtained from many Notorious Monsters to make the items "exclusive" to the recipient, meaning that the item literally cannot be sold or traded to other players.

Just as quickly as developers can alter the game conditions to try to thwart unfair competition, however, players will find new ways to achieve the desired result. For example, soon after Square Enix changed the "Leaping Boots" item that dropped from Leaping Lizzy (a rare lizard) to "Bounding Boots," which are exclusive to the recipient, players on Allakhazam.com noted that they had started to see other players camping Leaping Lizzy and shouting they would sell the "rights" for the Bounding Boots, once they had claimed Lizzy and killed her.[23] That meant the professionals or other enterprising players still intended to camp Leaping Lizzy, even if they didn't want the Bounding Boots for themselves. Instead, they would attempt to charge money from other players who wanted the Boots and weren't quick enough to "claim" Leaping Lizzy themselves.

Why is the gil-buying practice so viscerally despised by some players? One evening in late 2005, while I was taking a break from fighting, I took my avatar to "Lower Jeuno," a central gathering point for players. Standing at the Auction House was Kofgood, who is listed on Allakhazam.com's site as being a gold farmer (along with Kofnice and Kofboss). I was in the zone for a fair amount of time, and witnessed an almost endless stream of "/slap," "/poke," and other, rather more rude, emotes directed at him. Likewise, players were "/shouting" at Kofgood to stop ruining the game, and blaming gil sellers and real-money trade players for wrecking the economy. I did not notice any response from Kofgood, who continued about his business and eventually left the zone. Such outbursts demonstrate the frustration of players (which includes those who likely never post to or read game-related forums) regarding real-money trade and its practitioners.

Apart from concerns about the economy and the poor playing behavior of some alleged gil sellers (such as MPK-ing other players near them to eliminate the competition), many players see gil (or item) buying as cheating, no matter where the goods came from. Indeed, shortly after Sony announced its Game Exchange system, many *Final Fantasy XI* players were worried that a similar program might appear for Vana'diel.

Players who chastise other players for buying gil regularly scold them to "put in the time" or not play the game at all. They see the game as demanding of both time and skill, and have little patience for players short in supply of either commodity. Part of that is tied to gaming capital. *Final Fantasy XI* is similar to many fantasy-themed MMOs—it requires an ongoing commitment of time and energy. To achieve higher levels of success, dedication is demanded. It is a difficult game for "casual" players to enjoy, particularly past the first thirty levels. To do well demands the accumulation of a specific brand of gaming capital—that found in the world of MMOs and Vana'diel in particular.

Those who succeed at the game—and there are many different ways to succeed—are those who have learned how to play a job (or several) very well. They have figured out ways to earn the currency they need for the activities they enjoy—which could be leveling a job to 75, a craft to level 100, or exploring as many places as possible. Yet the game world is so large and intricate, no one player can go it alone. Players rely on other players for guidance, information, and participation in quests and activities to succeed as well as advance. Players begin by learning as much as possible and then, if successful enough, find themselves in a role reversal. The pupil can become the teacher, the receiver the giver, as one advances in skill. So I received help from higher-level characters in my linkshell when I fought a dragon to achieve rank 3. And I in turn assisted other linkshell mates to fight another dragon later on, when they needed the help.

It's all related to gaming capital. But what does that have to do with real-money trade? Economies suffer when two competing forms of currency exist. Which is dominant? How can they convert? What if one is vastly over- or undervalued in relation to the other? Gaming capital is squarely at odds with real-money trade as well as gil buying and selling. When both are at work, players become confused about how to value items or experiences—which is why some players react so strongly to gil buying. If a player has carefully acquired a significant amount of gaming capital, that capital might translate to a well-developed character with excellent armor (bought through the shrewd application of farming knowledge or countless hours spent camping Notorious Monsters), weapons, and abilities. And likewise, that image should "present" to other players just that type and amount of gaming capital.

Yet what if that top-notch character were purchased from PlayerAuctions.com? Or what if the "Sniper Rings +1" and Leaping Boots were bought using gil purchased from the International Gaming Exchange? Here, real-money trade is the currency system at work rather than gaming capital. And there is *no real way* to tell the difference. In the first case players could probably figure it out, if the character buyer has little actual skill for someone supposedly so advanced. Reputation does matter, particularly at high levels. In the second case, though, who's to know, unless the player says something? Unless that happens, other players are left to wonder which form of capital financed the purchase.

Summing Up

For players, practices such as real-money trade, botting, and power leveling likely fall along a spectrum of unfair advantage, according to their own individual feelings and beliefs about gameplay. Many players feel strongly about certain activities, but have little concern for others. Some object to any practice that is not as a game designer originally intended, while others only care about what affects them individually within the game. Yet no matter their personal leanings, many will go to great lengths to convince others of their views, often debating matters endlessly during a game or in forums devoted to the game. Some problems disappear due to designer influence, such as botting, while others live on, such as power leveling.

What matters, I think, is not that players ultimately reach agreement on what is cheating and what is not. Instead, they need space to determine the boundaries of acceptable play and ways to ensure that those stepping outside those bounds are punished. While some of that falls with game representatives, another important component can lie with players themselves, and is, I believe, critical to successful game spaces.

Player Revenge: Punishing the Cheat

Player responses to cheating in *Final Fantasy XI* are diverse and often quite creative. Many of the methods are practiced across online gaming communities, including the creation and publication of blacklists, shunning cheaters, and reporting egregious activities to the game administrators (referred to as Game Masters, as mentioned earlier).

One of the simplest ways that players respond to behavior they perceive as cheating is through telling others of the activities and the creation of blacklists. Such lists can be published on game chat boards found at sites like Killingifrit.com and Allakhazam.com as well as on the private boards for the game's many linkshells. The lists often contain the names of players accused of many activities, some of which may have nothing to do with cheating, and instead are poor behavior such as being consistently rude or abusive toward other players.

The act of naming poor players seems to be punishment enough for many posters. Of course, when players encounter a problem they believe has become widespread—or systematic—they do demand more, usually meaning intervention by the game administrators. But frequently, calling attention to cheaters (among others) stands as a main response to such activities.For instance, a player might post about a new "scammer" who has appeared on a server, describe the behavior, name the offender, and conclude with a line suggesting they desire no more than to have other players be aware in order to avoid the scammer. As an example, the following thread titled "Seanswann the moron" appeared on the Lakshmi server board on Allakhazam's site in 2005: "Tried to MPK my party 8 times. Each time he died and had to homepoint. Level 65 Death with no raise 8 times is like what 16,000 XP loss? Anyway he deleveled. After the second attempt I called a GM who came and watched as he tried over . . . and over. . . . Then suddenly Seanswann wasnt online anymore. priceless."[24] For such players, naming the behavior and associating the offender with the behavior publicly are "just" punishments.

Listings don't always remain uncontested, however, with accused players sometimes trying to either justify their actions or deny the behavior, and instead point the finger at the other poster. Such back-and-forth discourses are especially common when it is antisocial behavior being discussed, as these situations can be borderline cheating and offer the most room for multiple interpretations. For example, in a posting about a player being kicked out of a linkshell devoted to fighting Hyper Notorious Monsters (or high-level monsters that drop extremely rare items and only appear once or twice in a "real-life" twenty-four-hour period), the banished player alleges how the reason he was banished was for information he didn't reveal—concerning the "time of death" for certain monsters. The player goes on to explain how he couldn't have told the information to anyone, and other problems he experienced with the linkshell. In replies, other players, including the head of that linkshell (whose in-game name is Marinedeath), counter with accusations that the first player was actually on probation and there were other reasons the player was kicked out. Other players who know the players involved jump in and the story becomes one of "he said, she said." It does finally end, when the original poster writes:

I've talked with Marinedeath, we've agreed that i was wrongly accused and wrongly kicked, but thats beside the point. We both consider this matter closed and we've both agree that everyone would stop posting in this forum . . . including ds [acronym for the linkshell name] members.

In my defence, i'd like to say i don't know y u'd call me untrustworthy, because there r no grounds for it. Then there was a comment about me being selfish, which is bull. I publicly annouced in ls [linkshell] chat a couple of times that i would help anyone with any Zms [Zilart Missions], except 4&5, i had my fill of those after doing them twice to help a friend; nobody ever asked me to help.

I also tried helping dapunisher and kouryou out with Fenrir, but its fenrir, and we got our butts kicked. So respect marinedeath's order and my wish to close this.[25]

Such accusations and rebuttals can go back and forth until one player admits that the other is correct, or as above, when the disputing parties agree to each take a portion of the blame. Often, though, posters simply tire of discussing the matter and the thread eventually sinks from sight. But many posts alleging cheating behavior (such as gil-selling and MPK) are not contested, frequently because the alleged cheaters do not read the boards and possibly don't even speak English. Such posts can serve to alert other players—either to stay away from certain individuals or to beware of the latest scams circulating through the world.

Such warnings can help a "wronged" player feel she has a voice and she can influence the future fortunes of cheaters. Sometimes simply naming an activity or exposing a questionable character can be enough. Yet usually players demand more of a response, which often involves the player community on a particular server shunning certain individuals. For example, although "he" was never accused of cheating, the character known as "Intyoda" caused a great deal of trouble on the server in summer 2005 that resulted in many angry warnings and denunciations on Allakhazam:

DO NOT party with this person. I did party with him once in qufim and he kept booting people without warning that either 1) got lvl25 or 2) had a opinion. And when i say opinion i mean things like "I think we could try a pugil, we are all lvl24". It stayed like this and i went on with my life, being a whm i could get a party in Kazham at 24.

I had a few run ins with this guy with my new character. At the time he was playing a WHM [White Mage] in valkurm. He decided that turning in a sub job [quest] item was more important then keeping party members alive. He didn't warn us he was leaving, and thus, we died.

So the first time I saw Intyoda in my LS was midday right when we were having an LS eco-warrior [quest] run. I thought wow more people. (our LS has had a spike of new members recently). I couldn't participate in the eco run had to log for work but later that night me and 3 other ls mates including my close friend 'Oddsock went out to Kazham to party together.

I had turned off my LS for a while as our party got settled. Right when I switched it back on I saw this : <<Intyoda> Hey Odd SHUT UP U F'ING NOOB![26]

Although Intyoda tried to defend himself, there were so many independently confirmed stories about him that he was eventually forced to change his behavior. A couple of weeks after the posting started, I witnessed him "/shouting" in one of the main cities about his wish to start over and his request for everyone to give him another chance.

Of course shaming and blacklists don't always work, especially if individuals are making a profit from their activities, are cheating in ways that other players don't find out about, or have their own player community that supports or ignores the activity. Individuals who wish to respond to such cheaters, to punish them in some way, although smaller in number and options, have made various attempts to "get back at" and possibly end some cheating behaviors.

Beyond blacklists and calling Game Masters, some players decide to take matters "into their own hands" when it comes to cheaters. One tool some employ is MPK. As discussed previously in this chapter, normal *Final Fantasy XI* gameplay does not allow for PvP play, leaving players without the ability to fight other players. Players who then wish to attack other players (or see them die and have to leave the area, or be raised but slowed by "raise sickness") resort to attempts to lead aggressive monsters past the offenders, then leave the area in the hopes that the monsters will then attack the other players. The more monsters in a "train" the better, as it keeps the other players busy and could lead to their deaths.[27] Always a contested practice among players, this activity has been squashed by Square Enix, as during a 2006 update the company changed the method by which monsters follow players if those players zone or disappear from a certain region. After the change, when a player zones out of (or leaves) a region, any monsters following will automatically disappear and shortly after respawn at their original location, with their "aggro" reset to normal levels, meaning they won't automatically attack any nearby player.

Yet no matter the term, some players feel they are justified in attempting to kill other players. For them, cheating behavior can be met with responding cheatlike behavior. And they do not expect to be labeled as

cheaters for the retaliation. Instead, they often conceptualize it as necessary to curb the encroachment of those who don't respect the rules of the
game as they do, at least until they need to punish someone.

Conclusions

One way to think about the larger implications of cheating in virtual
worlds is to view it as a form of lying or deception. If practices are about
gaining unfair advantage, they often involve some level of deception—
either the claim is made to an accomplishment one did not earn, or one
hides how a particular item or goal was achieved. After all, if practices such
as botting or real-money trade were fully accepted and not thought of as
cheating, players would not need to hide such practices from either other
players or Square Enix—yet they do. The philosopher Sissela Bok writes
about lying in communities, and how societies will break down when deception becomes either a common or commonly perceived practice. She
explains that

all our choices depend on our estimates of what is the case; these estimates
must in turn rely on information from others. Lies distort this information and
therefore our situation as we perceive it, as well as our choices. . . . To the
extent that knowledge gives power, to that extent do lies affect the distribution
of power; they add to that of the liar, and diminish that of the deceived,
altering his choices at different levels.[28]

Likewise, psychologists have found that in game situations where
cheating is possible, if participants are not given the opportunity to punish
players they suspect of cheating, trust decreases and gameplay suffers.[29]
Clearly, deception and cheating have the potential to disrupt, if not ruin,
virtual worlds. Past practices have borne this out, with *Diablo* being one
example. Most commonly, developers have attempted to limit the actions
of cheaters, or what is considered cheating, through code and EULAs. Law
and architecture, to draw from Lawrence Lessig, are thus the principal bar-
ricades erected to stand against the accumulation of unfair advantage.[30]

Yet the work of psychologists as well as life scientists suggests another
viable option, one in line with notions of active players and cohesive, functional communities. The establishment of player-regulated social norms

may never curb some offenses and will always remain a dynamic system due to the evolving nature of online games. But by also giving players certain tools to combat cheating in active ways, we may develop virtual worlds and MMOs that hold individuals more accountable than was thought possible. So, for instance, if Square Enix, like the developers of *Habbo Hotel*, gave certain trusted players the ability to punish others found cheating, interesting things might happen.

First, given the power to actually impact others, players might develop a sense of ownership over the game space, rather than feel like residents of a company town owned and controlled entirely by Square Enix. If some players were deputized, they could confront abusive players or those who are acting in suspicious ways, such as moving too fast for a normal avatar or claiming mobs the split second that they spawn. Further, they could punish such players by reporting them, putting them in jail, or recommending that their accounts be suspended for a certain period of time. These are all activities currently entrusted to Game Masters, but by handing over or sharing such responsibilities with players, game developers like Square Enix could start to build trust and accountability into the system as well as the expectations for gameplay, rather than position law enforcement as a top-down, strictly hierarchical affair.

Such actions will of course pose challenges for developers, especially those who are more commercially oriented or have an international, multilingual player base. Yet we can pose these questions and potential solutions as ways to address the challenges of cheating, which are a perpetual moving target.

This chapter has examined the game design and play activity found in Vana'diel, at least on one server. Nevertheless, given the extensive cross-server posting on most game boards, my own conversations with players across servers, and the undifferentiated style of play offered on all *Final Fantasy XI* servers (all PvE and multilingual), I believe the experience I have described is a common one across the game world at large, at least for English-speaking players. That is an important caveat, as my Japanese is quite limited, and even though I have played with Japanese players and talked with some of them, it is impossible for me (at least) to answer the question of how Japanese players respond to such issues as power leveling, real-money trade, and bot use. Given that Square Enix is a Japanese company and is actively combating at least two of those activities, though, it may be safe to say that across all countries, there are many players who are unhappy with such practices.

More centrally, I believe that this study of an MMO demonstrates how ideas about cheating spring from the same concerns that players bring to single-player games. Players don't have an infinite amount of time or patience to play games. They also often, if not usually, play them for some sense of accomplishment, enjoyment, or fun, however we can define their goals. Just as when playing a single-player game, individuals get stuck, get tired, and lose interest. Cheating can be a way to get around a problem, however it is defined. That might be by rapidly leveling a character's tenth job through the "lowbie" areas to avoid that grind, or by paying twenty dollars for the gil to acquire a "Penitent's Rope" at level 60 (currently selling for two million gil) rather than spend days, if not weeks, trying to earn the gil in game through farming, crafting, or other means. To some this is cheating, and to others it is time and money wisely spent. What remains is a larger question: how significant is such quantitative invest- ment in the gameplay experience? Can there be ways for the grind-weary and the grind-accepting player to coexist on the same server? I'll examine such broader questions in the final chapter, which points to further ways to think about gameplay, cheating, and player activity.

Part III

Capital and Game Ethics

CAPITALIZING ON PARATEXTS: GAMEPLAY, ETHICS, AND EVERYDAY LIFE

On May 3, 2006, the founder of the popular MMO-themed Web site Allakhazam.com posted an announcement to let readers know that "we have added several new sites to our network and have joined them together to form the Zam.com Network which is now instantly the leading content destination for all MMO gamers. . . . Any changes we make will only be positive and will be ones that we think will make your site better."[1] The announcement went on to discuss how the Allakhazam site could now take advantage of greater resources, including faster servers, newly hired staff, and additional content.

What the initial post did not mention was the other parties involved in the business transaction. What site readers revealed in the discussion below the post, however, quickly turned the thread into a collective flash point for debate and anger, which then raged for days across the entire site and elsewhere on the Internet.[2] Allakhazam.com, long a proponent of fair gameplay and an opponent of real-money trade along with other forms of account buying and selling, had been bought out by a holding company that also owned the International Game Exchange, the largest real-money trade company in North America.[3] Many loyal readers were not pleased, to put it lightly.

While some readers professed not to care about the purchase, or adopted a wait-and-see attitude to determine whether the buyout would affect site content, many other readers were scathing in their response. One person's post spoke for many: "I hope you got a good contract from them [RPG Holdings], because it looks like it cost you your soul, even if you're too blind to see that. Two weeks left on premium then goodbye avatar, thanks for the ride."[4] The main thread dedicated to discussing the change (there were countless others) stretched over a period of weeks, with over a thousand posts made on the topic—suggesting no shortage of player feelings about this change in ownership.

It's too early to tell whether the readers' dissatisfaction will have any long-term effects on the Allakhazam site, yet a cursory glance at the Black Mages job forum page for *Final Fantasy XI* indicates that most of the original guides for obtaining gear and finishing difficult quests have not been deleted by upset writers, and the number of postings per day does not appear to have dropped off in any significant number. What's most interesting, though, is the sense of outrage that the announcement generated, and what it suggests about player communities, digital gameplay, cheating, and the future of paratextual industries.

As I argued in previous chapters, gameplay doesn't exist in a vacuum, nor do game developers or publishers exert the only forms of control over how to play, understand, or enjoy a game. Of course, players aren't free to play entirely as they wish, with no boundaries or limitations on their actions. Before they even pick up a controller, their expectations are shaped to some degree about what to expect and what it means to play a game. Players and game developers exist in a push-pull of interdependence, constantly exerting pressure on one another to gain control of the experience of gameplay as well as how to define that experience. Certainly, neither could exist without the other, and the perspectives of each inform the other. Added to that mix, and helping to define and extend that relationship, are the paratextual industries I've discussed here.

From *Nintendo Power* to the International Game Exchange, some companies that neither make nor sell games have worked diligently to shape how we think of games as well as how we should and shouldn't play them. In this book, I've concentrated on the commercial elements involved in this practice, thereby omitting a large piece of the puzzle. Player-created content—in the form of free walkthroughs, online guides, postings and discussions on game boards, and free or shareware programs to help players in their games to varying degrees—all are important influences on how we understand digital games. I'd like to spend some time exploring a few of those elements here, but even as they offer independent ways of understanding paratexts, many of the larger arguments I've made concerning their for-profit relatives offer similar experiences.

What's most critical now about such forms, I believe, is that many of the more successful indie paratextual efforts are now being incorporated into the profit-making enterprises. For example, will Allakhazam.com change because of its new owners? What sorts of changes might that mean? Did GameFAQs.com alter its approach after being purchased by CNET?

These questions not only explore the growing corporatization of the paratextual industries but also the concepts of gaming capital and what cheating means for gameplay as well as digital life. In particular, issues like cheating raise key ethical questions about the proper and improper, correct and incorrect ways to do things. From the beginning, I've taken the position that there is no clear-cut path and no objectively correct answer to what constitutes cheating in digital games. I've tried instead to describe cheating as a dynamic practice that players, game developers, and others have worked to define and shape, in games, over time, and across many different situations.

Cheating is fascinating because it shows us where we disagree about the limits of acceptable gameplay. If we all agreed on those limits, this would have been a short book. But we don't, and that's a valuable thing. As I conclude this book, I want to look at what sorts of ethical questions cheating and digital games demand we investigate. Because it's about more than finding a simple answer or concluding that to cheat in a game is of no real consequence—as John Pauly contends, let's take "popular culture seriously as a mode of moral imagination."[5]

Internet Gold: The Free Walkthrough

Before MMOs took hold of most of my free time, I was a dedicated single-player gamer, spending most of my time immersed in RPGs and a few action/adventure titles for good measure. And like many of my informants, the Internet was a gold mine for me in terms of finding places for reading about the latest games, previews of forthcoming games, and maybe most significantly, help to get through the game I was currently playing. While there are many individual and commercial sites dedicated to giving players more information about particular titles, one name kept getting recommended as the place to go to for the best in terms of walkthroughs and game help: GameFAQs.com.

GameFAQs.com is an aggregator of "gameFAQs," which literally stands for "game frequently asked questions," but is shorthand for walkthroughs, the detailed guides that can tell you the correct direction to go in when you enter the "Zanarkand Ruins" in *Final Fantasy X* as well as the right series of moves to make when battling the final boss in the first *Buffy the Vampire Slayer* videogame. Started by one person in 1995 and acquired by CNET Networks in 2003, not only is the GameFAQs site comprehensive, well-written, and player created, it has that one thing that the majority of game players demand most from their gameplay help: free access.

While GameFAQs.com has many elements including discussion boards, game reviews, and cheat codes, the heart of the site remains its walkthroughs. It contains more than 35,000 FAQs and guides, and "more than 600,000 unique gamers visit GameFAQs each day."[6] Visitors encountering the site will find a list of the "top ten" FAQ pages as well as the top ten "most wanted" FAQs. Writers are encouraged to be the first to provide an FAQ for new games, for which they'll receive gift certificates. Most games don't have that problem, instead listing multiple guides as well as reviews, cheat codes, and discussion boards.

Moving to the pages for individual games, readers can find a detailed list of guides, depending on the popularity of the game or the particular genre (RPGs tend to have more guides than other types of games, it seems). For example, the page for the game *Pikmin* lists ten general FAQs as well as four "in-depth" FAQs, two entries for "maps and charts," and five "foreign language FAQs" in Swedish, Dutch, Spanish, and Italian. In contrast, the page for the first *Kingdom Hearts* game lists fifteen general FAQs, thirty-three "in-depth" FAQs, four foreign language FAQs (in Norwegian, Portuguese, Spanish, and Dutch), and one "secrets" FAQ.[7] While the general FAQs are comprehensive guides to the entire game, in-depth FAQs will generally specialize in one area, such as a minigame, a particular level, one boss fight, or how to obtain a rare item or set of items. The general FAQs are the only ones rated by readers, allowing readers to see which FAQs are deemed more reliable or better presented than other guides.

As one reads through a general FAQ, it becomes obvious how much time and attention the creators have put into those documents. FAQs will list a revision number at the top, and for each revision, an explanation of what was updated in the text. FAQs also are divided into sections, usually corresponding with the progression of the game, and include lists of terms, items, weapons, and other things that players would find helpful. Most general FAQs are quite long, and when printed can run from dozens to hundreds of pages of text. Writers are spending countless hours producing such documents, all for no pay. What they do obtain, if the guide is good enough, is gaming capital and recognition.

What is remarkable about the diversity of guides that can be found on GameFAQs.com is, in one sense, their uniformity. Part of that is structural; in order to be accepted for listing on the site, FAQ creators must use particular conventions, such as sticking with plain text, not using special formatting commands, and listing the author name, version number, and date of the last update at the beginning of the document. Yet in addition to certain formatting requirements, many guide writers stick to particular ways of presenting information in guides, often drawn from commercial guides and walkthroughs.

For example, most FAQs will let readers know if they contain spoilers, and most will also claim to not include "too much" spoiler information—only the pieces necessary to get the player through the game. Guides to characters, specific bosses, and logical ways to progress through the game—all are generally included in both the free and commercial guides. What that suggests is that even as some individuals are creating guides for free, there are certain norms that game players have accepted for what constitutes a successful walkthrough or FAQ. "Free" guide writers know those conventions and learn to emulate them, usually even more success-fully than commercial publishers do.

A site such as GameFAQs.com serves as an aggregator not just for game help or player community formation but also for the creation and circulation of gaming capital. Successful FAQ writers gain a certain status, much like well-respected players in MMO games. And the site has capital-ized on that capital, especially with its 2003 acquisition by CNET. While FAQ writers retain the copyright to their work, the site itself has become part of a larger brand that seeks to organize, classify, and commodify various types of game information and gaming capital. When readers now read an FAQ for *Kingdom Hearts II*, say, they can also check prices around the Web for the game, go to the GameSpot Web site for further reviews, news stories, and screen shots, and even download a ringtone based on the game's theme music. Playing the game is almost superfluous.

Player-Created Content: But Is It Players Who Own It Anymore?

Just as GameFAQs.com is one site where the users provide a majority of the helpful content, other places exist around the Internet that do the same thing for other types of games. As I discussed at the beginning of this chapter, Allakhazam.com is another such site that relies heavily on input from individual readers. Allakhazam.com currently has game boards for *Final Fantasy XI, World of Warcraft, EverQuest, EverQuest 2, Dark Age of Camelot, Lineage 2, Star Wars: Galaxies*, and *EverQuest Online Adventures*. On the pages for *Final Fantasy XI*, which are some of the most extensive of those in the network, players contribute the majority of information, which ranges from general discussions of updates and periodic inflation, to intricate walkthroughs and strategies for almost every situation imaginable in the game.

For instance, when players in *Final Fantasy XI* decide they need to advance in rank for their home nation, there are a series of missions they must undertake. Each successive mission is increasingly difficult, of course, and usually also requires more help from other players. Players have posted extensive walkthroughs for all of the missions in each of the home nations, and below each walkthrough is usually an extended discussion of whether the information is correct, where the walkthrough needs more information, how things might have changed since an update, or alternate strategies to try. Thus, the knowledge found on Allakhazam.com is dynamic in a way that no printed guide or magazine could ever be—it adapts to changing conditions and player needs, and often provides multiple forms of advice and help. If a player has therefore recruited high-level player help (such as a level 75 Paladin and a level 74 Monk), one strategy might be tried, but if there are only a few lower-level characters of a particular job class attempting the mission, certain other ways of succeeding are offered.

Such detailed, useful information is again offered free of charge from a range of players, and the site welcomes contributions from anyone. Certain forms of information are "stickied" so they always remain as the top postings on the discussion boards—those are usually deemed the most valuable and timeless guides, which many players have rated (through the board's karma system) as the most useful overall. Posters' whose writing receives positive feedback can be identified in their posts as "sages," "scholars," and "gurus" by the board's rating system to indicate their helpfulness or value for other players. Such forms of gaming capital thus aid newer readers in identifying the most helpful information or people, in whatever forum they are looking in.

Such systems depend on individual player goodwill to succeed and prosper. The Allakhazam.com site is only as good as the information that its reader base has provided to it; there is no way the small staff of the site could supply that knowledge on its own. And it's that content that makes the site so valuable—a site by players, for players. Yet the site was sold in 2005 to a company that also owns the International Game Exchange. The question to ask is, will the site's readers continue to give away their content, particularly if they do not agree with the larger policies of the parent company or the International Game Exchange?

Founder Jeffrey Moyer had originally started the Allakhazam site as a one-page guide for *EverQuest* in 1999, and the site has grown to more than five million page views per day and more than half a million registered users.[8] Allakhazam.com offers free content provided mainly by its dedicated player communities, but if readers wish they can purchase a "premium" account each year for $29.99, thereby eliminating the banner ads from the site and offering access to extra features. So for *Final Fantasy XI*, readers can search all forums along with item and quest postings, which extend back to the beginning of the site. Given the limited way that most readers contribute financially to the site, the main way to respond to Allakhazam's announced buyout was to either declare that a person would stop visiting the site, cancel a premium membership once it expired, or possibly go through and edit prior postings to remove content. Time will tell what the response will be.

Places such as GameFAQs.com and Allakhazam.com point to the success of player-created content related to videogames found online. Such sites aggregate a large amount of information as well as individuals, making it easy for individual players to come together and create shared knowledge, if not community. The catch is that just as players can benefit from such accumulations of gaming capital, so too can larger corporations. Large media companies can acquire smaller start-up operations, offering them the scant resources they need to keep their sites flourishing. In return, corporations receive a vast amount of information and a (perhaps somewhat miffed) player base gathered in one area. Provided the majority of readers get past any initial discomfort with buyouts, business will return to normal soon enough, with the profits and control being centralized.

So here's another instance of a paratextual industry forming—one that some players may not wish to see come together. Others, of course, likely do not care as long as their central sources of information don't disappear, or place too many restrictions on their access or use. But this paratext is forming, and it is exerting a fair amount of influence on the rest of the game industry. The International Game Exchange states that the "2005 marketplace for virtual assets in MMOGs is approaching $900 million," and further, "some experts believe that the market for virtual assets will overcome the primary market—projected to reach $7 billion by 2009— within the next few years."[9]

If such predictions are even close to correct, the paratext is gaining ground on the primary text of the game industry, and is moving in particular ways to shape its future directions. Seen in that light, the paratext becomes critical to consider as a way to understand gameplay as well as the business of digital games.

Paratexts and the Game Industry

Paratexts surround, shape, support, and provide context for texts. They may alter the meanings of texts, further enhance meanings, or provide challenges to sedimented meanings. Paratexts are also anything but peripheral, and they grow more integral to the digital game industry and player community with every year. Game magazines taught players about the many ways to play a game and the components of a game to consider as important when trying to figure out what game to buy next. They also offered cheat codes to players, so they could have more fun with games that they might have put down already. Strategy guides let players pick those games back up and maybe actually finish them, having gotten stuck along the way before. And GameSharks let players unlock hidden areas and start the game later in the narrative than they had progressed to themselves.

Likewise, mod chips have let North American and European players enjoy Japanese games before they are released in their home countries (if they ever are), and they make players question the need for region lockout codes at all. Companies like IT GlobalSecure try to keep game code encrypted and thus multiplayer games fair, and Even Balance will label players as punks if they are found using certain hacks on its dedicated servers and then ban players from them. The International Game Exchange will sell in-game gold to players at a bargain price, while at the same time players on Allakhazam.com's boards will attempt to expose other players for that very purchase.

Those are only a few of the practices that the paratextual industries have supported or enacted as they've come into being. Their economic impact is growing, yet more important, as noted earlier, is the way that they shape players' expectations of what it means to play a game properly or improperly. Paratextual industries can support developer-imposed gameplay limitations or they may defy them. Mod chips, for example, challenge the practice of regional encoding, daring players to ask who should control what legitimately purchased games they can play on their own videogame console. Similarly, player communities such as those found on Allakhazam.com's site question the growing acceptance of real-money trade and wonder if they care to be affiliated with a site that is now partnered with a corporation they feel is ruining their gameplay experience.

Yet even as paratextual industries can challenge some practices, they also help to establish and firm up others. Game walkthroughs, whether free or for sale, now follow established conventions wherever they are found. Game players know what to expect from an FAQ, and how to go about finding one. Certain kinds of gameplay help are expected and demanded by players, usually instantaneously with a game's release. And that help can be found, for free or a price, with only a few clicks of a computer mouse.

To be successful the paratextual industries have had to be flexible, but I'm not suggesting there is an overarching centrality to their practices or organized activities. I've created somewhat of an illusion of coherence in order to demonstrate how different businesses and player activities have worked to shape, support, and challenge the business of the game industry. Increasingly, however, those businesses are coming together. Smaller deals like BradyGames working with Mad Katz to produce books of cheat codes are one thing; yet another is the purchasing of player Web sites and real-money trade businesses, and bundling them together.

Moreover, the integration of security software into games and players' computers raises important questions about the bounds of acceptable intervention, privacy, and control in games. So far, there aren't many people asking questions about those practices. But we need to know more, if we are going to let such activities continue.

Gaming Capital: Capitalizing on Knowledge

Tightly linked to the concept of the paratext is gaming capital. As a form of currency gaming capital is highly flexible, able to adapt to different types of gameplay, various games, and changing notions of what's important to know about games. Players can accumulate various forms of gaming capital not only from playing games but also from the paratextual industries that support them. And depending on a player's social circle, that capital can be quite valuable in building a reputation.

There's also a struggle here, as players, developers, and interested third parties try to define what gaming capital should be, and how players should best acquire it. Clearly, commercial entities have vested interests in commodifying as many elements of gaming culture as possible, to then sell those bits back to players as the most desirable forms of capital. In the beginning, much of that information came directly from game developers, and could be carefully controlled and dispensed to interested players. Yet with the development of the Internet, players began to individually create their own sites and spaces for circulating knowledge as well as creating their own forms of gaming capital.

Not to be deterred, though, the corporations are encroaching on those spaces, packaging and selling back to players their own hard work and effort. A player visiting GameFAQs.com is now not only looking for answers to complete *Dreamfall: The Longest Journey* but has also become a target demographic possessed of the correct amounts of gaming capital to take advantage of the many purchasing opportunities now appearing on the site.

Yet even as corporations work to commodify gaming capital, players resist at the same time. Players are the ones who ultimately judge what counts or not as such capital—so for many players, using an Action Replay is not a practice that will confer gaming capital, and neither is purchasing gold from the International Game Exchange. That might change over time or if game companies work out systems that make real-money trade legal within MMO games. But corporations and even small businesses can't individually dictate how players will judge what counts as gaming capital or not, what types are useful in their own situation, and how those forms change over time. It will always be a dynamic and contextual process that involves sedimentation, fluctuation, contradiction, and individual negotiation.

The Players

A large part of this study has focused on how individual players have defined and negotiated various activities that they may or may not view as cheating in their regular gameplay. As I have learned, many players define cheating in a fairly restrictive way and then proceed to break the rules with abandon. In a different context (like writing a paper for a school assignment), such rule breaking might be troublesome, but here something different is at play. While some players do certainly keep connections between the rules of their nongaming and gaming lives, others draw distinctions between them. For at least some players, the game world is a space apart where normal rules don't apply.

Such behaviors raise interesting questions about the role of games in our lives. For many players, playing games is, in some measure, a playing with rules and their boundaries. Games offer a bounded space (although some games are more bounded than others, depending on how many people are playing) for the exploration of actions and consequences as well as the ludic expression of activities deemed inappropriate (if not illegal) in regular life.

Many players cheat in (single-player and multiplayer) games to "play God" or have fun, without necessarily wanting to get ahead or defeat another human player. Such individuals have made a decision that while their activity may or may not be self-defined as cheating, such shortcuts or code alterations are acceptable in the space of the game. Johan Huizinga suggests that games are a "stepping out" of real life into a space apart.[10] Although more games are now following us into real life (Instant Messages from guildmates, phone calls from games themselves, or real-money trade that alters game economies), the space of the game itself instantiates particular rules that players must negotiate. And apart from breaking the terms of a EULA, there are few "real" consequences for breaking the rules of a game.

Similarly, many players cheat in games when they get stuck. Having reached a point where they cannot progress further without help, they turn to guides, codes, or friends to help them get past the difficulty. This is the most common and accepted form of cheating (some players don't see it as cheating at all), suggesting that the reaching of an impasse and the resulting request for help is not divorced from regular life.

Players also cheat in order to fast-forward through unpleasant or boring parts of a game, so as to reach its end point. That practice, found in single-player and multiplayer games (using cheat codes to skip levels or a power leveler in an MMO), is usually instrumental in nature, recognizing that a player wishes to complete a game yet not fully engage all aspects of it. Most of the time we can't fast-forward through our lives, and even if we could, we actively choose not to. Most students research and write papers rather than finding one on the Internet to download, and most drivers stop at deserted intersections, even if no police are in sight. Yet games offer us a space where we can experience that freedom, without significant consequences.

What is unfortunate is that popular discourse tends to judge in-game behaviors by the rules that operate in daily nongame life. I can see this in the way that many players have defended their actions, trying to reassure me that a particular code use was necessary to continued progress in a game. Players also state that "it's just a game" as a way to deflect criticism in advance of their actions. But why must players hold their actions in games to what is really a separate standard? Why don't players allow for more play and variation in games, permitting themselves to experiment with actions, identities, and practices that in real life are forbidden?

Individuals might find in games a space to explore the consequences of various actions, and challenge or reify their own beliefs about what are appropriate or inappropriate actions to take in specific circumstances. They can also play at taking what are normally the wrong actions for them in daily life, gaining perspective on other choices made. We expect children to play, but adults are considered juvenile when engaging in "childish" actions. Games are and can become even better at becoming spaces for exploration of not only fantastic worlds and rhetorics of power but also playing with rules and their boundaries.

A Future for Ethics and Gameplay

For the past six years, I've been asking game players how they define cheating in games, and how they negotiate and enact cheating practices. Some react as if I'm asking them to reveal their utter lack of ethics and values, and they then respond with clear denunciations that cheating is wrong and they would "never do anything like that." When asked "Like what?" the answers begin to fragment and lose moral certainty. Clearly, we need a better understanding of how ethics might be expressed in gameplay situations, and how we can study the ethical frameworks that games offer to players. Research in this area is getting started, but many interesting questions remain to be asked.[11]

As John Pauly argues, we need to "ground our ethical discourse in the understandings of our ordinary, everyday activity."[12] Digital games have become one of those activity spaces, a common part of contemporary culture. With millions of players engaging with virtual worlds alone as well as with others, we must see such spaces as important areas for learning about how we play, how we make decisions, and how we think about what is right and wrong for us, in different contexts and different situations. Examining cheating is only one possible way into studying those practices, and we need to continue that investigation in as many directions as possible.

We can look at players, games, and their intersection to ask many things: Do games pose interesting ethical questions for players to take up? What layers or levels are involved? For example, many games offer the player the opportunity to revert to a previously saved version of the game. So if I feel guilty about leaving my Sim zombie fenced up outside to die (which I did), I can revert back to a stage of the game where my zombie's still alive (which I didn't). How do players think about and engage with such choices? Are players seeing such opportunities in games to experiment with ethical decision making? Is Sim "murder" a common activity? What reasons do players construct for such actions? Furthermore, how has our larger culture(s) portrayed games, and what implications does that picture have for how we all approach (and judge) games?

So what is game ethics or what would it look like? To begin with, there are at least several layers that we can consider as a basis for asking questions. The actions and choices made as well as offered by game developers, game publishers, marketers, and game players, and the choices coded into the game itself, can all be analyzed. Here are just a few examples of where such questioning can lead.

In the game industry, for instance, we can look at the decisions made by a company such as Rockstar Games, the developer of a string of controversial titles such as the *Grand Theft Auto* series and *Manhunt*. What did the company's management consider when deciding to create such games? Was the potential for controversy and divisiveness considered? Was it considered a positive or negative component of each game's release? Does the company have any wider responsibility to the game development community? Do their games set precedents for legislation? Should the actions of one game company speak for all game companies?

Moving down a level, we can ask what game developers consider as they build games. How much violence and of what type is considered acceptable? Does that change with different player demographics? Do game developers even see their software coding in ethical ways? What about the design of individual characters—both central and peripheral avatars?

Finally, we can examine the individual player. How do players make choices about what they will or won't do in games? Do they follow rules in all circumstances or bend rules to achieve a greater good? Would a player shoot a dog in a game if that was the only way to win? How does a player justify murder in a game? Do players position the experience as "just a game" or a cathartic release from everyday pressures?

Such questions only scratch the surface of what we can investigate in relation to games and ethics. Yet they point to central issues and areas of interest. We need to move beyond the simplistic ideas of good and bad, legal and illegal, to the more interesting and relevant factors related to the process of making moral choices. How do developers, publishers, and players decide what is right and wrong? What do they conclude is right and wrong for them? And how does that play into or break through a magic circle into the everyday? We're only starting to ask such questions; the answers should prove fascinating.

Magic Circles and Play Boundaries

A final area to consider is the role of games and play in our lives, and how the spaces of games intersect with those of daily life. Huizinga felt that play and games were central experiences of human beings, and went so far as to assert that play constituted culture.[13] While games have always existed, they defy easy categorization—as games can be for fun or in deadly earnest (as in war games), with no stakes or high stakes involved. Games can involve escape, but not always. Huizinga, as mentioned earlier, believed that games were protected by a magic circle or bounded space set apart from the everyday (much like the difference between the sacred and the profane), with rules as a boundary system for maintaining them.

Yet is this indeed true, or is it a useful way to think of games? Is there some boundary that delimits the playing field, separating the game from other, nongame space? If we take this idea to be valid, what happens to our conceptions about games? In that scenario, games are walled off as a space apart—a space in which to create different rules, rewards, and punishments for the activities that take place within. Killing can be rewarded, or civilizations might best be taken over by "culture flipping" them to join your side. Players can experiment (to greater and lesser degrees) with potential actions, including exploring, socializing, empathizing, killing, being selfish, being silly, being inconsistent, or being all-powerful. The results of those actions will vary based on the game being played and its own particular rule set. Attempts to "game the game" can also provide players with elaborate, rich opportunities for exploration, experimentation, and greater knowledge.

If we acknowledge that games can provide such opportunities in "walled off" spaces, is it appropriate to judge games or game player actions by an external set of rules—rules that originate outside the magic circle? Games may reward players for specific actions—actions that would definitely not be rewarded in daily life. But should our standards for appropriate actions in daily life carry over to our game life? *The Sims* encourages players to create happy, successful families, but it also allows players to kill their Sims through neglect as well as indirect actions. Yet the player may be rewarded by the game for such violent actions (getting that family wrecker out of the home, for example). We should not be so quick to question such actions, if we do believe games really are a space apart, governed by a different set of rules.

What results when such judgments are applied is an infantilization of the game space. It suggests players cannot understand a separate set of rules and rewards, or that we can have no spaces where such alternate systems might function. A one-to-one mapping of values robs games of their unique character and rule set, creating a space derivative of real-life standards of behavior. When that happens, choices that might be interesting or significant within a game are diminished, and choices are robbed of their playful, experimental quality. And the game space becomes impoverished, leaving game players with two sets of rules to negotiate: the in-game rules for rewards, and the daily life rules that impose larger judgments on to their actions.

And what if we don't believe that games are a walled off space? As I've argued, games increasingly follow us around, as we surf the Web, talk with friends and family, and flip through magazines. Friends send me instant messages to ask me to log on to *Final Fantasy XI* to help with quests, and once in the game, I receive other instant messages from family, asking about my day at work. There's no easy boundary to let me know when I'm inside or outside that magic circle. Other game theorists have also convincingly maintained that we shouldn't make simplistic judgments such as that games are magic circles set apart from everyday life.[14] Yet if games aren't that space apart, does that negate the arguments I've just made?

I believe that while games are experiences we integrate into our daily activities, and there is no game space that's easily walled off, there are rules and rewards that apply to games, and these do form a boundary of some sort. While I may move fluidly between writing an academic paper and playing *Kitty Spangles Solitaire*, I also recognize that the rules for engaging each activity are different. I won't cheat while writing the paper but I might try to cheat in *Solitaire*. And just as I might (if I ever figure out how to) cheat in *Solitaire*, I've already decided that I'd never buy gold to advance my avatar in *Final Fantasy XI*. I've constructed boundaries around each activity, and for now, have negotiated what rules apply for each, and what sorts of gameplay I find acceptable, enjoyable, and right for me.

Where does such theorizing of play and games leave us in relation to ethics? Obviously, play and games are central parts of the human experience, and ethics are likewise centrally placed in our lives. How do the two come together? To suggest that games are a space apart from daily life and our normal rules for living is just as much of an ethical choice as making them part of our daily practices, which conform to and integrate with our daily codes of conduct. We cannot say that there are no ethics in games or that players bring no ethical frameworks to their gameplay; we simply leave the question unexamined, which is itself a choice. What we need to do instead is actively involve ourselves with the questions, seeking to determine how ethics fit, how we see them informing games and gameplay, and how we choose to integrate games into our lives.

Notes

Introduction: To Cheat or Not to Cheat

1. Gérard Genette, *Paratexts: Thresholds of Interpretation* (London: Cambridge University Press, 1997).
2. Dick Hebdige, *Subculture: The Meaning of Style* (London: Methuen, 1979).
3. Pierre Bourdieu, *Distinction: A Social Critique of the Judgment of Taste* (Cambridge, MA: Harvard University Press, 1984).
4. David Callahan, *The Cheating Culture: Why More Americans Are Doing Wrong to Get Ahead* (Orlando, FL: Harcourt, 2004).
5. J. Barton Bowyer, *Cheating: Deception in War & Magic, Games & Sports, Sex & Religion, Business & Con Games, Politics & Espionage, Art & Science* (New York: St. Martin's Press, 1982), 47.
6. Ibid., 3.
7. Sissela Bok, *Lying: Moral Choice in Public and Private Life* (New York: Vintage Books, 1978), 13.
8. Ibid., 19.
9. Ibid., 21.
10. Johan Huizinga, *Homo Ludens: A Study of the Play Element in Culture* (Boston: Beacon Press, 1950), 11.
11. Ibid., 11.
12. Bowyer, *Cheating*, 300.
13. Ibid., 428.
14. Ibid., 300–301.
15. Genette, *Paratexts*.
16. Peter Lunenfeld, ed., *The Digital Dialectic: New Essays on New Media* (Cambridge, MA: MIT Press, 1999).

Chapter 1: Creating the Market

1. Steven Kent, *The Ultimate History of Videogames* (Roseville, CA: Prima Publishing, 2001), 188.

2. Warren Robinett, foreword to *The Video Game Theory Reader*, ed. Mark J. P. Wolf and Bernard Perron (New York: Routledge, 2003), xvii.

3. Gérard Genette, *Paratexts: Thresholds of Interpretation* (London: Cambridge University Press, 1997); Martin Lister, *New Media: A Critical Introduction* (London: Routledge, 2003).

4. Pierre Bourdieu, *Distinction: A Social Critique of the Judgment of Taste* (Cambridge, MA: Harvard University Press, 1984), 6.

5. Karen Riggs, *Mature Audiences: Television in the Lives of Elders* (New Brunswick, NJ: Rutgers University Press, 1998).

6. I'd like to again thank Erica Butcher for suggesting the term gaming capital to capture this experience. It is better than terms such as games subculture or gaming culture at explaining the universe of games, game players, and the knowledge that circulates between the industry and gamers. It is also provocative that Bourdieu himself referred to culture as a game to be played. Bourdieu writes that "there is no way out of the game of culture," and "the games of culture are protected against objectification by all the partial objectifications which the actors involved in the game perform on each other" (*Distinction*, 6).

7. Public Broadcasting System, "Inside the Games: Classic Game Cheats," *The Video Game Revolution*, <http://www.pbs.org/kcts/videogame revolution/inside/cheats.html> (accessed September 7, 2004).

8. Ibid.

9. Elizabeth Weise, "Gay Programmer Fired for Adding Studly Guys to Computer Game," December 1996, <http://www.langston.com/Fun _People/1996/1996CFM.html> (accessed March 1, 2005).

10. Tom Odell, personal conversation, March 26, 2002.

11. Dmitri Williams, "A Brief Social History of Video Games," in *Playing Computer Games: Motives, Responses, and Consequences*, ed. Peter Vorderer and Jennings Bryant (Mahwah, NJ: Lawrence Erlbaum, 2005).

12. John Fiske, *Television Culture* (New York: Routledge, 1987).

13. Genette, *Paratexts*, 408.

14. Peter Lunenfeld, ed., *The Digital Dialectic: Essays on New Media* (Cambridge, MA: MIT Press, 1999), 19.

15. Angela McRobbie, *Jackie: An Ideology of Adolescent Femininity* (Birmingham, UK: Centre for Contemporary Cultural Studies, University of Birmingham, 1978); Myra McDonald, *Representing Women: Myths of Femininity in Popular Culture* (London: Edward Arnold, 1995).

16. By power gamer, I am referring to individuals who spend a considerable amount of money on games, play games on a regular basis, and are knowledgeable about general news in the game world. Such individuals may also be referred to as hard-core or enthusiast gamers, depending on the source. Most studies and people using the terms are hard-pressed to pin down specifics of this game-playing individual, and I'm no different.

But there is a difference between the occasional player of *Solitaire* and the regular player of *Metal Gear Solid*. That is the general difference I'm suggesting.

17. This section is limited largely to the world of console gaming and its peripherals market. During this same time, the computer game market was also growing and expanding, with its own stable of magazines and other peripherals. But due to the differences in demographics, marketing vehicles, and play styles, I have chosen to focus this analysis on the console game industry, which is actually the larger of the industries, revenue-wise. "Sales and Genre Data," *Entertainment Software Association*, <http://www.theesa.com/facts/sales_genre_data.php> (accessed August 8, 2005).

18. Ed Semrad, "CD-ROM: Is the Industry Ready for It?" *Electronic Gaming Monthly*, May 1992, 8.

19. Stephen Kline, Nick Dyer-Witheford, and Greig De Peuter, eds., *Digital Play: The Interaction of Technology, Culture, and Marketing* (Montreal: McGill-Queen's University Press, 2003), 130–132.

20. David Sheff, *Game Over: How Nintendo Conquered the World* (New York: Random House, 1993).

21. Kent, *Ultimate History*; Sheff, *Game Over*.

22. Kent, *Ultimate History*, 361.

23. Sheff, *Game Over*, 180.

24. Ibid.

25. "Little Nemo: The Dream Master," *Nintendo Power*, November–December 1990, 19.

26. "Super Mario Bros. 2," *Nintendo Power*, July–August 1988, 22.

27. "Counselor's Corner," *Nintendo Power*, February 1991, 78–79.

28. Agent #920, "Classified Information," *Nintendo Power*, February 1991, 34.

29. Ibid.

30. I discuss the "Classified Information" section later in this chapter in more detail. Briefly, it appeared as a section for readers to contribute to as Secret Agents by sending in codes and trick moves for recently released games.

31. "Power to the Player," *Nintendo Power*, February 1991, 66–69.

32. Such tactics are similar to the ratings that contemporary sites like GameFAQs.com can give for players' versions of tricks, codes, and walk-throughs.

33. It is hard to find exact, consistent figures, but some sources indicate that *Nintendo Power*'s circulation runs about five hundred thousand copies per month. By comparison, *Electronic Gaming Monthly*'s current circulation is around six hundred thousand copies per month. Readership figures are always higher, though, due to readers passing along their copies to

others. Jonah Weiland, "IDW and Konami Publicity Plan for '*Metal Gear Solid*' the Comic Book," ComicBookResources.com, <http://www.comicbookresources.com/news/newsitem.cgi?id=3872> (accessed October 12, 2004); Dan Hsu, personal conversation, October 12, 2004.

34. Or Nintendo's weakness, depending on your point of view.

35. In a recent comparison of the reviews of major gaming publications, however, *Game Daily* found that *Nintendo Power*'s reviews were only slightly more positive (1.5 percent) than the mean. By comparison, PSE2 magazine's reviews were 14.8 percent more favorable. "Grading on a Curve," *Game Daily*, <http://biz.gamedaily.com/features.asp?article_id=8370> (accessed November 30, 2004).

36. Hsu, conversation.

37. Because of the rapid proliferation of Web sites that offer cheat codes almost simultaneously with a game's release, some game magazines are slowly doing away with the inclusion of such codes and mini-strategy guides. Others, however, see it as a core part of their appeal.

38. "Media Kit," IDG Entertainment, <http://www.idgentertainment.com/mediakit/> (accessed November 1, 2004). It is interesting to note that *GamePro* is the only mass-market console magazine to actively promote its detailed strategy guide sections as a key feature in its media kit. In a crowded market, it is likely one way to differentiate itself from the competitors.

39. Ibid.

40. Synergies can extend only so far. While writing this chapter, GMR magazine went under and the fate of Xbox Nation is uncertain. "More on GMR and XBN," *Game Daily*, <http://biz.gamedaily.com/articles.asp?article_id=8548#8548> (accessed January 10, 2005).

41. "Media Kit 2004/2005," *Game Informer*, <http://www.gameinformer.com/OtherPages/Corporate/Advertising.htm> (accessed November 1, 2004).

42. There is some difference for computer game publications such as *Computer Gaming World*, which revealed in 2005 that its readership was now 15 percent female. Robert Coffey, "Hello, Ladies!" *Computer Gaming World* (July/August 2005), 106. Overall however, those are the highest demographic numbers for female readers.

43. "Gaming Enthusiasts," Ziff Davis Media, <http://www.ziffdavis.com/print_it.php?title=Gaming%20Enthusiasts> (accessed July 14, 2004).

44. Espen Aarseth, *Cybertext: Perspectives on Ergodic Literature* (Baltimore, MD: Johns Hopkins University Press, 1997).

Chapter 2: Guidance Goes Independent

1. Of course, magazines do vary in the amount of strategy and hint tips that they publish. *Nintendo Power* and *GamePro* magazines still include

strategy sections, while other publications such as *Electronic Gaming Monthly* and *Game Informer* have shrunk or eliminated such sections.

2. Nintendo remains distinct from other game companies in many areas, including its largely unique strategy of licensing multiple "official" guides to its major games as well as producing its own versions of the guides.

3. Stephen Kline, Nick Dyer-Witheford, and Greig De Peuter, eds., *Digital Play: The Interaction of Technology, Culture, and Marketing* (Montreal: McGill-Queen's University Press, 2003).

4. Prima Games is currently marketing eGuides for its games, which are PDF versions of their print guides. Yet they have attempted to sell different types of eGuides before. In 2002, Prima promoted a different type of eGuide on its site (for three games, *Tomb Raider: Chronicles*, *Tomb Raider: The Last Revelation*, and *Tribes*). Those guides promised "streaming video. Interactive maps. 3D VR rooms. Voice over instruction." Although it is unclear whether such guides were actually sold or not, Prima was interested in creating a more dynamic style of guide. The market was likely not ready at that time for such guides, as Prima ultimately abandoned such efforts and went instead with more static technologies (PDF) rather than the dynamics of Flash and Quicktime. Prima Games, <http://www.primagames.com> (accessed March 25, 2002).

5. As J. C. Herz points out, many players of *Myst* likely never made it very far, but were intrigued by the beautiful locations in the game and wanted something to use in their PC's new CD-ROM drive. A guide for *Myst* aided new game players to continue in their "armchair traveler" experience. J. C. Herz, *Joystick Nation: How Videogames Ate Our Quarters, Won Our Hearts*, and *Rewired Our Minds* (Boston: Little, Brown and Company, 1997), 150–151. There is some dispute about which game guide is the best-selling of all time. My research indicates that the official *Myst* guide is (at this time) the best-selling computer game guide, while the best-selling console game guide is for *Final Fantasy VII*. Sharon Belton, "A Segue into Publishing—Prima Publishing—Making It—Company Profile," *Nation's Business*, July 1998, <http://www.find articles.com/p/articles/mi_m1154/is_n7_v86/ai_20797631> (accessed July 26, 2004).

6. As a comparison, I was flipping through another strategy guide, for the game *Primal*, which I had not yet finished. Even in casually flipping, I saw the words "with his dying breath" on the last page of the guide, indicating some character would die at the end. Although it wasn't enough to spoil the game for me, it does irritate me that the guide creator couldn't go to a bit more trouble to hide such information.

7. Rick Barba and Rusel DeMaria, *Myst: The Official Strategy Guide* (Rocklin, CA: Prima Publishing, 1995), vii–viii (italics in original).

8. Ibid., viii.

9. Ibid., 96–97.

10. Ibid., 152.

11. Johan Huizinga wrote about the concept of the "magic circle" in relation to games and play, describing it as a place set apart from normal life, where the usual rules did not apply. It is an important concept in Katie Salen and Eric Zimmerman's work exploring theories of game design and development, *Rules of Play: Game Design Fundamentals* (Cambridge, MA: MIT Press, 2003). Some game researchers have problematized the term in relation to digital games, pointing to contradictions between games that are portable, MMOs that run around the clock, and the notion of a bounded, separate space. For more on this argument, see Ian Bogost, *Unit Operations: An Approach to Videogame Criticism* (Cambridge, MA: MIT Press, 2006). I am not here disputing or upholding the concept but instead pointing to how certain elements of the game industry and its paratext seek to keep some elements bounded or thematically consistent with each other.

12. Bryan Stratton, *URU: Ages beyond Myst: Prima's Official Strategy Guide* (Roseville, CA: Prima Games, 2003); Bryan Stratton, *Myst URU: Complete Chronicles: Prima Official Game Guide* (Roseville, CA: Prima Games, 2004).

13. Bart Farkas, telephone interview, September 23, 2003.

14. David Waybright, personal conversation, July 16, 2003.

15. Tim Bogenn, *The Hulk Official Strategy Guide* (Indianapolis, IN: BradyGames Publishing, 2003), 39.

16. Video Game Books Inc., *Playing Ms. Pac-Man to Win* (New York: Pocket Books, 1982); J. Douglas Arnold, *Compute's Nintendo Tips and Tricks* (Greensboro, NC: Compute Books, 1991).

17. Arnold, *Compute's Nintendo Tips*, 119.

18. Waybright, conversation.

19. Farkas, interview.

20. The attach rate is the percentage of guides to games sold for a particular title. Attach rates of about 15 percent are considered average, meaning that, for example, 15 percent of the people who bought the game *Primal* also bought the strategy guide for it. Waybright, conversation.

21. Mark Walker, telephone interview, September 9, 2003.

22. Farkas, interview.

23. Ibid.

24. Ibid.; Walker, interview; Andrew Rolleri, telephone interview, July 1, 2004.

25. Farkas, interview.

26. Rolleri, interview; Waybright, conversation.
27. During such crunches, one writer then falls into the old pattern of working for six hours, sleeping for three, working for six, and so on until the guide is done.
28. Waybright, conversation.
29. Rolleri, interview.
30. Rolleri, interview.
31. Susie Nieman, "BradyGames Sweeps Gaming Strategy Guide Industry in 2004," BradyGames.com, < http://www.bradygames.com/press/press _releases_detail.asp?promo=2226&rl=1> (accessed September 10, 2006).
32. Brady's approach echoes the game magazines' insider perspective on games and gameplay. The explicit claim about playing games supports the implicit knowledge that the company/publication therefore contains better information, produced by an insider rather than being a mass-produced entity. So both Brady and *Electronic Gaming Monthly* make greater appeals to the enthusiast gamer rather than other segments of the market.
33. Chris Kohler, *Power Up: How Japanese Video Games Gave the World an Extra Life* (Indianapolis, IN: BradyGames Publishing, 2005).
34. Kodak Video Programs, *How to Score More Points on Nintendo Games* (n.p., n.d. Pub); White Janssen Productions, *Secret Video Game Tricks, Codes, and Strategies*; Studio Video Productions, *Video Game Guide* (2002).
35. For the convenience of being able to electronically search these documents, however, the user gives up quite a few rights previously taken for granted. For instance, Prima e-guides only work on PC computers and cannot be printed. Furthermore, they cannot be shared (that is, they will not open on any other computer) or copied for backup.
36. Game Time Entertainment, *Official DVD Strategy Guide for Tom Clancy's Rainbow Six 3* (2003).
37. Although most strategy guides don't include cheat codes, there are a few that do so. For example, the *Quake: Authorized Strategy Guide* (Indianapolis, IN: Brady Publishing, 1996) contains information about the "Quake console," which "is a command interface into the engine behind the game" (116). Using the console allows the player to change attributes in the game, including giving the player all the weapons in the game, or being able to play the game in god mode.
38. Codes also often appear in compilation guides put out by strategy guide publishers as well as in codebooks published by game magazines. These too are designed to bring revenue back to the game and guide (plus magazine) publishers, and keep interest alive in older games.
39. In 1997, Nintendo went to court to seek a preliminary injunction against Prima Communications. Prima had released an unauthorized strategy

guide for the Nintendo 64 game *Goldeneye: 007* (which was perfectly legal), but Nintendo alleged that the guide included copyrighted maps used in Nintendo's own strategy guide for the title. The judge dismissed the case, stating that a map containing information about locations and such could not be infringing on a copyright (*Nintendo of America v. Prima Communications* [1997]). Ironically, Prima has gone on from this gaffe to create licensed, authorized guides for Nintendo, including guides for the recently released games *The Legend of Zelda: Wind Waker* and *Warioworld*.

Chapter 3: Genies, Sharks, and Chips

1. Nintendo's Game Boy line of handheld game systems has always allowed games from any region to play, meaning that I can load the latest Japanese *Hamtaro* (hamster) game on my U.S.-purchased Game Boy Advance SP.

2. David Sheff, *Game Over: How Nintendo Conquered the World* (New York: Random House, 1993). Although Galoob's Game Genie is credited in most places as the first cheat cartridge, there was a cartridge released prior to it, which only worked with computer games. The Konami Game Master was a cartridge designed to work with the Machines with Software eXchangeability computer standard, which was developed in 1983 by a Japanese company called ASCII Corporation. The standard was popular in Japan and Korea, but never caught on in the United States. The Konami Game Master cartridge let players alter certain Konami games, allowing them to start at different stages of the games, keep high scores on disc or tape, and play the game in slow motion, among other uses. For more information, see Old-Computers.com, <http://www.old-computers.com/museum/computer.asp?c=90> (accessed May 1, 2006). See also "Konami Game Master," Wikipedia, <http://en.wikipedia.org/wiki/Konami_game_master> (accessed May 1, 2006).

3. Howard Lincoln, quoted in Sheff, *Game Over*, 287.

4. Steven Kent, *The Ultimate History of Videogames*, (Roseville, CA: Prima Publishing, 2001).

5. *Lewis Galoob Toys, Inc v. Nintendo of America* (1992), <http://cyber .law.harvard.edu/openlaw/DVD/cases/Galoob_v_Nintendo.html> (accessed May 1, 2005).

6. Sheff, *Game Over*. Although Galoob's profits initially rose, the toy maker, founded in 1954, was ultimately acquired by Hasbro in 1998 for $220 million. By that time, its most profitable line was Star Wars figures and vehicles, and the production of Game Genies had likely ceased. Dan Fost, "Hasbro adds Galoob to Its Toy Chest," SF Gate.com, September

29, 1998, <http://www.sfgate.com/cgi-bin/article.cgi?file=/chronicle/archive/1998/09/29/BU88669.DTL&type=printable> (accessed August 23, 2004).

7. "Action Replay," Wikipedia, <http://en.wikipedia.org/wiki/Action_Replay> (accessed May 15, 2006).

8. "GameShark," Wikipedia, <http://en.wikipedia.org/wiki/game_shark> (accessed May 15, 2006).

9. "About Datel," Datel Design and Development Ltd., <http://www.datel.co.uk/about.asp> (accessed May 16, 2006).

10. "The Complete Not Just for Cheating," Codejunkies, <http://us.codejunkies.com/news_reviews.asp?c=US&cr=USD&cs=$&r=0&l=1&p=13&i=8191&s=8> (accessed September 17, 2004).

11. Ibid.

12. Jeff Gerstmann, "SOCOM: So Broken," GameSpot, <http://www.gamespot.com/gamespot/features/all/gamespotting/041303/2.html> (accessed July 8, 2003).

13. "Mad Katz Annual Report," 2005, <http://www.madkatz.com> (accessed June 1, 2006), 21.

14. "About Datel."

15. Aimee Mabe, "Mad Katz Announces GameShark Lineup at Electronic Entertainment Expo," GameShark.com, <http://www.gameshark.com/productinfo/articles/409700p1.html> (accessed July 11, 2003).

16. "Modchip," Wikipedia, <http://en.wikipedia.org/wiki/Modchip> (accessed May 15, 2006).

17. Ibid.

18. Ibid.

19. Ibid.

20. Randall Ramsay, "Australian High Court Rules Mod Chips Are OK," CNET, October 6, 2005, <http://www.cnet.com.au/games/ps2/0,39029672,40057408,00.htm> (accessed May 22, 2006); Rob Fahey, "Italian Court Rules Mod Chips Legal," Games Industry Biz, January 23, 2004, <http://www.gamesindustry.biz/content_page.php?section_name=ret&aid=2858> (accessed January 29, 2004).

21. Simon Carless, "Washington, DC, Game Stores Raided over Mod Chip Piracy," Gamasutra, December 8, 2004, <http://www.gamasutra.com/php-bin/news_index.php?sotry=4669> (accessed December 15, 2004).

22. Ibid.

23. John Lui, "Mod-Chipped Xbox? No Online Games for You," ZDNet Asia, <http://www.zdnetasia.com/news/internet/0,39044246,39157642,00.htm> (accessed January 20, 2004).

24. James Beniger, *The Control Revolution: Technological and Economic Origins of the Information Society* (Cambridge, MA: Harvard University Press, 1986).

25.   Here I refer to Stuart Hall's notion of preferred reading taken from his article "Encoding/Decoding," in *Culture, Media, Language: Working Papers in Cultural Studies, 1972–1979*, ed. Stuart Hall (London: Hutchinson, 1980).

Chapter 4: Gaining Advantage

1.   Or a computer, a keyboard, and a mouse.

2.   See Gareth Schott and Kristy Horell, "Girl Gamers and Their Relationship with the Gaming Culture," *Convergence* 6, no. 4 (2000): 36–53; Pam Royse, Joon Lee, Undrahbuyan Baasanjav, Mark Hopson, and Mia Consalvo, "Women Gamers: Technologies of the Gendered Self," in *New Media & Society* (forthcoming); T. L. Taylor, "Multiple Pleasures: Women and Online Gaming," *Convergence* 9, no. 1 (2003): 21–46.

3.   Hector Postigo, "Of Mods and Modders: Chasing down the Value of Fan-Based Video Game Modifications," in *Digital Games Industries*, ed. Jason Rutter (Manchester: Manchester University Press, forthcoming); Talmadge Wright, Eric Boria, and Paul Breidenbach, "Creative Player Actions in FPS Online Video Games," *Game Studies* (2002), <http://www.gamestudies.org/0202/wright/>.

4.   T. L. Taylor and Mikael Jakobsson, "The Sopranos Meet *EverQuest*: Socialization in Massively Multiuser Games," in *Command Lines*, ed. Sandra Braman and Thomas Malaby (forthcoming).

5.   Lawrence Lessig, *Code: And Other Laws of Cyberspace* (New York: Basic Books, 1999), 60.

6.   "Do You Use Cheat Codes or Not?" *Electronic Gaming Monthly* message boards, 2002, <http://boards.gamers.com/messages/message_view-topic.asp?name=egm&id=zrcdr>.

7.   Johan Huizinga, *Homo Ludens: A Study of the Play Element in Culture* (Boston: Beacon Press, 1950); Espen Aarseth, *Cybertext: Perspectives on Ergodic Literature* (Baltimore, MD: Johns Hopkins University Press, 1997). Elsewhere I critique the magic circle, as it suggests boundaries for gameplay that seem unrealistic in the contemporary world of games, where guides, fan fiction, and codes found in magazines (among other things) can appear and mediate gameplay at times apart from the actual playing of games. Yet the concept can still be helpful, I believe, in asserting that there is a boundary for games, which I believe are the rules of the game itself. Thus, the circle defines a conceptual rather than a spatial limit to games.

8.   Huizinga, *Homo Ludens*, 8.

9.   Aarseth, *Cybertext*, 124.

10.   Aarseth, *Cybertext*, 91.

11.   Oftentimes, even the guides themselves advise players to use them sparingly, in order to not spoil the excitement of figuring things out on

their own. One of the guides to *Myst* at GameFAQs.com admonishes players to try and play through the game without consulting the more detailed walkthrough, unless the player is absolutely stuck. Additionally, the commercial strategy guide for the Nintendo game *Legend of Zelda: Majora's Mask* actually seals the information about the final battle and end of the game in a separate envelope at the back of the guide.

12. J. Barton Bowyer, *Cheating: Deception in War and Magic, Games and Sports, Sex and Religion, Business and Con Games, Politics and Espionage, Art and Science* (New York: St. Martin's Press, 1982), 300–301.

13. Mike Laidlaw, "Cracking Pandora's Box," The Adrenaline Vault, <http://www.avault.com/articles/getarticle.asp?name=pandbox>.

14. Success is obviously a loaded term here, and could include grief players who measure success through the levels of discomfort they cause in others players as well as more traditional players who try to follow the game's various success markers.

15. Julian Kücklich, "Other Playings: Cheating in Computer Games" (paper presented at the Other Players conference, IT-University of Copenhagen, December 2004), 4.

16. Chek Yang Foo, "Redefining Grief Play" (paper presented at the Other Players conference, IT-University of Copenhagen, December 2004); Chek Yang Foo and Elina M. I. Koivisto, "Grief Play Motivations" (paper presented at the Other Players conference, IT-University of Copenhagen, December 2004).

17. Foo, "Redefining Grief Play"; Foo and Koivisto, "Grief Play Motivations."

18. Nightfreeze, "The Great Scam," <http://static.circa1984.com/the-big-scam.html> (accessed March 1, 2005).

Chapter 5: The Cheaters

1. Tony Ray, personal conversation, March 17, 2005.

2. Such players are generally easy to catch, and "calling their parents" is easily the best way to get them to stop cheating.

3. Jeff Morris, "Multiplayer Cheating: Dispatches from the Front" (paper presented at the annual meeting of the Game Developers Conference, San Jose, California, March 2006). Morris raises an interesting point when he questions the assumption that developers should "naturally" go after cheaters in multiplayer games. He points out that they are also paying customers, who are merely playing the game in a different way. By voiding their access keys or pressing charges against them, the developer is losing potential future sales from that customer. Ultimately, Morris concludes, each developer must decide whether or not the cost of going after cheaters is worth the expense, traded against the potential damage cheaters may be doing to the game and other players.

4. Ibid.

5. Thanks to Beth Barcus Novak for telling me about this particular strategy, which she has personally witnessed.

6. J. Barton Bowyer, *Cheating: Deception in War and Magic, Games and Sports, Sex and Religion, Business and Con Games, Politics and Espionage, Art and Science* (New York: St. Martin's Press, 1982).

7. Howard Rheingold, *Virtual Communities: Homesteading on the Electronic Frontier* (Reading, MA: Addison-Wesley Publishing, 1993); Mark Poster, "Postmodern Virtualities," in *Cyberspace/Cyberbodies/Cyberpunk*, ed. Mike Featherstone and Roger Burrows (Thousand Oaks, CA: Sage, 1995).

8. Allucquère Rosanne Stone, *The War of Desire and Technology at the Close of the Mechanical Age* (Cambridge, MA: MIT Press, 1995); Sherry Turkle, *Life on the Screen* (New York: Touchstone, 1995).

9. Richard Bartle, "Hearts, Clubs, Diamonds, Spades: Players Who Suit MUDs," <http://www.mud.co.uk/richard/hcds.htm> (accessed October 22, 2002).

10. Brad King and John Borland, *Dungeons and Dreamers: The Rise of Computer Game Culture from Geek to Chic* (New York: McGraw-Hill, 2003), 152.

11. Bowyer, Cheating; Lori Collins-Jarvis, "Discriminatory Messages and Gendered Power Relations in On-line Discussion Groups" (paper presented at the annual meeting of the National Communication Association, Chicago, November 1997).

12. Peter Ludlow, "Evangeline: Interview with a Child Cyber-Prostitute in TSO," *Alphaville Herald*, <http://www.alphavilleherald.com/archives/000049.html> (accessed June 1, 2006).

13. Chip Morningstar and Randall Farmer, "The Lessons of Lucasfilm's Habitat," in *Cyberspace: First steps*, ed. Michael Benedikt (Cambridge, MA: MIT Press, 1992), 293.

14. Miguel Lopez, "WoW Duping: Fact or Fiction?" *Gamespy*, July 20, 2005, <http://www.gamespy.com/articles/635/635262p1.html> (accessed May 1, 2006).

15. "List of Online Multiplayer Cheats," Wikipedia, <http://en.wikipedia.org/wiki/List_of_online_multiplayer_cheats> (accessed August 9, 2005).

16. Some of the gamers I talked with have explained that if they find a bug or related exploit in a game, they feel justified in taking advantage of it because the designer could have fixed it but did not. Similar views are expressed on many game discussion boards and in other player spaces.

17. "List of Online Multiplayer Cheats."

18. Duping can involve the exploiting of game bugs, but it can also be the result of hacking the game code. I talk about hacking code later in this section, but discuss duping mainly in this section.

19. "Battlenet Warnings!" Diabloii.net, <http://www.diabloii.net/battlenet/warnings.shtml#trading> (accessed August 11, 2005).

20. Ibid.

21. Noah Shachtman, "'Blizzard' of Cheaters Banned," *Wired News*, <http://www.wired.com/news/games/0,2101,55092,00.html?tw=wn_ascii> (accessed August 11, 2005); Bob Colayco, "Blizzard Closes and Bans Accounts and CD Keys Tied to the Use of Online Cheat Programs," Gamespot, <http://www.gamespot.com/pc/strategy/warcraft3reignofchaos/news_6024304.html> (accessed August 11, 2005).

22. In a later section as well as a later chapter, I discuss the breakdown of trust that can result as a consequence of such behaviors, and its impact on the wider game world.

23. Jennifer Sun, telephone interview, June 7, 2006.

24. Nightfreeze, "The Great Scam," <http://static.circa1984.com/the-big-scam.html> (accessed March 1, 2005).

25. "Gil Farming and Fishing Bots: Cheating in FFXI," MemoryCard <http://memorycard.blogs.com/memorycard/2004/08/gil_farming_and.html>.

26. David McCandless, "Make Cheats, Not War," *Guardian*, <http://www.davidmccandless.com/articles/make_cheats_not_war.htm>.

27. Ibid.

28. Eddo Stern, "A Touch of Medieval: Narrative, Magic, and Computer Technology in Massively Multiplayer Computer Role-playing Games," <http://www.eddostern.com/texts/Stern_TOME.html> (accessed June 1, 2006); ShowEQ Open Source Project Message Forums, <http://www.showeq.net/forums/faq.php?faq=seqfaq_gq#faq_seqfaq_gq_whatseq> (accessed May 3, 2006).

29. Ibid.

30. "WoW Glider," <http://www.wowglider.com/default.aspx> (accessed May 1, 2006).

31. "Frequently Asked Questions about Wow Glider," <http://www.wowglider.com/FAQ.aspx> (accessed May 1, 2006).

32. T. L. Taylor, "Becoming Player: Networks, Structured and Imagined Futures" (paper presented at the Beyond Barbie and Mortal Kombat: New Perspectives on Gender, Games, and Computing Conference, NSF Workshop, University of California at Los Angeles, May 2006); Nick Yee, "Maps of Azeroth" (paper presented at the Beyond Barbie and Mortal Kombat: New Perspectives on Gender, Games, and Computing Conference, NSF Workshop, University of California at Los Angeles, May 2006).

33. Robin Wilson, "A Hothouse for Women Scientists," *Chronicle of Higher Education*, May 5, 2006, <http://chronicle.com/weekly/v52/i35/35a01201.htm> (accessed May 10, 2006); Elizabeth Farrell, "Smith College's First Engineers Feel Like 'Rock Stars,'" *Chronicle of Higher*

Education, May 28, 2004, <http://chronicle.com/weekly/v50/i38/38a03401.htm>.

34. Susan Herring, "Gender and Power in Online Communication," CSI Working Paper, October 2001, <http://rkcsi.indiana.edu/archive/CSI/WP/WP01-05B.html> (accessed June 1, 2006).

35. Sun, interview.

36. Ibid.

Chapter 6: Busting Punks and Policing Players

1. Nick Yee, "Buying Gold," Daedalus Project, <http://www.nickyee.com/daedalus/archives/001469.php> (accessed May 15, 2006).

2. Chip Morningstar and Randall Farmer, "The Lessons of Lucasfilm's *Habitat*," in *Cyberspace: First Steps*, ed. Michael Benedikt, (Cambridge, MA: MIT Press, 1992), 288.

3. Dave Weinstein, "Cheating and Countermeasures in Multiplayer Games" (paper presented at the Austin Game Developers Conference, Austin, September 2003).

4. Michel Foucault, *Discipline and Punish: The Birth of the Prison* (New York: Pantheon, 1977).

5. "About Us," IT GlobalSecure, <http://www.itglobalsecure.com/en/company/c_overview.htm> (accessed May 15, 2006).

6. "Working with SecurePlay," IT GlobalSecure, <http://www.secureplay.com/product-docs/WorkingWithSecurePlay2.pdf> (accessed May 15, 2006).

7. "Protocol-Based Security and Software Security," IT GlobalSecure, <http://www.secureplay.com/papers/docs/ProtocolSecurtiyVsSoftwareSecurity2.pdf> (accessed June 1, 2006).

8. Steven Davis, personal conversation, July 24, 2003.

9. "Custom Anti-Cheating Solutions," IT GlobalSecure, <http://www.itglobalsecure.net.categories/gaming/service_custom_anticheating.htm> (accessed May 15, 2006).

10. Ibid.

11. "Cheating-Death," United Admins, <http://www.unitedadmins.com/index.php?p=content&content=Cheating-Death> (accessed May 15, 2006).

12. Ibid.

13. Ibid.

14. Ibid.

15. Banana, "Cheating-Death Is Dead," United Admins, March 20, 2006, <http://forums.unitedadmins.com/index.php?s=Cheating-Death66c57fbf6acbf9f3328671852ee83c&showtopic=47235> (accessed May 15, 2006).

16. Hiawatha Bray, "Game On: New Tools Will Defeat a Cheat," *Boston Globe*, November 5, 2003, E1; Don Clark, "Gamer Offers Form of

Instant Replay to Fight Cheating," *Wall Street Journal*, September 24, 2003, D4; Peter Wayner, "Do Cheaters Ever Prosper? Just Ask Them," *New York Times*, March 27, 2003, <http://www.nytimes.com/2003/03/27/technology/circuits/27chea.html?ei=5070&en=b35772c76e5251e5&ex=1069822800&pagewanted=print&position=top> (accessed November 24, 2003).

17. "Announcements," Even Balance, <http://www.evenbalance.com/index.php?page=announce.php> (accessed May 15, 2006).

18. Ibid.

19. "About Auto-MBL," Punksbusted.com, <http://www.punksbusted.com/forums/index.php?showtopic=41> (accessed May 20, 2006).

20. "Announcements."

21. Dave Pelland, "Hackers, Cheater Threaten Online Games' Business Model," KPMG Analysis, March 3, 2005, <http://www.kpmginsiders.com/display_analysis.asp?cs_id=126855> (accessed March 8, 2005); David McCandless, "Online: Make Cheats, Not War," *Guardian*, <http://www.davidmccandless.com/articles/make_cheats_not_war.htm>.

22. Alex Pham, "'Griefers' Bedevil Online Gamers," *Chicago Tribune*, September 9, 2002, <http://www.chicagotribune.com/business/chi-0209090015sep09.story> (accessed September 11, 2002).

23. Charles Porter, e-mail interview, June 1, 2006.

24. Ibid.

25. Will Leverett, telephone interview, November 4, 2004.

26. Porter, interview.

27. Ibid.

28. Ibid.; Leverett, interview.

29. Jennifer Sun, telephone interview, June 7, 2006.

30. Taodyn, Bannable Offenses, <http://bannable-offenses.blogspot.com/> (accessed May 1, 2006).

31. Taodyn, "Law and Order: SVU Must Be Joking," Bannable Offenses, <http://bannable-offenses.blogspot.com/2006/05/law-and-order-svumustbejoking.html> (accessed May 22, 2006).

32. Ernst Fehr and Simon Gächter, "Altruistic Punishment in Humans," Nature 415 (January 2002): 137–140.

33. Julian Dibbell, *My Tiny Life: Crime and Passion in a Virtual World* (New York: Holt and Company, 1999).

34. "Punkbuster for Players," Even Balance, <http://www.punkbusters.com/publications/aa-pl/index.htm> (accessed May 15, 2006).

Chapter 7: A Mage's Chronicle

1. Bruce Woodcock, "MMOG Charts," <http://www.mmogchart.com>.

2. Prior to this, Richard Bartle wrote about player types in "Hearts, Clubs, Diamonds, Spades: Players Who Suit MUDS," <http://www.mud.co

.uk/richard/hcds.htm> (accessed October 22, 2002). His taxonomy included killers, who have seemingly prefigured the cheating some players believe is part of PK. Bartle maintained that although many players disliked killers, a certain number of them were necessary for a properly balanced game.

3. See Brad King and John Borland, *Dungeons and Dreamers: The Rise of Computer Game Culture from Geek to Chic* (New York: McGraw-Hill, 2003).

4. Players of Diablo have written extensively about the player-versus-player (PvP) nature of the game and its resulting design ramifications. See, for example, Nathan Danylczuk, "The Political Economy of *Diablo II*," <http://www.Diabloii.net>; Micha Ghertner, "The Political Economy of *Diablo II*: A Critique," <http://www.Diabloii.net>; Samuel Kite, "The Political Critique of *Diablo II*: The Rebuttal," <http://www.Diabloii.net>; David Ko Leong, "Political Economy Synthesis," <http://www.Diabloii.net>.

5. See, for example, "Secrets to *Diablo*," <http://www.guardiansofjustice.com/diablo/Frames/Secrets.htm> (accessed February 5, 2005); "Interview of the Month: Bill Roper," <http://www.planetdiablo.com/features/articles/broper022702/> (accessed February 5, 2005); "*Diablo 2* Hints," <http://home.tula.net/sound/diablo2hints.html> (accessed February 5, 2005).

6. See T. L. Taylor, *Play between Worlds: Exploring Online Game Culture* (Cambridge, MA: MIT Press, 2006). See also Chek Yang Foo and Elina M. I. Koivisto, "Grief Play Motivations" (paper presented at the Other Players conference, IT-University of Copenhagen, December 2004); Chek Yang Foo, "Redefining Grief Play" (paper presented at the Other Players conference, IT-University of Copenhagen, December 2004).

7. See Mia Consalvo, "Zelda 64 and Video Game Fans: A Walkthrough of Games, Intertextuality, and Narrative," *Television and New Media* 4, no. 3 (2003): 321–334. Chuen-Tsai Sun, Holin Lin, and Cheng-Hong Ho, "Game Tips as Gifts: Social Interactions and Rational Calculations in Computer Gaming," in *Level Up: Digital Games Research Conference Proceedings*, ed. Marinka Copier and Joost Raessens (Utrecht: Utrecht University, 2003).

8. Ren Reynolds, "Playing a 'Good' Game: A Philosophical Approach to Understanding the Morality of Games," Gamasutra, <http://www.igda.org/articles/rreynolds_ethics.php>.

9. Gregory F. Lastowka and Dan Hunter, "The Laws of the Virtual Worlds," *California Law Review*, <http://ssrn.com/abstract=402860>.

10. Edward Castronova, *Synthetic Worlds: The Business and Culture of Online Games* (Chicago: University of Chicago Press, 2005).

11.   See Mia Consalvo, "It's a Queer World After All: Studying *The Sims* and Sexuality," Gay and Lesbian Alliance against Defamation, <http://www.glaad.org/publications>.

12.   T. L. Taylor, "Multiple Pleasures: Women and Online Gaming," *Convergence* 9, no. 1 (2003): 21–46.

13.   The game also allows players to complete missions and advance their avatar's "rank" (currently ranging from one to ten) in the world. That facilitates another level of differentiation and reputation between players, because even though an avatar's job may change, rank remains the same, at least as long as the player wishes to stay affiliated with one nation. A player, on reaching rank ten in one nation, may decide to change nationalities and restart rank missions. I'm unsure of the percentage of players who do this, but those who do so report they are mainly interested in seeing the story lines for each of the nations, which can often be quite detailed.

14.   In fall 2004, Square Enix added two servers or worlds (Remora and Hades) to make space for the growing population of Vana'diel. Players were told they could apply to migrate to a new server, although they could not specify which one. This is the only mass migration to take place so far in *Final Fantasy XI*.

15.   The translator must be manually engaged to work, but it is quite comprehensive in its scope. Yet players grouping together in parties across nationalities, especially North America and Japan, often feel that there are cultural differences impeding play as well. While I cannot go into depth on the scope of such issues here, I can note that on player boards, both Western and Eastern players (Japanese who can speak English, at least) tend to draw distinctions between the play styles of North American and Japanese players. For example, North American players were initially seen by Japanese ones as players who constantly begged in game for money and items, and when told how to improve their play style, responded rudely. As a counterpoint, North American players can feel that Japanese ones are overly concerned with experience point accumulation and treat the game as more like work than play. Of course these are generalizations, but they do suggest some of the problems that go beyond basic language translation in a global MMO.

16.   "Event Name: Ballista," Official Web Site of *Final Fantasy XI* Online, <http://www.playonline.com/ff11us/conflict/main/> (accessed June 1, 2006).

17.   This is usually done with aggressive monsters that attack on sight as well as monsters that "link" or will join other similar monsters in an attack. A player may begin by provoking one such monster, running away and letting it chase him/her, and taking that monster around an area to pick up other such monsters, thereby creating a chain of mobs. Once enough

monsters have joined the train, the player aims for an unsuspecting player, runs by, and hopes that some of the monsters break the train and attack the other player instead. This is best achieved if the player starting the train can leave a zone (monsters can't leave zones) and the targeted player is standing quite near the zone exit/entrance.

18. Quoted in King and Borland, *Dungeons and Dreamers*, 162.

19. For more information, reference the power-leveling service options on the International Game Exchange's Web site at <http://www.ige.com/wowus/accounts/worldofwarcraftus_en.html>.

20. It's highly likely that by the time you read this, at least one of these sites won't exist, yet many more will have taken its place. I should also point out that BuyGameCurrency is a metasite, offering players a means to comparison shop among competing gil sellers rather than a place to actually buy game currency.

21. This is in line with Vili Lehdonvirta's theoretical delineation of reasons for real-money trade relating to virtual assets. Lehdonvirta does not draw on primary data to support his perceptions, however, nor does he attempt to rank them. Vili Lehdonvirta, "Real-Money Trade of Virtual Assets: Ten Different User Perceptions" (proceedings of DAC 2005, IT-University of Copenhagen, December 2005), <http://www.hiit.fi/u/vlehdonv/publications/Lehdonvirta-2005-RMT-Perceptions.pdf>.

22. Nick Yee, "Buying Gold," Daedalus Project, <http://www.nickyee.com/daedalus/archives/001469.php> (accessed May 15, 2006).

23. Forum posting, Allakhazam.com, <http://ffxi.allakhazam.com/forum.html?forum=10&mid=1138755398179122268#113876339668505230>.

24. The preceding quote probably means nothing to you, if you are not a regular player of *Final Fantasy XI*. In translation, then, this post is saying the following:

Seanswann tried to kill everyone in my party eight times by luring groups of powerful monsters to us, in hopes that they'd attack us when he disappeared. But every time he did that he died and had to return to his home point, a location far away from us, and then travel back. Each time he died, he lost 10 percent of his accumulated experience points, or about sixteen thousand of them. As a result, he went down from level 65 to level 64. After his second try at killing us, I called a game representative, who came and watched as this guy tried the same thing over and over. And then, the game representative must have thrown the guy in jail, as he wasn't online anymore. Troille, "Seanswann the moron," <http://ffxi.allakhazam.com/forum.html?forum=46&mid=1122867158235623230&num=4>. Interestingly, one night in 2006 I ended up in an experience points party with a person who said in group chat that his other character was named "seanswann." I watched this person carefully for the next few hours of gameplay, and noticed nothing troublesome about his attitude or gameplay. Maybe he had learned a lesson, or at least learned that those types of activities didn't pay off.

25. To translate roughly, the poster is relating a problem he had with other members of his linkshell, and his version of events. The poster announced he would help anyone with their ZM, or Rise of the Zilart missions, except the fourth and fifth ones, which he was tired of. He also tried helping a couple of members fight Fenrir, one of the avatars that summoners must defeat in order to acquire their use in regular gameplay, but due to its difficulty, they were defeated. <http://ffxi.allakhazam .com/forum.html?forum=46&mid=1119862414165339863&num=30>.

26. Forum posting, Allakhazam.com, <http://ffxi.allakhazam.com/forum .html?forum=46&mid=1120010736375822635&num=120>.

27. Another name for this activity is "kiting" or killing-in-transit. Some players use the term kiting in different ways, however, such as to refer to the "puller's" job of luring a mob to camp. The mob often trails behind it like a kite, and like a kite, if it gets too far away, might be lost.

28. Sissela Bok, *Lying: Moral Choice in Public and Private Life* (New York: Vintage Books, 1978), 19.

29. Ernst Fehr and Simon Gächter, "Altruistic Punishment in Humans," *Nature* 415 (January 2002): 137-140.

30. Lawrence Lessig, *Code: And Other Laws of Cyberspace* (New York: Basic Books, 1999).

Chapter 8: Capitalizing on Paratexts

1. Allakhazam Defender of Justice, "Zam.com Q & A," Allakhazam.com, <http://www.allakhazam.com/forum.html?forum=3;mid=114668646932 202500;num=0;page=1> (accessed May 10, 2006).

2. Mr. Rasputin, "Allakhazam Sells Out to IGE. No, Really. And IGE Andraste Is Savant," Corporation, <http://www.corpnews.com/node/ 133?PHPSESSID=8fbd6994b6b279ab38185ef5de62ec19> (accessed June 1, 2006); Taodyn, "Change Is Never Good," Bannable Offenses, <http://www.blogger.com/comment.g?blogID=25324432&postID=114 677231212075299> (accessed May 12, 2006).

3. In a forum outside the Allakhazam site discussing the MMO Vanguard, Allakhazam posted in part, "I can assure you that Allakhazam.com never has had and never will have any association with IGE [the International Game Exchange]. No amount of money will change that. We are players ourselves and disagree with everything they stand for. I've turned down their advances so many times in so many ways over the years that I think they have finally given up on us." Allakhazam, "Loss of Affiliated Fan Sites." Vanguardsoh.com, <http://www.vanguardsoh.com/forums/ showpost.php?p=190819&postcount=260> (accessed June 11, 2006).

4. Bigkillian, responding in "Zam.com Q & A" thread.

5. John Pauly, "*La Femme Nikita* and the Ethics of Organizational Life" (paper presented at the annual International Communication Association conference, New Orleans, May 2004), 1.

6. "GameFAQs," CNET Networks, <http://www.cnetnetworks.com/advertise/properties/gamefaqs.html> (accessed June 1, 2006).

7. "Pikmin FAQs," GameFAQs.com, <http://www.gamefaqs.com/console/gamecube/game/516498.html> (accessed June 1, 2006); "Kingdom Hearts FAQs," GameFAQs.com, <http://www.gamefaqs.com/console/ps2/game/516587.html> (accessed June 1, 2006).

8. "About the Site," Allakhazam.com, <http://www.allakhazam.com/Staff_Bios.html> (accessed June 1, 2006).

9. "About Us," International Game Exchange, <http://www.ige.com/about> (accessed June 1, 2006).

10. Johan Huizinga, *Homo Ludens: A Study of the Play Element in Culture* (Boston: Beacon Press, 1950).

11. Ren Reynolds, "Playing a 'Good' Game: A Philosophical Approach to Understanding the Morality of Games," Gamasutra. <http://www.igda.org/articles/rreynolds_ethics.php>.

12. Pauly, "*La Femme Nikita*."

13. Huizinga, *Homo Ludens*.

14. T. L. Taylor, *Play between Worlds: Exploring Online Game Culture* (Cambridge, MA: MIT Press, 2006).

References

Aarseth, Espen. *Cybertext: Perspectives on ergodic literature*. Baltimore, MD: Johns Hopkins University Press, 1997.

"About Auto-MBL." Punksbusted.com. <http://www.punksbusted.com/forums/index.php?showtopic=41> (accessed May 20, 2006).

"About Datel." Datel Design and Development Ltd. <http://www.datel.co.uk/about.asp> (accessed May 16, 2006).

"About the site." Allakhazam.com. <http://www.allakhazam.com/Staff_Bios.html> (accessed June 1, 2006).

"About us." International Game Exchange. <http://www.ige.com/about> (accessed June 1, 2006).

"About us." IT GlobalSecure. <http://www.itglobalsecure.com/en/company/c_overview.htm> (accessed May 15, 2006).

"Action replay." Wikipedia. <http://en.wikipedia.org/wiki/Action_Replay> (accessed May 15, 2006).

Allakhazam. "Loss of affiliated fan sites." Vanguardsoh.com. <http://www.vanguardsoh.com/forums/showpost.php?p=190819&postcount=260> (accessed June 11, 2006).

Allakhazam Defender of Justice. "Zam.com Q & A." Allakhazam.com. <http://www.allakhazam.com/forum.html?forum=3;mid=114668646932202500;num=0;page=1> (accessed May 10, 2006).

"Announcements." Even Balance. <http://www.evenbalance.com/index.php?page=announce.php> (accessed May 15, 2006).

Arnold, J. Douglas. *Compute's Nintendo tips & tricks*. Greensboro, NC: Compute Books, 1991.

Banana. "Cheating-Death is dead." United Admins. March 20, 2006. <http://forums.unitedadmins.com/index.php?s=Cheating-Death66c57fbf6acbf9f3328671852ee83c&showtopic=47235> (accessed May 15, 2006).

Barba, Rick, and Rusel DeMaria. *Myst: The official strategy guide*. Rocklin, CA: Prima Publishing, 1995.

Bartle, Richard. "Hearts, clubs, diamonds, spades: Players who suit MUDs." <http://www.mud.co.uk/richard/hcds.htm> (accessed October 22, 2002).

"Battlenet warnings!" Diabloii net. <http://www.diabloii.net/battlenet/warnings.shtml#trading> (accessed August 11, 2005).

Belton, Sharon. "A segue into publishing—Prima Publishing—making it—company profile." *Nation's Business*, July 1998. <http://www.findarticles.com/p/articles/mi_m1154/is_n7_v86/ai_20797631> (accessed July 26, 2004).

Beniger, James. *The control revolution: Technological and economic origins of the information society*. Cambridge, MA: Harvard University Press, 1986.

Bogenn, Tim. *The Hulk official strategy guide*. Indianapolis, IN: BradyGames Publishing, 2003.

Bogost, Ian. *Unit operations: An approach to videogame criticism*. Cambridge, MA: MIT Press, 2006.

Bok, Sissela. *Lying: Moral choice in public and private life*. New York: Vintage Books, 1978.

Bourdieu, Pierre. *Distinction: A social critique of the judgment of taste*. Cambridge, MA: Harvard University Press, 1984.

Bowyer, J. Barton. *Cheating: Deception in war & magic, games & sports, sex & religion, business & con games, politics & espionage, art & science*. New York: St. Martin's Press, 1982.

Bray, Hiawatha. "Game on: New tools will defeat a cheat." *Boston Globe*, November 5, 2003, E1.

Callahan, David. *The cheating culture: Why more Americans are doing wrong to get ahead*. Orlando, FL: Harcourt, 2004.

Carless, Simon. "Washington, DC, game stores raided over mod chip piracy." Gamasutra. December 8, 2004. <http://www.gamasutra.com/php-bin/news_index.php?sotry=4669> (accessed December 15, 2004).

Castronova, Edward. *Synthetic worlds: The business and culture of online games*. Chicago: University of Chicago Press, 2005.

"Cheating-Death." United Admins. <http://www.unitedadmins.com/index.php?p=content&content=Cheating-Death> (accessed May 15, 2006).

Clark, Don. "Gamer offers form of instant replay to fight cheating." *Wall Street Journal*, September 24, 2003, D4.

References

Coffey, Robert. "Hello, ladies!" *Computer Gaming World*, July–August 2005, 106.

Colayco, Bob. "Blizzard closes and bans accounts and CD keys tied to the use of online cheat programs." Gamespot. <http://www.gamespot.com/pc/ strategy/warcraft3reignofchaos/news_6024304.html> (accessed August 11, 2005).

Collins-Jarvis, Lori. "Discriminatory messages and gendered power relations in on-line discussion groups." Paper presented at the annual meeting of the National Communication Association, Chicago, November 1997.

"The complete not just for cheating." Codejunkies. <http://us.codejunkies .com/news_reviews.asp?c=US&cr=USD&cs=$&r=0&1=1&p=13&i=8191&s =8> (accessed September 17, 2004).

Consalvo, Mia. "Gil farming and fishing bots: Cheating in FFXI." MemoryCard. <http://memorycard.blogs.com/memorycard/2004/08/gil _farming_and.html>.

Consalvo, Mia. "It's a queer world after all: Studying *The Sims* and sexuality." Gay and Lesbian Alliance against Defamation. <http://www.glaad.org/ publications>.

Consalvo, Mia. "Zelda 64 and video game fans: A walkthrough of games, intertextuality, and narrative." *Television and New Media* 4, no. 3 (2003): 321–334.

"Custom anti-cheating solutions." IT GlobalSecure. <http://www.itglobal secure.net.categories/gaming/service_custom_anticheating.htm> (accessed May 15, 2006).

"*Diablo 2* hints." <http://home.tula.net/sound/diablo2hints.html> (accessed February 5, 2005).

Dibbell, Julian. *My tiny life: Crime and passion in a virtual world*. New York: Holt and Company, 1999.

"Event name: Ballista." Official Web site of *Final Fantasy XI* online. <http:// www.playonline.com/ff11us/conflict/main/> (accessed June 1, 2006).

Fahey, Rob. "Italian court rules mod chips legal." Games Industry Biz. January 23, 2004. <http://www.gamesindustry.biz/content_page.php?section_name =ret&aid=2858> (accessed January 29, 2004).

Farrell, Elizabeth. "Smith College's first engineers feel like 'rock stars.'" *Chronicle of Higher Education*, May 28, 2004. <http://chronicle.com/weekly/ v50/i38/38a03401.htm>.

Fehr, Ernst, and Simon Gächter. "Altruistic punishment in humans." *Nature* 415 (January 2002): 137–140.

Fiske, John. *Television culture*. New York: Routledge, 1987.

Foo, Chek Yang "Redefining grief play." Paper presented at the Other Players conference, IT–University of Copenhagen, December 2004.

Foo, Chek Yang, and Elina M. I. Koivisto. "Grief play motivations." Paper presented at the Other Players conference, IT–University of Copenhagen, December 2004.

Fost, Dan. "Hasbro adds Galoob to its toy chest." SF Gate.com. September 29, 1998. <http://www.sfgate.com/cgi-bin/article.cgi?file=/chronicle/archive/1998/09/29/BU88669.DTL&type=printable> (accessed August 23, 2004).

Foucault, Michel. *Discipline and punish: The birth of the prison*. New York: Pantheon, 1977.

"Frequently asked questions about Wow Glider." <http://www.wowglider.com/FAQ.aspx> (accessed May 1, 2006).

"GameFAQs." CNET Networks. <http://www.cnetnetworks.com/advertise/properties/gamefaqs.html> (accessed June 1, 2006).

"GameShark." Wikipedia. <http://en.wikipedia.org/wiki/game_shark> (accessed May 15, 2006).

"Gaming enthusiasts." Ziff Davis Media. <http://www.ziffdavis.com/print_it.php?title=Gaming%20Enthusiasts> (accessed July 14, 2004).

Genette, Gérard. *Paratexts: Thresholds of interpretation*. London: Cambridge University Press, 1997.

Gerstmann, Jeff. "SOCOM: So broken," GameSpot. <http://www.gamespot.com/gamespot/features/all/gamespotting/041303/2.html> (accessed July 8, 2003).

"Grading on a curve." *Game Daily*. <http://biz.gamedaily.com/features.asp?article_id=8370&section=media&e-mail=> (accessed November 30, 2004).

Hall, Stuart. "Encoding/decoding." In *Culture, media, language: Working papers in cultural studies, 1972–1979*, ed. Stuart Hall. London: Hutchinson, 1980.

Hebdige, Dick. *Subculture: The meaning of style*. London: Methuen, 1979.

Herring, Susan. "Gender and power in online communication." CSI Working Paper, October 2001. <http://rkcsi.indiana.edu/archive/CSI/WP/WP01-05B.html> (accessed June 1, 2006).

Herz, J. C. *Joystick nation: How videogames ate our quarters, won our hearts, and rewired our minds*. Boston: Little, Brown and Company, 1997.

Huizinga, Johan. *Homo ludens: A study of the play element in culture*. Boston: Beacon Press, 1950.

"Interview of the month: Bill Roper." <http://www.planetdiablo.com/features/articles/broper022702/> (accessed February 5, 2005).

Kent, Steven. *The ultimate history of videogames*. Roseville, CA: Prima Publishing, 2001.

King, Brad, and John Borland. *Dungeons and dreamers: The rise of computer game culture from geek to chic*. New York: McGraw-Hill, 2003.

"Kingdom Hearts FAQs." GameFAQs.com. <http://www.gamefaqs.com/console/ps2/game/516587.html> (accessed June 1, 2006).

Kline, Stephen, Nick Dyer-Witheford, and Greig De Peuter, eds. *Digital play: The interaction of technology, culture, and marketing*. Montreal: McGill-Queen's University Press, 2003.

Kohler, Chris. *Power up: How Japanese video games gave the world an extra life*. Indianapolis, IN: BradyGames Publishing, 2005.

"Konami game master." Wikipedia. <http://en.wikipedia.org/wiki/Konami_game_master> (accessed May 1, 2006).

Krissel, Richard. *The ultimate strategy guide to Super Mario Bros*. New York: Signet, 1991.

Kücklich, Julian. "Other playings: Cheating in computer games." Paper presented at the Other Players conference, IT–University of Copenhagen, December 2004.

Laidlaw, Mike. "Cracking Pandora's box." The Adrenaline Vault. <http://www.avault.com/articles/getarticle.asp?name=pandbox>.

Lastowka, Gregory F., and Dan Hunter. "The laws of the virtual worlds." *California Law Review*. <http://ssrn.com/abstract=402860>.

Lehdonvirta, Vili. "Real-money trade of virtual assets: Ten different user perceptions." Proceedings of DAC 2005, IT–University of Copenhagen, December 2005. <http://www.hiit.fi/u/vlehdonv/publications/Lehdonvirta-2005-RMT-Perceptions.pdf>.

Lessig, Lawrence. *Code: And other laws of cyberspace*. New York: Basic Books, 1999.

Lewis Galoob Toys, Inc v. Nintendo of America (1992). <http://cyber.law.harvard.edu/openlaw/DVD/cases/Galoob_v_Nintendo.html> (accessed May 1, 2005).

Lister, Martin. *New media: A critical introduction*. London: Routledge, 2003.

"List of Online Multiplayer Cheats." Wikipedia. <http://en.wikipedia.org/wiki/List_of_online_multiplayer_cheats> (accessed August 9, 2005).

Lopez, Miguel. "WoW duping: Fact or fiction?" *Gamespy*, July 20, 2005. <http://www.gamespy.com/articles/635/635262p1.html> (accessed May 1, 2006).

Ludlow, Peter. "Evangeline: Interview with a child cyber-prostitute in TSO." *Alphaville Herald*. <http://www.alphavilleherald.com/archives/000049.html> (accessed June 1, 2006).

Lui, John. "Mod-chipped Xbox? No online games for you." ZDNet Asia. <http://www.zdnetasia.com/news/internet/0, 39044246,39157642,00.htm> (accessed January 20, 2004).

Lunenfeld, Peter, ed. *The digital dialectic: New essays on new media*. Cambridge, MA: MIT Press, 1999.

Mabe, Aimee. "Mad Katz announces GameShark lineup at Electronic Entertainment Expo." GameShark.com. <http://www.gameshark.com/productinfo/articles/409700p1.html> (accessed July 11, 2003).

"Mad Katz annual report." 2005. <http://www.madkatz.com> (accessed June 1, 2006).

McCandless, David. "Make cheats, Not war." *Guardian*. <http://www.davidmccandless.com/articles/make_cheats_not_war.htm>.

McDonald, Myra. *Representing women: Myths of femininity in popular culture*. London: Edward Arnold, 1995.

McRobbie, Angela. *Jackie: An ideology of adolescent femininity*. Birmingham, UK: Centre for Contemporary Cultural Studies, University of Birmingham, 1978.

"Media kit." IDG Entertainment. <http://www.idgentertainment.com/mediakit/> (accessed November 1, 2004).

"Media kit 2004/2005." *Game Informer*. <http://www.gameinformer.com/OtherPages/Corporate/Advertising.htm> (accessed November 1, 2004).

"Modchip." Wikipedia. <http://en.wikipedia.org/wiki/Modchip> (accessed May 15, 2006).

"More on GMR and XBN." *Game Daily*. <http://biz.gamedaily.com/articles.asp?article_id=8548#8548> (accessed January 10, 2005).

Morningstar, Chip, and Randall Farmer. "The lessons of Lucasfilm's *Habitat*." In *Cyberspace: First steps*, ed. Michael Benedikt. Cambridge, MA: MIT Press, 1992.

Morris, Jeff. "Multiplayer cheating: Dispatches from the front." Paper presented at the annual meeting of the Game Developers Conference, San Jose, California, March 2006.

Mr. Rasputin. "Allakhazam sells out to IGE. No, really. And IGE Andraste is Savant." Corporation, <http://www.corpnews.com/node/133?PHPSESSID =8fbd6994b6b279ab38185ef5de62ec19> (accessed June 1, 2006).

Nieman, Susie. "BradyGames Sweeps Gaming Strategy Guide Industry in 2004." BradyGames, <http://www.bradygames.com/press/press_releases _detail.asp?promo=2226&rl=1> (accessed September 10, 2006).

Nightfreeze. "The great scam." <http://static.circa1984.com/the-big-scam.html> (accessed March 1, 2005).

Old-Computers.com. <http://www.old-computers.com/museum/computer .asp?c=90> (accessed May 1, 2006).

Pauly, John. "*La Femme Nikita* and the ethics of organizational life." Paper presented at the annual International Communication Association conference, New Orleans, May 2004.

Pelland, Dave. "Hackers, cheater threaten online games' business model." KPMG Analysis. March 3, 2005. <http://www.kpmginsiders.com/display _analysis.asp?cs_id=126855> (accessed March 8, 2005).

Pham, Alex. "'Griefers' bedevil online gamers." *Chicago Tribune*, September 9, 2002. <http://www.chicagotribune.com/business/chi-0209090015sep09.story> (accessed September 11, 2002).

"Pikmin FAQs." GameFAQs.com. <http://www.gamefaqs.com/console/ gamecube/game/516498.html> (accessed June 1, 2006).

Poster, Mark. "Postmodern virtualities." In *Cyberspace/cyberbodies/cyberpunk*, ed. Mike Featherstone and Roger Burrows. Thousand Oaks, CA: Sage, 1995.

Postigo, Hector. "Of mods and modders: Chasing down the value of fan-based video game modifications." In *Digital games industries*, ed. Jason Rutter. Manchester: Manchester University Press, forthcoming.

"Protocol-based security and software security." IT GlobalSecure. <http:// www.secureplay.com/papers/docs/ProtocolSecurtiyVsSoftwareSecurity2.pdf> (accessed June 1, 2006).

Public Broadcasting System. Inside the games: Classic game cheats. *The video game revolution*. <http://www.pbs.org/kcts/videogamerevolution/inside/cheats .html> (accessed September 7, 2004).

"PunkBuster for players." Even Balance. <http://www.punkbusters.com/ publications/aa-pl/index.htm> (accessed May 15, 2006).

Quake: Authorized strategy guide. Indianapolis, IN: Brady Publishing, 1996.

References

Ramsay, Randall. "Australian high court rules mod chips are ok." CNET. October 6, 2005. <http://www.cnet.com.au/games/ps2/0,39029672,40057408,00.htm> (accessed May 22, 2006).

Reynolds, Ren. "Playing a 'good' game: A philosophical approach to understanding the morality of games." Gamasutra. <http://www.igda.org/articles/rreynolds_ethics.php>.

Rheingold, Howard. *Virtual communities: Homesteading on the electronic frontier.* Reading, MA: Addison-Wesley Publishing, 1993.

Riggs, Karen. *Mature audiences: Television in the lives of elders.* New Brunswick, NJ: Rutgers University Press, 1998.

Robinett, Warren. Foreword to *The video game theory reader*, ed. Mark J. P. Wolf and Bernard Perron. New York: Routledge, 2003.

Royse, Pam, Joon Lee, Undrahbuyan Baasanjav, Mark Hopson, and Mia Consalvo. "Women gamers: Technologies of the gendered self." In *New Media & Society.* Forthcoming.

Salen, Katie, and Eric Zimmerman. *Rules of play: Game design fundamentals.* Cambridge, MA: MIT Press, 2003.

Schott, Gareth, and Kristy Horell. "Girl gamers and their relationship with the gaming culture." *Convergence* 6, no. 4 (2000): 36–53.

"Secrets to *Diablo*." <http://www.guardiansofjustice.com/diablo/Frames/Secrets.htm> (accessed February 5, 2005).

Semrad, Ed. "CD-ROM: Is the industry ready for it?" *Electronic Gaming Monthly*, May 1992, 8.

Shachtman, Noah. "'Blizzard' of cheaters banned." *Wired News.* <http://www.wired.com/news/games/0,2101,55092,00.html?tw=wn_ascii> (accessed August 11, 2005).

Sheff, David. *Game over: How Nintendo conquered the world.* New York: Random House, 1993.

ShowEQ Open Source Project Message Forums. <http://www.showeq.net/forums/faq.php?faq=seqfaq_gq#faq_seqfaq_gq_whatseq> (accessed May 3, 2006).

Stern, Eddo. "A touch of medieval: Narrative, magic, and computer technology in massively multiplayer computer role-playing games." <http://www.eddostern.com/texts/Stern_TOME.html> (accessed June 1, 2006).

Stone, Allucquère Rosanne. *The war of desire and technology at the close of the mechanical age*. Cambridge, MA: MIT Press, 1995.

Stratton, Bryan. *URU: Ages beyond Myst: Prima's official strategy guide*. Roseville, CA: Prima Games, 2003.

Stratton, Bryan. *Myst URU: Complete chronicles: Prima official game guide*. Roseville, CA: Prima Games, 2004.

Sun, Chuen-Tsai, Holin Lin, and Cheng-Hong Ho. "Game tips as gifts: Social interactions and rational calculations in computer gaming." In *Level up: Digital games research conference proceedings*, ed. Marinka Copier and Joost Raessens. Utrecht: Utrecht University, 2003.

Taodyn. Bannable Offenses. <http://bannable-offenses.blogspot.com/> (accessed May 1, 2006).

Taodyn. "Change is never good." Bannable Offenses. <http://www.blogger .com/comment.g?blogID=25324432&postID=114677231212075299> (accessed May 12, 2006).

Taodyn. "Law and order: SVU must be joking." Bannable Offenses. <http:// bannable-offenses.blogspot.com/2006/05/law-and-order-svumustbejoking .html> (accessed May 22, 2006).

Taylor, T. L. "Multiple pleasures: Women and online gaming." *Convergence* 9, no. 1 (2003): 21–46.

Taylor, T. L. "Becoming player: Networks, structured and imagined futures." Paper presented at the Beyond Barbie and Mortal Kombat: New Perspectives on Gender, Games, and Computing Conference, NSF Workshop, University of California at Los Angeles, May 2006.

Taylor, T. L. *Play between worlds: Exploring online game culture*. Cambridge, MA: MIT Press, 2006.

Taylor, T. L., and Mikael Jakobsson. "The Sopranos meet *EverQuest*: Socialization in massively multiuser games." In *Command Lines*, ed. Sandra Braman and Thomas Malaby. Forthcoming.

Turkle, Sherry. *Life on the screen*. New York: Touchstone, 1995.

Video Game Books Inc. *Playing Ms. Pac-Man to Win*. New York: Pocket Books, 1982.

Wayner, Peter. "Do cheaters ever prosper? Just ask them." *New York Times*, March 27, 2003. <http://www.nytimes.com/2003/03/27/technology/circuits/ 27chea.html?ei=5070&en=b35772c76e5251e5&ex=1069822800&pagewanted =print&position=top> (accessed November 24, 2003).

Weiland, Jonah. "IDW and Konami publicity plan for 'Metal Gear Solid' the comic book." ComicBookResources.com. <http://www.comicbookresources .com/news/newsitem.cgi?id=3872> (accessed October 12, 2004).

Weinstein, Dave. "Cheating and countermeasures in multiplayer games." Paper presented at the Game Developers Conference, Austin, September 2003.

Weise, Elizabeth. "Gay programmer fired for adding studly guys to computer game." December 1996. <http://www.langston.com/Fun_People/1996/1996CFM.html> (accessed March 1, 2005).

Williams, Dmitri. "A brief social history of video games." In *Playing computer games: Motives, responses, and consequences*, ed. Peter Vorderer and Jennings Bryant. Mahwah, NJ: Lawrence Erlbaum, 2005.

Wilson, Robin. "A hothouse for women scientists." *Chronicle of Higher Education*, May 5, 2006. <http://chronicle.com/weekly/v52/i35/35a01201 .htm> (accessed May 10, 2006).

Woodcock, Bruce. "MMOG Charts." <http://www.mmogchart.com>.

"Working with SecurePlay." IT GlobalSecure. <http://www.secureplay.com/product-docs/WorkingWithSecurePlay2.pdf> (accessed May 15, 2006).

"WoW Glider." <http://www.wowglider.com/default.aspx> (accessed May 1, 2006).

Wright, Talmadge, Eric Boria, and Paul Breidenbach. "Creative player actions in FPS online video games." *Game Studies* (2002). <http://www.gamestudies .org/0202/wright/>.

Yee, Nick. "Buying Gold." Daedalus Project. <http://www.nickyee.com/daedalus/archives/001469.php> > (accessed May 15, 2006).

Yee, Nick. "Maps of Azeroth." Paper presented at the Beyond Barbie and Mortal Kombat: New Perspectives on Gender, Games, and Computing Conference, NSF Workshop, University of California at Los Angeles, May 2006.

Index